# Goddesses, Whores, Wives and Slaves

*Women in Classical Antiquity*

## SARAH B. POMEROY

THE BODLEY HEAD
LONDON

1 3 5 7 9 10 8 6 4 2

The Bodley Head, an imprint of Vintage,
20 Vauxhall Bridge Road,
London SW1V 2SA

The Bodley Head is part of the Penguin Random House group of companies
whose addresses can be found at global.penguinrandomhouse.com.

Penguin
Random House
UK

First published in the USA by Schocken Books Inc, 1975
First published in Great Britain by Pimlico, 1994
Reissued by The Bodley Head, 2015

www.vintage-books.co.uk

A CIP catalogue record for this book
is available from the British Library

ISBN 9781847923837

Printed and bound by Clays Ltd, St Ives plc

MIX
Paper from
responsible sources
FSC
www.fsc.org    FSC® C018179

Penguin Random House is committed to a sustainable future
for our business, our readers and our planet. This book is
made from Forest Stewardship Council® certified paper.

# CONTENTS

*Illustrations follow p. 148*

# CHRONOLOGICAL TABLE

*(Many dates are approximate)*

(all dates are B.C.)

| | | | |
|---|---|---|---|
| BRONZE AGE | 3000 | | *Greece* |
| | 1200 | | |
| | | 1184 | Traditional date of the fall of Troy |
| | | | Fall of Mycenae |
| DARK AGE | | 1000–900 | Protogeometric Pottery |
| | | 900–700 | Geometric Pottery |
| | 800 | | Phoenician alphabet |
| | | | Homer |
| | | 700 | Hesiod |
| ARCHAIC | | | Semonides |
| | | | Sappho |
| | | 594 | Archonship of Solon |
| | | 545–510 | Tyranny of Pisistratids |
| | 500 | | |
| | | 490–479 | Persian Wars |
| | | 458 | Aeschylus *Oresteia* |
| | | 451/450 | Citizenship Law of Pericles |
| | | 441 | Sophocles *Antigone* |
| | | | Aspasia |
| | | 431–404 | Peloponnesian War |
| | | 411 | Aristophanes *Lysistrata* |
| CLASSICAL | | 405 | Death of Euripides |
| | | 459–380 | Lysias |
| | | 429–347 | Plato |
| | | 428–354 | Xenophon |
| | | | Demosthenes, Aristotle |
| | *regnum* | 359–336 | Philip II of Macedon |
| | | | Praxiteles' Aphrodite of Cnidus |
| | *regnum* | 336–323 | Alexander |
| | 323 | | |
| | | 316 | Death of Olympias |
| HELLENISTIC | | 270 | Death of Arsinoë II |
| | 30 | 30 | Death of Cleopatra VII |
| | | | *Rome* |
| | 753 | | |
| | | 753 B.C. | Traditional date of the founding of Rome |
| ARCHAIC | | | by Romulus |
| | 509 | | |
| | | 509 B.C. | Expulsion of kings, founding of Republic |
| | | 493 B.C. | Cult of Ceres on the Aventine |
| | | 451–450 B.C. | Traditional date of the Twelve Tables |
| | | 264–241 B.C. | First Punic War |
| REPUBLIC | | 234–149 B.C. | Cato the Elder |
| | | 218–201 B.C. | Second Punic War |
| | | 195 B.C. | Repeal of Oppian Law |
| | | 169 B.C. | Voconian Law |

| | | |
|---|---|---|
| | 133 B.C. | Tribunate of Tiberius Gracchus, beginning of one hundred years of civil discord |
| | 106–43 B.C. | Cicero |
| | 95–46 B.C. | Cato the Younger |
| LATE REPUBLIC | 84–54 B.C. | Catullus |
| | 70–19 B.C. | Virgil |
| | | Propertius, Tibullus, Sulpicia, Livy |
| | 44 B.C. | Assassination of Julius Caesar |
| | 43 B.C.–A.D. 17 | Ovid |
| | 42 B.C. | Oration of Hortensia |
| | 31 B.C. | Defeat of Antony and Cleopatra at Actium |
| 27 | regnum 27 B.C.–A.D. 14 | Augustus (formerly known as Octavian) |
| | A.D. 14 | |

(all dates are A.D.)

| | | |
|---|---|---|
| | regnum 14–37 | Tiberius |
| | 29 | Death of Livia, widow of Augustus |
| | | Valerius Maximus |
| | regnum 37–41 | Gaius (Caligula) |
| | regnum 41–54 | Claudius |
| | 50–120 | Plutarch |
| | regnum 54–68 | Nero |
| | 59 | Assassination of Agrippina, mother of Nero |
| | 61–112 | Pliny the Younger |
| | regnum 69–79 | Vespasian |
| | regnum 79–81 | Titus |
| | 79 | Destruction of Pompeii and Herculaneum |
| | regnum 81–96 | Domitian |
| | | Tacitus |
| | | Juvenal |
| EMPIRE | regnum 96–98 | Nerva |
| | regnum 98–117 | Trajan |
| | | Soranus |
| | regnum 117–38 | Hadrian (wife, Sabina) |
| | | Apuleius |
| | regnum 138–61 | Antoninus Pius (wife, Faustina the Elder) |
| | | Aulus Gellius |
| | regnum 161–80 | Marcus Aurelius (wife, Faustina the Younger) |
| | regnum 180–92 | Commodus |
| | regnum 193–211 | Septimius Severus |
| | regnum 211–17 | Caracalla |
| | 217 | Death of Julia Domna |
| | regnum 218–22 | Elagabalus |
| | 222 | Death of Julia Soaemias |
| | regnum 222–35 | Severus Alexander |
| | 226 | Death of Julia Maesa |
| | regnum 285–305 | Diocletian |
| | regnum 306–37 | Constantine |
| | regnum 527–65 | Justinian |

# INTRODUCTION

THIS BOOK was conceived when I asked myself what women were doing while men were active in all the areas traditionally emphasized by classical scholars. The overwhelming ancient and modern preference for political and military history, in addition to the current fascination with intellectual history, has obscured the record of those people who were excluded by sex or class from participation in the political and intellectual life of their societies.

The "glory of classical Athens" is a commonplace of the traditional approach to Greek history. The intellectual and artistic products of Athens were, admittedly, dazzling. But rarely has there been a wider discrepancy between the cultural rewards a society had to offer and women's participation in that culture. Did his wife Xanthippe ever hear Socrates' dialogues on beauty and truth? How many women actually read the histories of Herodotus and Thucydides? What did women do instead? Most important, why was it necessary for the Athenians to make such a distinction between the culture of men and that of women? When pagan goddesses were, in their way, as powerful as gods, why was the status of human females so low?

The "grandeur of Rome" is another axiom of ancient history. The focus of Roman history has also tended to be on the political deeds of male society—winning and governing an empire. Roman women were not in practice excluded from participation in social, political, and cultural life to the same extent as Greek women. Yet the prevailing scholarly opinion that some Roman women, at least, were emancipated likewise needs revision. In comparison to Athenian women, some Roman woman appear to have been fairly liberated, but never did Roman society encourage women to engage in the same activities as men in the same social class.

This book spans a period of more than fifteen hundred years. The Greek section begins with Bronze Age mythology and legends surrounding the fall of Troy, traditionally fixed at 1184 B.C., and proceeds through the Dark Age and Archaic period to the Classical world of the fifth century B.C. and the Hellenistic period. The Roman section covers the Roman Republic and the transition to Empire with the advent of Augustus in 31 B.C., and ends with the death of Constantine in A.D. 337, but concentrates on the late Republic and early Empire. My aim was to write a social history of women through the centuries in the Greek and Roman worlds. There is no comprehensive book on this subject in English.

I have had to make some difficult decisions concerning the ancient sources which were appropriate for use in this study. The available evidence is archaeological and literary.

The literary testimony presents grave problems to the social historian. Women pervade nearly every genre of classical literature, yet often the bias of the author distorts the information. Aside from some scraps of lyric poetry, the extant formal literature of classical antiquity was all written by men. In addition, misogyny taints much ancient literature. The different genres of ancient poetry vary in reliability for the social historian. How much of what satirists or rejected lovers pour out in elegaic poetry about women can be acceptable evidence for the modern historian? I believe it is also necessary to avoid drawing conclusions about Greek women of the Classical period from the depiction of Bronze Age heroines in Greek tragedy. Tragedies have been examined to provide insight into the attitudes of particular poets toward women—in them the poet reveals his ideals and fantasies about women—but tragedies cannot be used as an independent source for the life of average women. Greek comedy, on the other hand, of both the Classical and Hellenistic periods, shows ordinary people rather than heroes and heroines, and is a more reliable source for the social historian.

Among prose authors, ancient historians, biographers, and orators provide the soundest and most extensive information about women. Although Herodotus and Thucydides are poor sources for the lives of Greek women, later historians and biographers were frequently fascinated by the activities and personalities of famous women. Of course, many ancient historians, influenced by their ideal of womanhood, were led to bitter disapproval of the actual women who were being described. The numerous orations surviving from antiquity also provide a wealth of material about women's roles and legal status, although, of course, their bias is polemical. Lastly, the writings of ancient philosophers are useful, for most of them propound moral views on women rooted in contemporary society, whether they accept or reject them. In addition to history, biography, oratory, and philosophy, for the Roman period there are extensive collections of legal texts and judicial commentary. Among Latin prose literature, the letters of Cicero and Pliny are fruitful sources for the private lives of women in their social class.

Ancient history, to a considerable degree, has been basically the study of the ruling classes. The women who are known to us from the formal literature of antiquity are mainly those who belonged to or associated with the wealthy or intellectually elite groups of society. It must also be recognized that there is more information available on women who were famous—whether for good or evil. I have felt that my task was to examine the history of all women, and to avoid the emphasis on the upper classes and their literature. There is not much material available, but I was greatly aided in the Roman section especially by the recent publication of several scholarly works by historians who included women and the lower classes in their studies.

Evidence from the fine arts, including sculpture, vase painting, frescoes, mosaics, and depictions of women on tombstones and coins, as well as objects used by women—e.g., ornaments, kitchen utensils, looms, and furniture—are useful in reconstructing the private life of women. Written evidence that would not be classified as formal literature can be found in the graffiti on ancient buildings as well as in the inscriptions on ancient monuments. Documents written on papyrus are a most important primary source for studying the economic, legal, and social aspects of women's lives in the Hellenistic and Roman periods. Since most of the extant papyri come from Egypt, these texts record the activities of Greek, Roman, and Egyptian women living in that country. Among the papyri are letters, legal documents, prayers, and charms written by or for women. These texts are the ancient equivalent of the private letters and diaries which have proven prime sources for the lives of women in later eras.

The story of the women of antiquity should be told now, not only because it is a legitimate aspect of social history, but because the past illuminates contemporary problems in relationships between men and women. Even though scientific technology and religious outlook clearly distinguish ancient culture from modern, it is most significant to note the consistency with which some attitudes toward women and the roles women play in Western society have endured through the centuries.

Originally the book was planned as something more definitive, but as I began to write I became increasingly aware that most of the standard references in the field of Classics did not include women in their purview. For example, the major works of the social historian M. I. Rostovtzeff *(The Social and Economic History of the Roman Empire* and *The Social and Economic History of the Hellenistic World)* have splendidly detailed indexes, but neither has an entry for "Women." His utter blindness to women led to such absurdities as his noticing only two unenfranchised classes in Greece: the resident aliens and the slaves.[1] This last observation appears in a short history of Greece, and was left unchanged when the book was revised by E. J. Bickerman in 1962. It is obviously impossible in a single book to fill all the gaps in the history of ancient women. Indeed, it would be demeaning of the subject to attempt to do so.

In ancient history there are few certainties. We are trying to assemble a puzzle with many pieces missing. In a period when the history of men is obscure, it naturally follows that the documentation for women's lives is even more fragmented. On questions where there is substantial debate—for example, the status of women in Classical Athens—I have tried to present the evidence and the various interpretations of other scholars; I have also attempted to indicate reasons for the divergence in opinion. But on issues where the evidence seemed to me to be insufficient to justify choosing one viewpoint and rejecting another, I have generally refrained from indicating a preference and arguing for it. Thus, many of the conclusions voiced in this book are more tentative than some readers might wish.

I have tried to give some guidance to the reader interested in women's history who is not a classicist. Notes have been kept to a minimum, but for the benefit of the classicist there is limited documentation of controversial items. All translations, except where attributed to others, are my own. Readers who wish to consult the complete ancient texts from which passages are excerpted can find translations of most Greek and Latin authors in the Loeb Classical Library series published by Harvard University Press, which, where appropriate, indicate the line and section numbers of the Greek or Latin text. An interested reader can engage in further research by consulting annotated editions of the ancient authors, using the line or section numbers in the Loeb editions as a guide.

The writing of the book began as an undergraduate course of lectures at Hunter College. I am very grateful to my students from whom, over the years, I have had a large amount of helpful criticism. They have forced me to continually take a fresh look at many issues.

Acknowledgments are due to the American Council of Learned Societies, the Ford Foundation, the National Endowment for the Humanities, and the Nooney Fund of Hunter College for financial support which facilitated the writing of this book. I am also grateful to the Fondation Hardt pour l'Etude de l'Antiquité classique for its hospitality during the summer of 1974. However, the conclusions, opinions, and other statements in this book are solely those of the author.

This study covers a long period of history and a wide range of topics. I am grateful to have been able to discuss some of the issues with other scholars, though it should not be assumed that they concur with all my views. I should like to express my thanks to J. P. Sullivan for reading the entire manuscript; to Froma Zeitlin for reading the chapters on myth, religion, and Athenian literature; to William V. Harris, W. K. Lacey, and Martin Ostwald for reading the chapters on Greek women; to Susan Treggiari for reading Chapter IX; and to Robert E. A. Palmer for reading the Roman chapters. I have also enjoyed the use of the incomparable slide collection of my colleague Claireve Grandjouan. Warm thanks are also due to Judith Peller Hallett, Marylin Arthur, Flora Levin, and Robert Rowland for translating some of the passages that appear in this book. I am indebted to Beverly Colman and Christopher Kuppig of Schocken Books for editing the manuscript.

Lastly, I must thank my husband and children for their support. Without them the life of a scholar would have been a lonely one.

# I

## GODDESSES AND GODS

CLASSICAL MYTHOLOGY provides the earliest glimpse of male-female relationships in Greek civilization. Myths are not lies, but rather men's attempt to impose a symbolic order upon their universe. Some myths are so primordial as to be undatable, and we are haunted by the question of whether women could have participated in their creation. These myths and others evolving from actual historical events were later recounted and systematized by poets. An investigation of how myths arose and of their connection to external and psychological realities is an essential prelude to the study of the history of women, for the myths of the past molded the attitudes of successive, more sophisticated generations and preserved the continuity of the social order.[1] Hence we begin with myths about women both mortal and divine.

### The Genealogy of the Gods

Since Homer, the earliest extant Greek poet, does not deal to any great extent with the generations of gods preceding the rule of Olympian Zeus, we have to look to the works of a slightly later poet, Hesiod, for information about them. Hesiod was a dour, bitter poet and farmer living in Boeotia in approximately 700 B.C. His views of gods and humankind not only shaped but probably corresponded to the ideas held by the population as a whole, and thus the *Theogony* became the standard Greek version of divine evolution. Hesiod details the divine progression from female-dominated generations, characterized by natural, earthy emotional qualities, to the superior and rational monarchy of Olympian Zeus. Whether this corresponds to a historical change in Greek religion from emphasis on the worship of female divinities to that of male divinities is unclear, although more will be said later about the possibility of such worship. It is highly probable that misogyny was one of several factors that motivated Hesiod to organize the dark, evil divinities and their monstrous offspring in the early generations, to be overthrown by the civilizing Zeus.

Ge is the first reigning earth goddess. Her children are primarily deifications of the features of the physical world, while her grandchildren include some of the most dreadful monsters to haunt mythology. Ge's husband Uranus (who is also her son) hates his children and so hides them deep within Ge. She then persuades her son Cronus to castrate his father with a sickle.

The story repeats itself in the next generation of gods, when King Cronus swallows his children by Rhea, Ge's daughter. Finally, aided by Ge, Rhea helps her son Zeus to overthrow his father.

Zeus eventually puts an end to the successive overthrowing of kings by conspiracies of wives and sons. Establishing a patriarchal government on Olympus, Zeus introduces moral order and culture by fathering the Hours, the Fates, the Muses, and the Graces. But he denies power to females, even taking away their sole claim to consideration as bearers of children when he gives birth to Athena through his head and to Dionysus from his thigh.

Zeus's subordination of the female power thus exalted into public philosophy Hesiod's private unsympathetic view of women. This view is clearly expressed in the story of the creation of the first woman, Pandora.[2] Her name is ambiguous. It can mean "giver of all gifts," making her a benevolent fertility figure, or "recipient of all gifts." Hesiod chooses the latter interpretation in order to attribute to the first woman the woes of mankind.

> And when Zeus made the lovely curse, the price
> For fire's boon, to other gods and men
> He brought her, thrilled with Athena's array.
> Amazement seized both gods and mortal men
> To see the snare, a futile thing for men.

From her has sprung the race of womankind,
The deadly race and tribes of womankind,
Great pain to mortal men with whom they live,
Helpmeets in surfeit—not in dreadful need.
Just as in ceilinged hives the honeybees
Nourish the drones, partners in evil deeds,
And all day long, until the sun goes down,
They bustle and build up white honeycombs,
While those who stay inside the ceilinged hives
Fill up their bellies from the others' work,
So women are a curse to mortal men—
As Zeus ordained—partners in evil deeds.
For fire's boon he made a second curse.

Then, angry, spoke Zeus, gatherer of clouds:
"Prometheus, the shrewdest one of all,
You've gladly stolen fire and cheated me,
Which will cause pain to you and men to come.
For fire I'll give them evil, and they all
Will cheer their hearts embracing this foul thing."
The sire of men and gods spoke, then he laughed.
He ordered famed Hephaestus to make haste:
Mix earth with water, add a human voice
And strength, a face like deathless goddesses',
A maiden's form—desirable and fair.
Athena was to teach her weaving skills,
And Aphrodite drench her head in grace,
And sore longing, and cares that gnaw the limbs.
To add a bitch's thoughts, and wily ways.
Zeus ordered Hermes, Slayer of Argus.
The gods obeyed the lord Zeus, Cronus' son.
Renowned Hephaestus molded out of earth
A modest maiden's likeness—as Zeus bid.
Gray-eyed Athena clothed and girded her.
Persuasion and the Graces draped her flesh
In golden necklaces, and for a crown
The fair-haired Seasons wove the flowers of spring.
In her breast the guide, Slayer of Argus,
Put lies and crooked words and wily ways,
As loud-thundering Zeus had bid. A voice
The gods' herald bestowed, and then a name,
Pandora (since all Olympian gods
gave a gift)—a pain to hard-toiling men.[3]

Pandora is comparable to the temptress Eve. and the box she opened may be a metaphor for carnal knowledge of women, which was a source of evil to men.

## The Olympians

With Zeus's defeat of his father, the Olympians take over. This anthropomorphic family included six chief goddesses: Athena, Artemis, Hestia, Aphrodite, Hera, and Demeter. In many ways female immortals resemble their human counterparts, except, of course, that divinities never grow old or die. Both literature and visual arts indicate that the goddesses are clearly differentiated among each other in function, appearance, personality, and in their relationships to both mortal and immortal males.

The most complex of the goddesses is Athena (Roman Minerva). Her activities are better documented than those of other goddesses since she plays an important role in the works of Homer and in the art and literature of the city that derived its name from hers, a city with the richest heritage in Greece. Athena is a masculine woman; some might label her androgynous. She is female in appearance and associated with the handicrafts of women and the fertility of the olive, but many of her attributes are those traditionally associated with males. She is a patroness of wisdom, considered a masculine quality by the Greeks. She is also a warrior goddess, protector of the citadel, armed with shield, spear, and helmet. In this capacity she is patroness of a number of mortal warriors and heroes. At times she disguises herself as a man to facilitate personal contact with her favorites; so she appears to Odysseus and his allies:

Athena, daughter of Zeus, came near them, making herself resemble Mentor in appearance and voice. Seeing her, Odysseus rejoiced, and greeted her, saying, "Mentor, defend me, remember your dear friend who did good things for you. We two were boys together." These were his words, but he suspected he was addressing the warrior goddess Athena.[4]

Athena is the archetype of the masculine woman who finds success in what is essentially a man's world by denying her own femininity and sexuality.[5] Thus Athena is a virgin—and, what is more, a virgin born not of woman but of man. While her mother was pregnant, Zeus swallowed her and, in time, at the stroke of the ax of Hephaestus, Athena was born, as befits a goddess of wisdom, out of the head of Zeus, fully armed and uttering her war cry. Because she herself was born of man, Athena is able to affirm that the father is the true parent of any child. This belief is strengthened by the birth of Aphrodite (Roman Venus), who, according to Hesiod, was born out of the foam of the sea from the castrated genitals of the sky god Uranus, and by the birth of Dionysus. In male–female antagonisms related in tragedy and epic, Athena always sides with the male, even hinting that she is suspicious of the motives of the virtuous Penelope.[6]

As patroness of Athenian industry, Athena presides over crafts, sharing her rule with her half-brother Hephaestus. In this sphere, involving practical knowledge rather than abstract thinking, she can interact with both men and women. A woman's skill in spinning and weaving is attributed to the grace granted her by Athena.

In contrast to the sociable Athena, Artemis (Roman Diana) is a huntress who shoots arrows from afar. She prefers to spend her days in mountains and forests in the company of wild beasts, remote from gatherings of men and gods. (Atalanta and the Amazons are mortal byforms of Artemis. Atalanta had been exposed to die in infancy because her father wanted a son, and was raised in the forest by a bear. She was a huntress who joined men in legendary expeditions and devised numerous schemes to avoid marriage, but finally yielded to a suitor who had the aid of Aphrodite.) The Amazons worshiped Artemis and resembled her. Both goddess and Amazons wore short tunics, were archers, and avoided the company of males. An apparent exception to Artemis' principle of shunning mortal men was Hippolytus, the son of the Amazon Hippolyte. Hippolytus was a devotée of Artemis, not only because of his mother's influence but especially because chastity was not to be found among male divinities. For the Greeks, chastity was a virtue only in women. Thus a youth like Hippolytus, who valued chastity, was forced to worship this quality in a female divinity.

In her relationships with humans, Artemis is primarily concerned with females, especially the physical aspects of their life cycle, including menstruation, childbirth, and death, however contradictory the association of these with a virgin may appear. (She is also cited as the reason for the termination of female life: when swift death came to a woman, she was said to have been shot by Artemis.) The Artemis of classical Greece probably evolved from the concept of a primitive mother goddess, and both she and her sister Athena were considered virgins because they had never submitted to a monogamous marriage. Rather, as befits mother goddesses, they had enjoyed many consorts. Their failure to marry, however, was misinterpreted as virginity by succeeding generations of men who connected loss of virginity only with conventional marriage. Either way, as mother goddess or as virgin, Artemis retains control over herself; her lack of permanent connection to a male figure in a monogamous relationship is the keystone of her independence.

The third virginal Olympian goddess is Hestia (Roman Vesta), sister of Zeus. She was

> a queen whom both Poseidon and Apollo courted. But she was completely unwilling to marry, and stubbornly refused. Touching the head of aegis-bearing Zeus, she, that shining goddess, swore a great oath which truly has been fulfilled that she would be a virgin forever. Zeus gave her a high honor instead of marriage, and she holds a place in the middle of the house and the richest share. In all the temples of the gods she has a portion of honor, and among mortals she holds first place among the goddesses.[7]

There is little myth about Hestia, for she was the archetypal old maid, preferring the quiet of the hearth to the boisterous banquets and emotional entanglements of the other Olympians. Moreover, she is seldom depicted in the visual arts, for instead of having an anthropomorphic conception, Hestia is commonly envisioned as the living flame.

The fourth major goddess, Aphrodite (Roman Venus), represents physical beauty, sexual love, and fertility. According to Hesiod, she, like Athena, was born of man, not of woman. Her origin in sexual organs and the sea—suggestive of amniotic fluid—underlines Aphrodite's nature as a fertility figure.[8]

Much of Aphrodite's seductiveness lies in her frivolous, deceitful character, for these appear to be the qualities of sexually attractive females. Thus these attributes are found in Pandora and in Helen, both Aphrodite's favorites. She, the most beautiful goddess, is married to the ugliest immortal, the lame Hephaestus. Perhaps this unfortunate union gives her an excuse for marital infidelity. Of all the goddesses, only Aphrodite commits adultery, an indiscretion considered only mildly censurable in a love goddess who is sacred to prostitutes.

The Romans traced their rulers' descent from Venus' (Aphrodite's) son Aeneas. In philosophical discussions on the nature of love in Plato's *Symposium,* Aphrodite is said to have a dual nature.[9] Aphrodite Urania, born of Uranus without a mother, represented intellectual, nonphysical love. Aphrodite Pandemos, said to have been created by the union of Olympian Zeus and the sky goddess Dione, was the patroness of prostitutes, and represented common or vulgar love. Vulgar love could be either heterosexual or homosexual, but intellectual love could be found only in a relationship between two males. The dichotomy between the two sorts of love survived through the Neoplatonism of the Renaissance to the present. In the late Renaissance the concept of intellectual or heavenly love came to be applied to heterosexual relationships as well.

Hera (Roman Juno), queen of the gods, is a mature female married to her brother Zeus. Both Zeus and Hera are fertility divinities. Zeus, in his aspect of fertility god, exercises the patriarchal prerogative of promiscuous intercourse and fathers numerous offspring; Hera, although outproducing the other fertility goddesses of her generation—Demeter and Aphrodite—bears only four children. The daughters of Hera are the colorless Hebe, cupbearer to the gods, and Eileithyia, goddess of childbirth. Her sons are more interesting, though remarkably lacking in celestial qualitities. Ares is stupid and bloodthirsty, a war god who positively delights in bloodshed (unlike the more civilized warrior goddess Athena). That Ares is the product of Zeus and Hera is emblematic of the bellicose nature of their union.

The domination of Zeus over Hera, as well as over the other divinities, is constantly threatened. Hera—as her husband's sister—is his equal, and is never totally subjugated. Far from omnipotent, Zeus is frequently affected and deceived by such females as Aphrodite and Thetis, and most of all by Hera. According to Hesiod, when Zeus produced Athena from his head, Hera, in jealousy, parthenogenically gave birth to Hephaestus. The pathos of her rebellion is demonstrated by the fact that Hephaestus is a buffoon and, of all the Olympians, the only cripple. Homer, on the other hand, relates that Zeus threw Hephaestus out of heaven for taking his mother's side in the quarrel with Hera; or, inconsistently, that Hera threw her son out in shame at his deformity.[10]

Hera not only persecutes her own son; she is a wicked step-mother as well. She is continually hostile to her husband's paramours—often young virgins—and to their progeny. Her victims include Hercules, Dionysus, Io, Callisto, and Leto.

Myth describes Hera's own marriage as a kind of permanent war, with brief interludes in bed, but in cult Hera was the guardian of human marriage.

The goddesses of Olympus appear in myth never to have had more than narrowly restricted functions, despite the major importance of their cults to Greek cities. On the other hand, gods enjoyed a wider range of activities. Thus Zeus and Apollo are examples of male deities who function as rulers, intellectuals, judges, warriors, fathers, and sexual partners in both homosexual and heterosexual affairs. These gods may engage in any activity available to mortal males. Among the gods there are no virgins, and sexual promiscuity—including rape—was never cause for censure even among the married ones.

In contrast, three of the five Olympian goddesses are virgins. Athena is warrior, judge, and giver of wisdom, but she is masculinized and denied sexual activity and motherhood. Artemis is huntress and warrior, but also a virgin. Hestia is respected as an old maid. The two nonvirginal goddesses come off no better: Aphrodite is pure sexual love, exercised with a pronounced irresponsibility. Hera is wife, mother, and powerful queen, but she must remain faithful and suffer the promiscuity of her husband.

The goddesses are archetypal images of human females, as envisioned by males. The distribution of desirable characteristics among a number of females rather than their concentration in one being is appropriate to a patriarchal society. The dictum of Pseudo-Demosthenes in the fourth century B.C. expresses this ideal among mortals: "We have mistresses for our enjoyment, concubines to serve our person, and wives for the bearing of legitimate offspring." [11] In reality, in any era only a wealthy man could afford to surround himself with a number of women, each playing a different role in his life. However, the Olympian pattern survived as the ideal.

A fully realized female tends to engender anxiety in the insecure male. Unable to cope with a multiplicity of powers united in one female, men from antiquity to the present have envisioned women in "either-or" roles. As a corollary of this anxiety, virginal females are considered helpful, while sexually mature women like Hera are destructive and evil. The fact that modern women are frustrated by being forced to choose between being an Athena—an intellectual, asexual career woman—or an Aphrodite—a frivolous sex object—or a respectable wife-mother like Hera shows that the Greek goddesses continue to be archetypes of female existence. If the characteristics of the major goddesses were combined, a whole being with unlimited potential for development—a female equivalent of Zeus or Apollo—would emerge.

In spite of their specialized functions, goddesses were very active in a wide range of human affairs. But the careers of goddesses do not reflect a less-limited scope for women, at least in historical times. Except for those outside the pale of respectability, the lives of mortal women were circumscribed by domesticity. Goddesses, on the other hand, even if married, were not constrained by familial obligations: Hera defied her husband and Aphrodite ignored hers. The other major goddesses chose not to marry at all. Certainly few mortal women would have made—or even been offered—such a choice. This does not mean that goddesses had nothing at all to do with mortal women. In discussing the relationships of goddesses to mortal females, myth must be distinguished from cult. Myths represent goddesses as hostile to women, or show them pursuing many activities foreign to the experience of mortal women. In cult, on the other hand—that is, in the ceremonial veneration of these divinities by women—attention is paid both to the fulfillment of women's needs and to the delineation of their proper roles in society. Thus, for women, Athena's patronage of weaving, Hera's of marriage, and Artemis' of childbirth were of supreme importance, but these qualities are not emphasized in myth. Some of the cults in which women participated will be described in Chapters IV and X.

## *Immortals and Mortals: Patterns of Interaction*

Both Olympian and lesser goddesses had relationships with mortal men, which could be either erotic or inspirational. In the case of erotic affairs, such as Aphrodite had with Anchises and Adonis or Circe and Calypso had with Odysseus, the gods become jealous and sometimes take revenge. Thus Zeus killed Iasion by lightning in punishment for his affair with Demeter; Tithonus was awarded immortality without eternal youth for his affair with Aurora; and Adonis, who was loved by Aphrodite, was killed by either Hephaestus or Ares. In such cases one can discern the double standard among the immortals: immortal females are expected to fornicate with males of similar rank—that is, gods—while immortal males may enjoy females of the lower, or mortal, status. Similarly among their human counterparts, a man had sexual access to a legitimate wife as well as to the female slaves in his household, while his wife was expected to be faithful to him.

When the relationship between a goddess and a mortal was inspirational or protective, we often find that the goddess was a virgin. Psychoanalytic criticism of classical literature suggests that the very fact of asexuality provides the reason for Athena's constructive and friendly relationships with most of the major Greek heroes, including Odysseus, Hercules, Perseus, Bellerophon, and Achilles. According to this theory, the fear of mature female sexuality meant that these men could feel secure only with a virgin. This idea is very tantalizing, and applicable to the Greek males' attitudes toward mortal women as well.

Ariadne, who helped Theseus slay the Minotaur; Medea, who aided Jason in his quest for the Golden Fleece; and Nausicaa, the advisor of Odysseus, were all virgins. Yet, when the relationships of another virgin goddess, Artemis, are examined, it becomes clear that virginity in itself is not the only significant factor in fostering the relationships of goddesses and mortals. Rather, personality and inclination lead Athena to be close and helpful to mortals, while her half-sister Artemis coolly maintains her distance.

The mature goddesses are less helpful to men than the virgins. Like Calypso and Circe, they are more likely to detain a hero through their sexual magic. Or, like the monstrous Harpies or Sirens, they may actually devour him. However, Hera guides Jason, and goddesses help their mortal sons. Thus Thetis helps Achilles at Troy, and Aphrodite aids Aeneas. With the exception of the rescue of Ariadne by Dionysus, we do not find the reverse situation of a male god going out of his way to aid a mortal female.

The relationships of male mortals and female immortals fared slightly better than those between gods and earthly women, possibly because the status of the mortals—frequently heroes—approached more closely that of the goddesses. Nevertheless, it is interesting to note that in these relationships, the female, being a divinity, remains dominant.

We only rarely find similar nonerotic relationships between male gods and female mortals. Most frequently, such relationships involve a sexual liaison terminating with the suffering or destruction of the woman and the birth of an extraordinary child.

Thus Zeus pays regular visits to Semele, a Theban princess, and has intercourse with her. When forced to reveal his identity to her, his fiery thunderbolts destroy her. She was then seven months pregnant. Zeus rescues the embryo and sews it into his thigh. Two months later, the god Dionysus is born from Zeus. Similarly, Zeus impregnates Danaë with his golden rain and she gives birth to the hero Perseus. Other offspring produced by Zeus's affairs with mortal women include Hercules, born of Alcmene; Helen and Pollux, born of Leda; and Epaphus, born of Io. Io's suffering, due to the jealousy of Hera, is so severe that the female chorus of Aeschylus' *Prometheus Bound* was led to pray that Zeus may never take a fancy to any of them.[12] In studying other male gods, it becomes evident that Zeus's role as a fertility god was not the only reason for his multiple liaisons, but rather that patriarchal mores condoned the male god's exploitation of females.

Apollo's amatory adventures with human females—and males as well—are even more destructive than those of his father Zeus, for he is not only lustful but vengeful as well. To win Cassandra and Sibyl, Apollo offers both women the gift of prophecy. When they continue to refuse his advances, he punishes Cassandra by causing her prophecies to be always disbelieved, and Sibyl by making her immortal without granting her eternal youth. Daphne, who may have been immortal herself, actually escapes from Apollo's lust by being metamorphosed into a laurel tree. Cassandra, Sibyl, and Daphne are all destroyed by Apollo's attention. But looking at their fate from another point of view, these women, like Athena and Artemis, refused to yield to a male and attained a triumph of self-assertion.

Apollo's actual seduction and betrayal of Creusa causes the child of the union to reflect that the gods maintain a lower standard of morality than mortals.[13] Coronis, while pregnant by Apollo, has an affair with a mortal. When her divine lover learns of her infidelity, he sends his sister Artemis to kill her. He rescues his unborn son Asclepius from the corpse of Coronis on the pyre. Apollo, otherwise renowned for his rationality and moderation, loses these qualities when rebuffed by women.

Analysis of the amours between gods and mortal women reveals the vulnerability of the woman; the wretched helplessness of the unwed mother; the glory awarded her, sometimes posthumously, for bearing a divine child; and the passivity of the woman in that she never enticed or seduced the god but instead was the victim of his spontaneous lust. Poseidon was not as active a lover of mortal women as his brother Zeus, but the sole divine exception to male dominance and exploitation of mortal females was Dionysus. After Ariadne, the Cretan princess, has been seduced and abandoned by Theseus on the island of Naxos, Dionysus rescues her, marries her, and remains a faithful husband. Dionysus, of course, was a popular rather than an aristocratic god.

The two gods most frequently involved in sexual liaisons with mortal women were Zeus and Apollo, the most powerful figures in the Greek pantheon. But the discrepancy between the status of male and female partner had led to the exploitation and destruction of the powerless by the powerful.

The endless catalogue of rape in Greek myth includes some merely attempted and other fully consummated attacks of gods not only on mortal women, but also on goddesses. The grim picture, one would presume, was painted by men. But the erotic fantasies of modern women give us another perspective from which to view the rape myths. According to current psychology, women frequently enjoy the fantasy of being overpowered, carried away, and forced to submit to an ardent lover. Helene Deutsch claims that such erotic images are but another indication of the innate masochism of women. Karen Horney agrees that these fantasies are a symptom of masochism, but adds that the fantasies, like the masochism, are the result of women's repression by society. We will never know whether Greek women dreamed of being Leda enfolded in the soft, warm caress of Zeus, or flattered themselves that they were as desirable as Europa, who was carried off by a most intriguing Zeus—masquerading as a bull. Perhaps they alleviated their anxieties by fantasizing that, like Danaë, they avoided suffering penetration and were impregnated by a golden shower; or perhaps they freed themselves from the guilt attendant on an adultery fantasy by imagining that they were Alcmene, and innocently accepted Zeus as a lover because the king of the gods had disguised himself as their husband.

There are a few instances of erotic relationships between mortal men and gods. The story of Ganymede, who caught the fancy of Zeus, has a happy ending, for the boy ends up on Olympus as the cupbearer of the gods. Hyacinthus, on the other hand, is loved by

Apollo and by Zephyrus. Apollo accidentally slays his beloved with a discus which Zephyrus jealously directs against the boy. There is little to conclude from so few examples except that the existence of sexual attraction between males was recognized in myth. Other than the stories about the Amazons, there are no classical myths alluding to female homoerotic associations.

## Mother Goddesses

The inspirational, nurturant, and sexual relationships of some goddesses with mortal men may be reminiscent of the tradition of mother goddess and male consort. Mother goddesses were prominent in the Bronze Age cults of Minoan Crete. Numerous statuettes from the Bronze Age and earlier periods that may represent the mother goddesses and their worshipers or priestesses have been found. Minoan statuettes of females wearing flounced skirts and blouses revealing the breasts, as well as fresco painting of the period, allude to the primacy of the female in the religious sphere. Mother goddesses appear later in Greek myth as Ge, Rhea, Hera, Demeter, and Cybele. These goddesses were primarily fertility powers, the fertility of the female being associated with agricultural productivity.

It has been thought that fertility goddesses were worshiped in Crete as well as by an autochthonous matriarchal population on the mainland of pre-Bronze Age Greece.[14] Greek-speaking invaders brought with them the worship of Zeus, with its emphasis on male dominance and patriarchal law. The invaders, to consolidate their conquests, married their gods to the native goddesses. The numerous sexual liaisons of Zeus have been interpreted as attempts to unite the worship of the invading god with the cults of the female divinities of the native population. The male-female tension in Greek myth, manifest at its most trivial level in the frequent bickering between Hera and Zeus, can be explained as the result of a forced marriage between the conquering god and a formerly powerful but vanquished goddess. Their marriage was not modeled on human marriage. As described by Homer, the relationships of Hector and Andromache, Hecuba and Priam, and Alcinous and Arete were far more tranquil than that of Zeus and Hera.[15]

The existence of the mother goddess in prehistory has been

seriously challenged by scholars in recent years. In a study of anthropomorphic figurines from late neolithic Crete—the period postulated for the dominance of the mother goddess—it was discovered that 37.3 per cent were female, 9.2 per cent male, 40.7 per cent sexless, and 12.8 per cent indeterminate.[16] Some scholars claim that to attempt to connect a hypothetical earth mother of prehistory to mother goddesses of classical mythology is fallacious. Modern anthropology has also demonstrated that anthropomorphic figurines can serve a wide variety of functions, and that female figurines emphasizing buttocks and breasts in ways similar to prehistoric figurines can be used for pubertal rites, rather than as representations of goddesses.

While some steatopygous neolithic figures, particularly those from Çatal Hüyük in Anatolia, emphasize the sexual features of the female, those from the western Mediterranean do appear to stress her fatness in a comforting teddy-bear fashion. Perhaps hunger was more of a concern than sexuality in the latter case. The historian Moses Finley concludes that the primacy of the mother goddess is only a "remarkable fable," and unequivocally attacks the notion of female dominance in prehistory.[17] Yet the mother goddess theory and its corollary—that female dominance in religion may indicate a feminine force in other spheres of a society—continue to find some support.[18]

Jungian psychology transfers the theory of the mother goddess from the realm of objective historical existence to the sphere of the psychic development of the individual. Erich Neumann, a disciple of Jung, analyzing ancient mythology in terms of modern psychology, considers that the mother goddess is an archetypal figure, dominating the ego of the child, who, in turn, experiences the world of his youth as a matriarchy.[19] According to Neumann, the Great Mother can be a good mother, giving food and nurture to the child, but she can also be a devouring, seductive, and castrating mother, evoking retributive hostility in the child. These speculations belong to the realm of modern psychology rather than to classical studies or ancient history. The Great Mother, viewed by a modern Jungian, may well be an appropriate archetype in the evolution of the individual consciousness. But the archetypes of the masculine intellectual goddess, or the huntress, or the mature woman whose guardian yields to her preference not to wed, imply nothing about the existence of a flesh-and-blood Athena, Artemis, or Hestia in antiquity.

Accordingly, a historian could only very cautiously and tentatively attempt to interpret prehistory—a time for which we know very little about family organization or social systems—in Jungian terms. On the other hand, the notion that the Great Mother is also a subjective archetype does not eliminate the possibility that she may have played an important role in communal cults in prehistory.

Modern feminists find the theory of female dominance in religion as well as in other areas of prehistoric culture attractive, as though what had happened in the past could be repeated in the future. This popular view is understandable, since, if women were not subordinate in the past, we have *ipso facto* proof that they are not so by nature. Therefore, the question of the role of females both divine and mortal in prehistory has become an emotional issue with political implications as well as a topic of scholarly debate.

For the classical scholar, the mother goddess theory provides a convenient, if unprovable, explanation of the following puzzles: Why are there more than four times as many neolithic female figurines as male ones? Why do females predominate in Minoan frescoes? Why does Hesiod describe earlier generations of divinities as female-dominated, while the last generation, the Olympian, is male-dominated? However, to use the mother goddess theory to draw any conclusions regarding the high status of human females of the time would be foolhardy.[20] Later religions, in particular Christianity, have demonstrated that the mother may be worshiped in societies where male dominance and even misogyny are rampant.

If Moses Finley and others of his opinion are correct, and it is impossible to draw any conclusions about social systems in prehistory in the absence of written documents from the time or with the archaeological evidence now available, then we must recognize that it is as foolish to postulate masculine dominance in prehistory as to postulate female dominance. The impartial scholar will be forced to confess that the question is open and may never be answered.

# II

## WOMEN IN THE BRONZE AGE
## AND HOMERIC EPIC

> Certainly there is no cause to blame Trojans and well-greaved
> Achaeans if they endure lengthy hardships for such a woman. In her
> face she is amazingly like the immortal goddesses. Still, even though
> she is like this, let her return in the ships, and not stay here as a plague
> to us and our descendants.[1]

THESE ARE the sentiments of the Trojan elders about the beautiful
Greek queen Helen, in the tenth year of a war in which many of their
sons had been killed and which was to culminate in the destruction
of their city. The epic poem—the *Iliad*—from which this passage is
taken is the earliest extant work of European literature; the dramatic
date is 1184 B.C., the later Bronze Age. Without a doubt, there is no
period in Greek history for which our evidence of the experience of
women is more fascinating or as contradictory.

Bronze Age societies are reflected in an oral tradition of epic
poems sung by illiterate bards. Succeeding generations of poets
preserved the basic outline and formulaic vocabulary of the epics,
but each gave his own flavor to the retelling. Thus, through the ages,
the traditional elements of the epics have not only been preserved,
but have also taken on the values, mores, and biases of each generation of poets. As far as women are concerned, this ahistorical oral
tradition has produced a rich portrait—though filled with inconsistencies.

There were many epic cycles about the Bronze Age, several of which served as the bases for tragedies, histories, and other literature written by later Greek authors. Tradition tells us that a blind bard of exceptional talent, Homer, who was familiar with the legends surrounding the capture of Troy and the return of the victorious Greek heroes, shaped the tales into the monumental epics known as the *Iliad* and the *Odyssey*. Homer himself was illiterate. According to the most plausible theory, he worked in the eighth century B.C.; his poems continued to be transmitted orally by bards from generation to generation until sometime in the sixth century B.C. when they were set down in written form. Although the vagaries of the transmission of these epics need not concern us here, it should be remembered that, because they were oral documents, the *Iliad* and the *Odyssey* cannot profitably be regarded as accurate histories of the late Bronze Age. They are ultimately poetic legends derived from the actual historical event of the capture of Troy, but they are also poetic reflections of the evolving societies and cultures of Greece.

## The Royal Woman of Greece and Troy

Of course, the personage of Helen stands apart in the Trojan epic—the most beautiful woman in the world, for whom a war was fought. But the Bronze Age legends are pervaded with powerful female figures,[2] such as Clytemnestra, Hecuba, Andromache, and Penelope, who figure prominently in the war between Greece and Troy. Among the Greek queens are Helen, her sister Clytemnestra, and Penelope. Similar themes can be traced in the lives of all three. They were all married: Helen to Menelaus in Sparta, Clytemnestra to Menelaus' brother Agamemnon in Mycenae, and Penelope to Odysseus in Ithaca. Helen abandoned Menelaus and sailed off with the handsome Trojan prince Paris. Led by Agamemnon, the Greeks made war against the Trojans for ten years in order to punish them, and also to bring Helen back.

This is the traditional explanation for the war, based on the apparently fictional belief that Helen's father had made all her suitors, before they were even allowed to woo her promise to bring her back should she ever be stolen. But Greek historians of the Classical period found it incredible that men would fight a protracted war over a woman—even if she were the most beautiful woman in the world. Herodotus, writing in the fifth century B.C., contended that the Trojans would not have been so foolish as to fight ten years for the sake of a foreign woman. Following an alternative lyric tradition, found in the work of Stesichorus, a poet of the mid-sixth century B.C., Herodotus suggested that Helen was not present in Troy at all, but rather in Egypt, and that the besieging Greeks would not be dissuaded by the Trojans' protests that Helen was not within their walls.[3] Likewise, Thucydides in the fifth century B.C.—generally a period of depressed prestige for Greek women—did not recognize that marriage to a woman like Helen might have had political and economic implications. He rejected the story that the loss of Helen was the primary cause of the war and took the position that the Greeks fought the Trojans to extend their political and economic domination over the eastern Mediterranean world.[4]

Though a definitive analysis of the causes of the Trojan War is impossible from this vantage point, the significance of Helen and the other royal women of the Bronze Age in the popular mind—transmitted through the centuries as integral elements of the epic tradition—is undeniable. But the dramatic importance and emotional influence of women should not at all be mistaken for evidence of their equality; the political power of even the queens of ancient Greece was a sometimes transient, nearly always double-edged blessing.

## Motives for Marriage

Heroic Greek society differed from that of later periods in many interesting ways, which in turn shaped the roles of women within the society. Politically, the major concern of that time was defense: military preparedness and strength were vital for survival. Men served their families and citadels as warriors; women were expected to bear and rear future warriors. Thus heroic Greek society demanded that all mature women be married, and destined all young women for that end. In the *Odyssey*, upon meeting the princess Nausicaa, who is of marriageable age, Odysseus almost immediately expresses the polite wish that she find a husband and enjoy a harmonious marriage.[5]

Marriages could serve as links between powerful families. In the case of a marriage between residents of different localities, where the couple would live was determined by tradition and by a complex variety of economic, political, and military considerations which took into account the advantages to both parties to the marriage agreement. Thus the two patterns of marriage, which coexisted, were the patrilocal and the matrilocal.

In the patrilocal pattern the suitor brought back a bride to his own house, and the bride was used as a bridge in a new alliance between the houses of her husband and of her father. Brides were not purchased by grooms, but gifts were customarily exchanged on the occasion of a wedding. Hence Penelope's father and brothers urged her to marry the suitor who presented the most gifts.[6] Marriage by capture was a variant of patrilocal marriage. For instance, Briseis was enslaved during the Trojan War and became the property of Achilles. He referred to her as his "bedmate," but she was led to expect to celebrate a ceremony of legal marriage with him when the couple returned to Achilles' home in Greece.[7]

In the matrilocal pattern it was often a roving warrior who married a princess and settled down in her kingdom. The husband was attracted by the expectation of inheriting his bride's father's realm; hence the succession to the throne in this case was matrilineal. Sometimes fathers gave their daughters in marriage to notable warriors to obtain them as allies. Achilles boasted that he had his choice among the daughters of many Greek chieftains.[8] Since the prize was the kingdom, the princess' father often held a contest for her hand, thereby assuring himself that he found the strongest or most clever son-in-law. Thus Odysseus participated in athletic competitions with the young men of Scheria for the hand of the princess Nausicaa—although he ultimately rejected her; Penelope herself decided to marry the victor of the contest of the bow; and Neleus arranged a prenuptial contest for the hand of his daughter.[9]

In other Bronze Age sagas not narrated by Homer, the marriages of Hippodamia, Atalanta, and Jocasta also illustrate matrilineal succession to the throne. Pelops won the hand of Hippodamia by defeating and killing her father in a chariot race. Similarly, Atalanta married Hippomenes when he defeated her in a footrace. Jocasta married Oedipus when he successfully competed in the prenuptial ordeal of finding the answer to the riddle of the sphinx, demonstrating he had the excellence necessary to defend the royal house.

Marriage by capture or by contest were clearly two patterns in which the bride's wishes could not be consulted. Homer does not usually indicate the bride's views, but it was implied that Nausicaa would have some choice in the selection of her husband;[10] and despite the attempts of her male relatives to influence her, Penelope retained the prerogative of choosing among her suitors, or of not remarrying at all. Clytemnestra and Helen freely chose to abandon Agamemnon and Menelaus, and their subsequent marriages to new husbands were regarded as genuine.

Though free choice of husbands was not always a part of Greek marriage customs, the matrilineal and matrilocal pattern of marriage did give the woman the benefit of remaining within the strongly supportive environment of her close relatives and friends, while her husband was essentially an alien. Moreover, the woman who became queen in her father's land would seem to have been in a strong position compared to her brothers. There are alternative versions of many of our succession myths, but if we accept the stories that show that the throne could pass to the warrior who marries the princess of the realm despite the presence of her brothers—e.g., Helen had two brothers, Jocasta one, and Nausicaa several—we are led to suppose that the princess was a person of prestige not only to her husband but to her brothers. Familial blood ties figure prominently in many of the ancient epics. The power of the mother's brother and the close bond between brother and sister—common features of matrilineal societies—appear most significantly in the Oedipus myth. Jocasta's brother Creon ruled as regent between his sister's marriages, and Antigone, daughter of Jocasta and Oedipus, risked her life because of her affection for her brother.

## Husbands and Wives in Homer

Knowledge of the marriage patterns prevalent in Bronze Age Greece allows us to return to the Homeric epics better prepared to understand the social and political functions that marriage and women as wives served in that age. For instance, the marriage of Menelaus and Helen was matrilocal and matrilineal. Since Menelaus is red-haired in Homer, it is evident that he was a northerner, while Helen was the daughter of Tyndareus, the reigning king of Sparta. Helen was the most beautiful woman in the world, and Menelaus naturally was insulted that she preferred Paris to him. However, we can be fairly certain—knowing the political stakes of a matrilineal marriage—that the Trojan War was provoked by more than Menelaus' personal jealousy. Since Menelaus was king by virtue of his position as Helen's husband, he might lose the throne if he lost her. Therefore he refused to accept the validity of her change in husbands and determined to recover her, as the essential prerequisite to his claim to the throne of Sparta. When Troy was captured, Menelaus could not take vengeance on Helen, although she had behaved treacherously toward the Greeks. Thus Helen, who was responsible for the war, ironically suffered the least. We meet her again in the *Odyssey* enjoying a mature married life with Menelaus. But Homer tells us that she knew of drugs that would cause men to forget pain. These potions, along with her fabulous beauty, must have been useful in regaining the favor of her original husband.

A similar pattern may be observed in the case of Helen's sister Clytemnestra. When her husband Agamemnon went to Troy, he left Clytemnestra in the care of a herald. Incensed because Agamemnon had slaughtered their oldest daughter Iphigenia as a requisite sacrifice for the expedition against Troy, she got rid of the herald and took Agamemnon's cousin Aegisthus as a new husband. Homer, in a formulaic passage, reports that "Aegisthus took her off to his own house," but all the stories show them living together in the palace. When Agamemnon returned from Troy, they killed him, and Aegisthus, as Clytemnestra's husband, became king.

On the other hand, Penelope's marriage to Odysseus was patrilocal. She remained faithful to her husband for twenty years, but was besieged by suitors as though she were a prisoner in her house. Odysseus' aged father was powerless, his mother had died, Penelope's male relatives were not near at hand, and her son was immature. The plight of Penelope and Telemachus in the absence of a man of heroic stature in the house to defend them is comparable to the wretched widowhood envisioned by Hector's wife Andromache. Andromache also married in a patrilocal arrangement and was stranded after Hector died. When she laments her husband's death, she compares the life of her son to that of a boy whose parents are still living.[11] Evidently "parents" really means father, for without a father the son loses his friends, his share in the men's banquets, and the lands he stands to inherit.

Homer's attitude toward women as wives is obvious in his regard for Penelope and Clytemnestra. Penelope wins the highest admiration for her chastity, while Homer entrusts the ghost of Agamemnon to describe Clytemnestra's infidelity in reproachful terms. Even the virtuous members of the sex are to be forever sullied by Clytemnestra's sin.[12] This generalization is the first in a long history of hostility toward women in Western literature.

However, it is by no means certain that Homer's judgments on Clytemnestra and Penelope reflect the attitude of Bronze Age Greece in general toward women. Above all, the Bronze Age citadel was in constant need of defense against raids and conquest, and in the politically unstable climate of society a heroic leader was requisite for its survival.[13] The citadel of Mycenae under the rule of Clytemnestra and Aegisthus was far more secure than Ithaca in the hands of Penelope alone. Odysseus, whose intelligence prompted him to resist joining the Trojan expedition, returned from the war to find his palace in chaos, most of his slaves unfaithful, and his possessions depleted.

The problem of strong, effective leadership brings up the intriguing question of matriarchy during the Bronze Age. Although the two concepts are distinct, ever since the influential writing of the social philosopher John Jacob Bachofen in the nineteenth century matriarchy has often—and wrongly—been associated with matriliny. Matriarchy can be loosely defined to cover a fairly wide range of situations—from that in which women dominate men outright to a more or less egalitarian relationship between the sexes. Because of the aristocratic bias of Greek epic, the only formal marriages that we can consider occur between kings and queens, and within the Homeric epics there are only two instances where matriarchy seems possible. In the kingdom of Scheria, Nausicaa, in her determination to help Odysseus, advises him to approach and supplicate her mother Arete before he goes to her father, the king.[14] In the subsequent narrative it is apparent that Arete exercises considerable power, giving judgments to the people and taking measures concerning Odysseus. No doubt in peaceful societies like that of Scheria, women might have exercised more influence than in a besieged city, where martial prowess was a more significant quality of leadership for the survival of a group. Still, even Arete's prestige is only noteworthy when compared with "other women who keep house subordinate to their husbands." [15]

Another place where the queen may exercise power greater than or equal to that of the king is in the home town of Andromache, Thebe under Place. Andromache's mother was said to rule (*basileuō*), although her father was also said to have been lord (*anassō*).[16] Tablets from Mycenean Greece refer to a great king as *anax,* while a subordinate ruler is called *basileus.* On the other hand, Homer does use the verb *basileuō* to describe ruling by kings in other instances. Just possibly we have here a conflict between a tradition reporting the reign of a queen, and an addition by a poet who could not conceive of a female ruling a city. Yet, whether the example of a powerful queen like Arete or Andromache's mother had any implications for other women in the domain is simply not known. No one would call Renaissance Britain a matriarchy just because of the reigns of Mary Stuart, Mary Tudor, and Elizabeth. Accordingly, the question of Bronze Age matriarchy remains the subject of tantalizing speculation.

Concern for the continuity of strong leadership probably contributed to the decline in matriliny by the end of the Bronze Age. Menelaus, for example, insisted on a male heir even though he already had a legitimate daughter. The succession in Ithaca was also ambiguous. Penelope's suitors originally sought to marry her and succeed to Odysseus' place as king. However, when Telemachus matured the suitors' intent changed: they began to speak of either taking Penelope back to their own palaces or challenging Telemachus directly to assert his right to his father's title and possessions.

A special pattern of matriliny occurs in the Greek epics—that of heroes who trace their descent through the union of a mortal woman with a god. In reality, the custom may have served the social function of legitimizing the offspring of extramarital relationships—a necessary response to the moral fluidity and personal autonomy characteristic of the age. The best-known Homeric example is Sarpedon, the child of Laodamia and Zeus. Many gods had offspring, and in general it appears that women of heroic status could have children outside of marriage and claim a god as the father. But that they might simply not be believed is shown in the non-Homeric myth describing the scorn heaped on the unwed Semele when she was pregnant with Dionysus, even though she claimed Zeus as her child's father.

## Amazons: Women as Warriors

Matriarchal societies—in the sense of totally female, rather than female-dominated, societies—are described in Greek literature and art of all periods. The Amazons, a group of warrior women, were said to live in northern Anatolia, or even farther east in the barbarian world. One explanation of their name is that it is derived from *a* (without) *mazos* (breast). According to this fanciful etymology, they cut off their right breasts in order to draw their bows more easily. They resorted to men of neighboring tribes for sexual intercourse. Females were reared, but male children were sent away, or crippled to be used as servants. Many Bronze Age heroes are said to have fought against them, in all cases successfully. Achilles slew the Amazon queen Penthesilea, who had come to Troy as Priam's ally. Bellerophon and Priam fought against them once.[17] One of Hercules' labors was to obtain the girdle of an Amazon queen. The Athenian hero Theseus similarly had to campaign against and vanquish the Amazons. According to Plutarch's *Life of Theseus,* the Amazons even followed Theseus to Athens and engaged him in battle. Theseus married one of their queens (either Antiope or Hippolyte), but slew her when she became enraged at his plan to discard her in favor of a new marriage to Phaedra.

Whether the Amazons had a historical existence is unprovable. It appears not to be beyond the realm of possibility that exclusively female societies existed. Herodotus relates that the Amazons succumbed to the Scythians, whose historical reality has never been questioned, and that the Amazons and Scythians together thus became the ancestors of the Sauromatae. The Amazons yielded to the Scythians partially because they preferred sex to victory. Herodotus adds the interesting detail that the women were able to learn the language of the men, but the men could not understand the Amazons' language.[18]

On the other hand, the fact that many Greek heroes had to test their strength against them leads one to suspect that the Amazons could have been either a totally mythical fiction or a group whose eccentricities inspired many false tales. Thus we find that Alexander the Great consorted with an Amazon, and that even in the twelfth century A.D. Adam of Bremen was still writing about Amazons living in the East.

Amazons appear frequently in the visual arts, where they are shown in short tunics of the type worn by the goddess Artemis, or in loose Oriental trousers, sometimes with one breast bare but never with one missing. [Plate 1] The figure of the Amazon was an idiom through which the Greek artist could portray young athletic females without offending sensibilities by suggesting they were Greeks.

There are many representations of battles of Greeks against Amazons, called amazonomachies, scattered throughout the Greek world. Often, as on the Parthenon metopes, an amazonomachy is paired with a sculptural representation of a battle of Greeks against Centaurs. The Centaurs were lustful creatures with the heads of men and the bodies of horses. There were, practically speaking, only male Centaurs, but no females, at least until the fourth century. Perhaps the Greek mind, with its penchant for combining symmetry and alternatives, may have fictionalized the two groups, the Centaurs male and lustful, the Amazons female and chaste.

Another exclusively female society supposedly existed for a brief period in the Bronze Age on the island of Lemnos. The Lemnian women had been shunned by their husbands because they were cursed with an offensive odor. With the sole exception of Hypsipyle's rescue of her father, the women killed every man on the island in one night. They welcomed the Argonauts, who were passing through, and bore many children to repopulate the island. Like some Amazons, the Lemnian women were so delighted by the Greek heroes that they tried to detain them. However, the Argonauts ranked duty above pleasure, and continued their quest for the Golden Fleece.

## Women in a Man's World

The society depicted by Homer and his comments upon it clearly reflect a strong system of patriarchal values, but the code of behavior is less rigid than in some later Greek societies. In an atmosphere of fierce competition among men, women were viewed symbolically and literally as properties—the prizes of contests and the spoils of conquest—and domination over them increased the male's prestige.

Women, free or slave, were valued for their beauty and accomplishments. Thus Agamemnon announced that he preferred Chryseis to Clytemnestra, for the slave girl was in no way inferior in figure, bodily stature, intelligence, and accomplishments.[19] We see that contests for valuable women provoked murderous quarrels among men.

Interestingly, it was a quarrel with Agamemnon over a valuable slave woman that precipitated Achilles' withdrawal from the fighting at Troy and provided the theme for the *Iliad.* The Trojan elders undeniably saw Helen as a worthy cause for fighting, though they recognized the cost of keeping her, while on the Greek side the loss of Helen spurred the soldiers not only to destroy the Trojans' city but also to savor the rape of their wives in requital.[20] In less monumental contests related by Homer, a skilled slave woman was offered as the prize in a footrace honoring Patroclus, and Eurymedousa was selected by the Phaeacians as a special trophy for King Alcinous.[21] In the sense of conquest, an extra measure of prestige accrued to the warrior who possessed a slave who was once the wife or daughter of a man of high status. Thus, after the fall of Troy, the women of the Trojan royal family were allotted as special prizes to the heroes of the Greek army.

Generally, when towns were conquered or raided, male prisoners were either ransomed by their relatives or put to death by the victors, but women and children were enslaved (in this context the ransoming of Andromache's mother was very unusual).[22] Hence there were large numbers of female slaves in the camp of the Greek army, who were brought home to serve their conquerors in Greece. The picture given by Homer is confirmed by Mycenaean tablets listing large numbers of women and children, sometimes with their places of origin.[23] The women and children are probably slaves, and males are recorded as sons of the women, indicating that they were born in an informal union. The fathers may have been male slaves, when such unions were countenanced by the owners. However, it is more likely that the fathers were free men who consorted with the slave women for pleasure.

The availability of slave women facilitated a sexual double standard in epic society. Kings were heads of patriarchal households which included slave concubines available for their own use or to be offered to itinerant warriors to earn their support. When Agamemnon returned to Clytemnestra after a ten-year absence, he fully expected her to welcome his concubine as well as himself. He had, moreover, kept at least one slave concubine in the camp at Troy. We are also told that Menelaus, desiring an heir, managed to father a son, Megapenthes, on a concubine. The fact that Laertes did not consort with his slaves from fear of his wife was considered worthy of comment: Laertes was partial to Eurycleia, but did not sleep with her because he feared his wife. However, Eurycleia must have given birth to a baby somehow, without incurring her master's displeasure.

for she became wetnurse to Laertes' son Odysseus, and in her old age remained on affectionate terms with Odysseus' family.[24]

Needless to say, women were not permitted the same sexual liberties as men. As we have noted, the infidelity of Helen and Clytemnestra produced critical political threats to their kingdoms. As is customary in patriarchy, the virginity of unmarried girls and their good reputations were prized possessions. Nausicaa slept with a handmaiden guarding her on either side, and Penelope and Nausicaa both took pains to avoid becoming the subject of gossip.[25] On the other hand, the penalties for the loss of virginity were not so severe as they were later to become in Greece. Homer mentions without criticism two girls who had illegitimate babies, claiming impregnation by immortals. The girls subsequently married heroes, with the usual honors.[26] A slave of either sex was actually the property of the master and was not permitted sexual relationships without the master's consent. This restriction was in force throughout antiquity. Thus it is not surprising that after Odysseus killed Penelope's suitors, he brutally executed twelve of his slave women who had been fornicating with them. Homer does not indicate that the slaves had any choice, but he does acknowledge that they could have feelings. The lamentation of Briseis at leaving Achilles for Agamemnon is famous. Less well known but equally interesting is the story of Phoinix's quarrel with his father. The father had fallen in love with a concubine, and Phoinix's mother urged Phoinix to have intercourse with the girl first so that she would detest the older man. He followed his mother's suggestion, and earned his father's curses.[27]

The same patriarchal structure that has been seen in the Greek royal families can be found among the Trojans, with some interesting minor variations. Women were monogamous, men were polygamous. King Priam had numerous wives and concubines, the foremost of whom was his wife Hecuba. In general, the offspring of concubines were free, but of lower status in the heroic hierarchy. We have noted, however, the efforts of Menelaus to bequeath his throne to his illegitimate son, since Helen had borne him only a daughter. But according to a tale told by Odysseus, an illegitimate son was allotted a smaller share of an inheritance than the sons of a freeborn wife.[28] The fate of illegitimate daughters is not specifically indicated, either in Greece or Troy.

Thus it is Hecuba's children—among them Hector, Paris, Troilus, Polyxena, and Cassandra—who play the leading roles in the Trojan myths. She had nineteen children, but Priam's household included a total of fifty sons, with their wives, in addition to his twelve daughters and their husbands. Here we may observe an interesting combination of matrilocal and patrilocal marriage.

The value of the son in the eyes of both parents, a primary symbolic feature of patriarchal society, is emphasized in both the *Iliad* and the *Odyssey*. Penelope's protectiveness of Telemachus is evident in her concern for his embarking on the dangerous voyage described at the beginning of the *Odyssey*. Similarly, she devised the contest of the bow when she began to suspect that her suitors were plotting against her son's life. But maturity requires a reversal of this protectiveness—Telemachus first asserted his manhood by ordering Penelope from the public rooms of the palace, also indicating to the suitors his intention to assert his claim to his father's throne.[29] The dependence of mothers on their sons' devotion to them is made clear elsewhere in Homer, as in Anticleia's statement that she died not of illness but of longing for her son Odysseus.[30] Hecuba displayed the depth of her love for her son Hector by baring her aged breasts in an attempt to dissuade him from entering battle, again when she entreated him to rest and refresh himself, and vengefully when she expressed her wish to eat Achilles' liver after he had slain Hector.[31]

The strength of father–son relationships is clear, for example, in the immediate rapport that develops between Telemachus and Odysseus upon the latter's return to Ithaca, even though they have not seen each other for twenty years. More brutally, the affinity between father and son receives Homer's praise even in the case of Orestes, who avenged his father's death by killing his mother.[32] On the other hand, relationships between parents and their female progeny, for example between Nausicaa and her parents or Priam and Hecuba and their daughters, show less dependence of the elder generation on the younger.

Although women suffered disabilities under the patriarchal code, they were not considered inferior or incompetent in the Homeric epic. When Agamemnon and Odysseus sailed to Troy, they had no qualms about leaving their wives to manage their kingdoms in their absence, although Agamemnon did leave a herald to look after Clytemnestra. Likewise, in Scheria, Queen Arete gave judgments to the people, and her opinions were heeded. Hector was concerned by what the Trojan women would think of him, since his overambitious strategy had resulted in heavy casualties.[33] Yet the dependency of women on men is unequivocally stated. Penelope's need for Odysseus and her feeling that she has been besieged by the suitors in her own house are poignantly expressed when Homer compares her feelings on being reunited with Odysseus to the sensation of a shipwrecked person upon viewing land.[34] This simile is a dramatic indication that Odysseus, though shipwrecked literally, has been more comfortable on his travels than Penelope has been at home with her suitors.

In Troy we see women in a besieged city and in an army camp, certainly a situation where women would be dependent on their warrior sons and husbands, and on other male protectors. Andromache and Briseis declare their dependence on Hector and Achilles as complete because of the deaths of all other members of their families.[35] Andromache begs her husband not to make her a widow and wishes to die after Hector's death. Yet Andromache reveals her strength, independence, and competence when she actually offers Hector some practical advice on military strategy. She tells Hector to draw up the Trojan troops near the fig tree, where the walls were weakest and where, it had been prophesied, the enemy would break through. Hector, however, reminds Andromache that war is the business of men, and that she should go back to her house and work on the loom.[36] Hector was not insulting Andromache but stating a fundamental fact about the separation of male and female spheres in antiquity.

## Daily Life in the Bronze Age

In their daily lives, royal women and female slaves were engaged in similar tasks, the significant distinction being that royal women worked of their own volition, while slaves worked under compulsion. The distinction between free men and male slaves is more definitely demarcated: free men may engage in the same chores as slaves, but only free men carry weapons and defend their cities. The duties of women revolve around the household. The Homeric epithet "white-armed" and Bronze Age frescoes that show women with white skin and males with suntanned flesh both testify to the indoor orientation of women's work. The lady of the house managed the household. The households of Alcinous and Odysseus had many female slaves.[37] There was a much smaller number of male slaves, and these worked outdoors. All food was prepared in the house by slave women and served by them.

Clothing was made, from start to finish, in the home, and in this task royal women and even immortals were engaged, as well as slave women. Mature women customarily sat by the hearth as they wove or spun. The hearth was in the center of the main room of the house. Thus, as the obvious examples of the Homeric queens Helen, Penelope, and Arete indicate, sitting by the hearth meant that a woman was totally involved in whatever was happening in her entire household. It is quite common to find a royal woman weaving while entertaining her guests, much as women today knit or embroider in public. In some instances, the ceaseless weaving acquires a magical quality, as though the women were designing the fate of men. Arete, though a queen, was able to recognize that clothing worn by Odysseus had been made in her own household.[38] The Nausicaa episode demonstrates that even a princess considered the laundering of clothes an obligation as well as an accomplishment that would earn praise.

Women were also in charge of bathing and anointing men. Homer's lack of prudishness is nowhere more obvious, for this task was not reserved to slave women, nor to females like Calypso who were intimate with the men they bathed. Polycaste, Nestor's virginal young daughter, bathed Telemachus and massaged him with olive oil, and Helen relates that at Troy she herself had bathed and anointed the disguised Odysseus.[39]

Independent historical evidence also bears testimony to the usual chores of Bronze Age women. Tablets from Pylos written in the Mycenaean Linear B script list among the tasks of women fetching water and furnishing baths, spinning, weaving, grinding corn, and reaping. They also tell us that the food allotment for men was two and a half times the ration of women.[40]

Compared with subsequent Greek literature, epic gives a generally attractive impression of the life of women. They were expected to be modest, but were not secluded. Andromache and Helen walk freely through the streets of Troy, though always with escorts, and women are shown on the shield of Achilles helping to defend a city's walls.[41] The rendezvous of a boy and girl outside the walls of Troy is referred to.[42] Wives, notably Helen, Arete, and Penelope, may remain within the public rooms in the presence of male guests without scandal. Not only concubines but legitimate wives are considered desirable, and there is little trace of the misogyny that taints later Greek literature.

# III

## THE DARK AGE
## AND THE ARCHAIC PERIOD

ANCIENT HISTORY comes to us in a haphazard succession of periods for which we have useful documentation interspersed with periods that remain obscure due to their dearth of written records. The art of writing disappeared at the close of the Bronze Age, with the fall of Mycenae; accordingly, there is little information available to us for the four centuries following the Trojan War (ca. 1200–800 B.C.), and the period has aptly become known as the Dark Age. What little knowledge we have is based on archaeological finds, on some passages from Homer which seem to date from this time, and on inferences from the literature of later periods.

By 800 B.C. writing had been reintroduced into the Greek world, by adapting the Phoenician alphabet to the requirements of the Greek language, though even for this Archaic period (800–500 B.C.) we have but fragmentary remains of the literature. However, our picture of this era is broadened somewhat by evidence from the visual arts, notably sculpture and vase painting.

Our scraps of information come from diverse sources spread over a wide geographical area, yet for each city we consistently know more about the aristocracy than about the lower classes. It would be foolhardy to draw more than the most tentative conclusions on the basis of this sketchy evidence, but there are noticeable similarities in the behavior of aristocrats in various cities.

Among the upper classes can be discerned the survival of attitudes and patterns of behavior that had been preeminent during the

Bronze Age. Sex roles where men are ideally warriors and women are childbearers received clear affirmation in the later periods, regardless of either specific locale or the diversity of social and political structures to be found throughout the Greek world. Thus, the role of women—because it was biologically determined—displayed a continuity throughout these obscure times, despite the upheavals that changed men's lives.

## Motives for Marriage in Unsettled Times

The pre-Classical period was a time of great change, characterized by class struggles and transformations in governmental patterns. The city-state (*polis*) as an institution was created during this era. Intramural animosities, as well as population pressure, caused the Greeks to found new cities or colonies on almost any unclaimed land around the Mediterranean.

A few women performed a rather mysterious function in the interests of colonization. Often the oracle of Apollo at Delphi was consulted on important matters, such as the undertaking of a colonizing expedition. The god Apollo spoke at Delphi through the medium of a prophetess called the Pythia. That a woman was the mouthpiece of a male deity may be explained by the hypothesis that Delphi was formerly the site of a female chthonic cult, although in historical times no woman but the Pythia was admitted to the temple. A male prophet put the questions to her. Her responses were delivered in a state of frenzy, and interpreted by male priests. Ironically then, although the Delphic oracle was supreme in Greece, the woman through whom the god communicated with mortal men served merely as a courier of sorts and had no direct influence on the meaning of the prophesies.[1]

The objectives of colonization during this time reveal that the Greeks' motives for foreign expeditions were no longer the same as those of the Argonauts and other Bronze Age adventurers whose sexual liaisons during their travels were limited to temporary amours with exotic foreign women. The goal of colonists during the later periods was to establish themselves and their descendants permanently in some far-off quarter, rather than merely to reap the spoils of foreign conquests and return with booty to their ancestral homes. Consequently, when colonizing expeditions were predominantly or totally male, the colonists were often forced to find wives among the native population.

One particularly violent episode is related by Herodotus: Athenian colonists did not bring women with them to Miletus, but rather seized the native Carian women and killed their male relatives outright. To revenge this homicide, the daughters of the abducted Carian women swore an oath that was passed down to their female descendants never to dine with their husbands or call them by name. Herodotus also reports the strange practice that developed between the male colonizers of Thera and their native wives at the time the city of Cyrene was founded: the husbands found that their wives had completely different tastes in food, so the men and women in that colony continued to maintain separate diets.[2]

The Bronze Age mores that judged marriage to be more important to the growth and the strengthening of the *polis* and the family than to the fulfillment of the individuals involved carried over into the pre-Classical periods in more ways than one. While some colonists in distant reaches of the expanding Greek world literally captured their wives by force, the upper classes in the established centers of power arranged marriages among sons and daughters to aggrandize their political and economic standing much as they had during the Bronze Age. After the mid-seventh century B.C. a number of Greek cities were ruled by extraconstitutional monarchs known as tyrants. Greek tyrants, aristocrats, and foreign rulers were linked by means of a complex matrix of dynastic marriages. This situation implies, of course, that the relationship between husband and wife in these cases did not supplant their relationships with blood relatives. Rather, the wife served primarily as a material bond between her father—and implicitly his political and economic power—and the power of her husband's family. The benefits of marriage were such that some tyrants were bigamous.[3]

Elements of Bronze Age prenuptial rivalry were preserved in the lively competition that was generated for the daughters of influential fathers. The extremes to which suitors went to prove their worth is illustrated in the stories surrounding the marriage of Agariste, daughter of Cleisthenes, who reigned as tyrant in Sicyon from 600 to 570 B.C. After Cleisthenes was victorious in the games at Olympia, he proclaimed that he would entertain suitors for his daughter's hand. Thirteen illustrious suitors from twelve cities entered the competition. Cleisthenes entertained the suitors for a year—they feasted as royally as the suitors of Penelope—and rated them according to their lineage, their manly virtues, their prowess at running and wrestling, their family connections, and other criteria. Hippoclides was chosen, but when he behaved in a ridiculous fashion by dancing at his betrothal feast, he was quickly replaced by Megacles, one of the Alcmaeonidae, a powerful Athenian family.[4] Thus the runner-up in the competition was suddenly elevated to the prized status and the marriage of Agariste was celebrated with due extravagance.

A few marriages in ruling families were influenced more by sentiment than by politics. Pisistratus arranged a marriage between his daughter and a young man who loved her so much that he kissed her when he happened to meet her on the street. The marriage of Periander, tyrant of Corinth, and Melissa was also an affair of the heart. Periander first caught sight of Melissa, daughter of the ruler of Epidaurus, when she was pouring wine for workmen in a field, wearing a revealing Dorian-style dress not covered by a cloak. (It is interesting to note that these two young daughters of tyrants were not kept secluded but in fact mingled with men: one on a city street, the other on a farm.) Periander married Melissa, but later in a fit of jealousy he murdered her. His passionate attachment was so strong that he had intercourse with her dead body. When her spirit returned and complained that she was cold and naked, since the clothes that had been buried with her had never been burned, Periander ordered all the women in Corinth to gather in the temple of Hera wearing their best clothing. He stripped them and burned the garments for Melissa.[5]

Women of wealth—even if they lacked prestigious fathers—were also desirable. In the latter part of the sixth century B.C., Theognis of Megara wrote: "Even the finest man does not mind marrying the bad daughter of a bad father, if he gives much wealth; nor does a woman refuse to be the bedmate of a bad but wealthy man, for she would rather be wealthy than good." [6]

## Dorian Women: Sparta and Gortyn

Because the law codes of Sparta and Gortyn, a city in Crete, were established relatively early, there is more written information about the lives of their women than there is for Athenian women in pre-Classical times. But much of our knowledge of the Spartans is derived from non-Spartan authors of later periods, who attempted to emphasize the difference between Dorian Sparta and Ionian Athens, and the role of women was an index of the contrast between the two ways of life.

The Spartan regime, developed in the seventh century B.C., was traditionally attributed to the lawgiver Lycurgus. This archaic code remained nominally unchanged throughout Spartan history.[7] Bearing children was the most important function of Spartan women, since the state was constantly at war and the production of warriors was of highest priority. Accordingly, the law of Lycurgus on burials forbade the inscription of the name of the deceased on a tomb except for a man who had died at war or a woman who had died in childbirth.[8] Because the biological role of the mother in reproduction was seen as at least as important as the role of the father, a program with a goal of physical fitness for girls was prescribed. Unlike the Athenian, the Spartan girls were as well nourished as the boys.[9] Housework and the fabrication of clothing were left to women of inferior classes, while citizen women were occupied with gymnastics, music, household management, and childrearing.

There is some doubt about whether the girls exercised in the nude. However, Spartan art of the Archaic period portrays the nude female body, while the art of other Greek cities does not.[10] Spartan women's dress was appropriate to their life style. They wore the Dorian *peplos,* with slit skirts which bared their thighs and permitted a freedom of movement impossible to women dressed in the voluminous Ionian *chiton.* Ancient opinions varied on whether their scanty costume encouraged chastity or licentiousness. Herodotus states that at one time all Greek women wore the Dorian dress, which was fastened at the shoulders with broochpins. However, the Athenian women once used these pins as weapons on a man who brought them news of their husbands' deaths, and were then punished by the men and forced to dress in the Ionian *chiton,* which, being stitched, did not require pins.[11]

In Sparta the interests of the community prevailed over those of private citizens. A newborn male was examined to determine if he would become a strong warrior. If he passed the test, he was permitted to live. All girls, apparently, were reared, for Plutarch reports that they were merely handed over immediately after birth to the care of the women.[12] The state had no interest in whether any child was born of the husband of its mother, so long as the father was a

Spartan citizen. But when at the end of the eighth century B.C. the Spartan men were absent on a campaign of long duration, the women resorted to intercourse with unfree men known as helots.[13] It may well be that the state encouraged relations with the helots so that there would be a new crop of young men if there were heavy casualties and the army did not return.[14] The children of these unions were euphemistically termed "children of unmarried mothers," but they were not recognized as Spartan citizens when the army did return home successful from the war. They were sent off to found the city of Tarentum.

Adultery was not as strictly defined as in some societies. Various Athenian writers report on wife-sharing among the Spartans, viewing extramarital relationships in terms of the husband's lending his wife to another man when that man needed an heir to his estate. The Athenians' interpretation of Spartan behavior may have been influenced by their own strictly monogamous society. It is difficult to believe that Spartan women, who were notoriously outspoken—so much so that there is an anthology of their witticisms attributed to Plutarch—passively submitted to being lent by their husbands as childbearers to others. While there is no firm evidence to confirm the hypothesis, I find it easier to believe that the women also initiated their own liaisons, whether purely for pleasure or because they accepted the society's valuation of childbearing. This would not have been difficult when a husband was off on a campaign. The Archaic Spartans may have actually had no particular interest in curtailing extramarital sexual unions, with the proviso that both partners be healthy Spartan citizens, since more frequent intercourse would tend to produce more children who were potential warriors.

Marriage was encouraged at Sparta as the most desirable basis for procreation, however, and bachelors were ridiculed and suffered legal disabilities. Spartan marriage customs were unusual among the Greeks, although the basic pattern was the familiar marriage by capture. One novel way this was accomplished was by shutting up young men and women in a dark room, each man leading home whichever woman he caught—sight unseen.[15] Another way, more frequently practiced, was for the groom to carry off his bride in secret. Here the marriage by capture was not a display of real force, but rather a symbolic enactment of a previous engagement. The bride was dressed for her wedding in man's clothing, with her hair cut short in a mannish style. Whether this transvestitism was to signify her entrance upon a wholly new way of life, or whether—as psychoanalytic interpretation would have it—the groom, accustomed to homosexual involvements in his army career, would find it easier to relate to his bride if she looked somewhat masculine, is uncertain. The husband went on living with his army group until the age of thirty and visited with his wife by stealth. Since Spartan youths were wed at eighteen, married couples did not live together for the first twelve years of their marriage. Lycurgus supposedly made this regulation so that when the couple were together they were never satiated, and their offspring were thought to be as vigorous as their desire. Spartan marriage, then, was a kind of trial marriage, the purpose being to determine whether the woman was capable of conceiving. If the bride did not become pregnant, the marriage— which was held in nearly complete secrecy—could be inconspicuously nullified without public dishonor. The fact of a trial marriage implies that the bride could marry again with the hope of proving her fertility with a different husband.

The simplicity and rigorousness of life in Sparta during the Archaic Age gradually gave way to a more relaxed and luxurious way of living. Greek and Roman writers tend to blame the women for this corruption of the earlier regime. Aristotle states that the Spartan women had never really accepted the laws of Lycurgus from the time of their first promulgation.[16] Women were not directly responsible for the declining vigor of Sparta after the Peloponnesian War, but they adapted readily to a less archaic and less demanding mode of life.

For women, abandoning the Lycurgan regime meant abdicating their role as child-producers.[17] Economic conditions in the society as a whole also encouraged individuals to limit the size of their families, for if the population increased, wealth would have to be divided into very small parcels. As a result of this change of attitude, the Spartan population began to dwindle after 479 B.C., and fell catastrophically in the fourth century B.C.[18]

The conspicuous prosperity of women while the state was floundering provoked criticism. Formerly women were not permitted to wear jewelry, cosmetics, perfume, or dyed clothing. By the fourth century B.C. they controlled by means of their dowries and inheritances two-fifths of the land and property in Sparta, and some spent their money on expensive racehorses and fancy clothing.

In the mid-third century B.C. King Agis attempted to restore the Lycurgan discipline. According to Plutarch, who gently disapproves of the freedom enjoyed by Spartan women, the reforms failed due to the refusal of the women to give up their ease and luxury in favor of the earlier ideals.[19] Aristotle also criticized Spartan women, linking various elements in the decline of Sparta with the degeneracy of its women.[20] Here Aristotle anticipated the Roman tendency to connect the vigor of the state with the virtue of the women, and political weakness with moral degeneracy—particularly of women.

Aristotle also noted that the physical absence of men, who were abroad for extended periods owing to military obligations, was largely responsible for the freedom enjoyed by Spartan women. The separation between the sexes and the relative freedom of women can be documented also for the Dorian city of Gortyn during the Archaic period. However, at Gortyn the geographic separation between the sexes was less marked, warfare was not as constant, and, as a result, the powers of the women of Gortyn were less than those of Sparta. Parts of the law code of Gortyn, dating from the seventh or sixth century B.C. and preserved in a fifth-century inscription, have a large number of provisions pertinent to women—many of which are notably liberal. Some scholars believe the Gortynian code represents a stage in the evolution of increasing freedom for women. Others, including those who believe in the existence of matriarchal and matrilineal systems in Bronze Age Crete, suggest that the code documents a gradual restriction of female freedom but retains traces of the earlier patterns.[21]

Social structures at Gortyn are comparable to those at Sparta. The lives of free men centered around all-male groups in which they were trained for warfare and slept and ate together. Homosexual relationships were not discouraged. The age at which a married man could live at home in Gortyn is not known, but Aristotle suggests that the separation of men and women was encouraged in order to reduce the birthrate.[22]

Since the men concentrated on their military duties, the women were involved in managing the home and property. Thus, at Gortyn, free women had the right to possess, control, and inherit property, though the inheritance of a daughter was less than that of a son. Upon divorce a wife took her own property and half the produce of the household, and if the husband was at fault, he paid a small fine.

A woman's work was recognized as producing wealth which ought to be evaluated, and there are stipulations in the code indicating the fraction of what she has "woven" that a divorced or widowed woman could take with her. Women not only controlled their own property, but when a father, husband, or son violated the regulations concerning the property of children, the control passed to the mother or wife.

Since the code recognized homosexual relations as valid, there were rules about rape in which the penalty for raping a free person, male or female, was the same: a monetary fine. The penalty was doubled if committed by a slave against a free person, but there was also a penalty for raping a household slave. Elsewhere in Greece the punishment for adultery was severe (for example, at Italian Locri the punishment was blinding), but in Gortyn the penalty was only monetary.[23] The fine for adultery was doubled if the act took place in the home of the woman's father, brother, or husband. No penalty is named for adultery between a free man and a nonfree woman.

If a free woman married a nonfree man and lived in his house, the children were not free, but they were considered free if he lived in her house. Thus, under Gortynian law a woman could have both free and nonfree children. On the other hand, in the provision concerning a baby born after divorce, the child belonged first to the father. The mother was required to present the child to its father; he could accept or reject it. If he rejected the child, the mother could rear it or get rid of it (*apoballo*—"to throw away"—is the verb employed). Hypergamy was possible only for males; there is no mention of marriage between a free male and a nonfree female. Of course, no Greek state needed to regulate sexual relations between a free man and a nonfree woman, since the children of such a union would not be considered the father's heirs.

Regulations regarding the *patrōïōkos*—a fatherless girl without brothers—are interesting in the Gortynian case, especially in comparison with the Athenian stipulations concerning the equivalent *epiklēros*. The primary obligation for such a girl was to perpetuate her father's line by bearing a child, and thus to keep her inheritance within the paternal tribe. Her paternal uncles, beginning with the eldest, were first in the order of succession to her hand. They were followed by their sons—her paternal cousins—also ranking by age, and finally by any man within her father's tribe. Marriage to a *patrōïōkos* may have not been highly desired, especially if she were not particularly wealthy, because she continued to manage her own property after marrying and did not become part of her husband's family. Instead, in an inversion of usual dynastic practice, her husband eventually became an instrument in the perpetuation of his late father-in-law's household. Gortynian law also afforded the *patrōïōkos* some measure of choice in her marriage. In the case that she did not wish to wed a member of the tribe who presented himself, the *patrōïōkos* could escape the obligation by paying him a monetary compensation from her inheritance and then marry freely. If no one from the tribe requested her hand, she was also allowed free choice of a husband. The one irony here—a stray matrilineal element in the midst of an otherwise patrilineal tradition —was that although the paternal uncles of the *patrōïōkos* looked after her property, her maternal uncles were entrusted with her upbringing.

The rearing of young women was likely to have been a short-lived responsibility, however, as *patrōïōkoi,* and perhaps all girls, were considered marriageable at the age of twelve. In Gortyn, the regulations concerning adultery in the house of a girl's father, then of her brother, and finally of her husband may indicate that a bride did not move out of her parental home until she was of a competent age to manage her own household.[24]

For Gortyn, though unfortunately not for Sparta, we also have legal regulations governing the women of the lower classes—serfs and slaves. Marriage, divorce, birth, and possession of chattels were subject to laws rivaling in complexity and comprehensiveness those affecting the upper classes. Extensive regulations were required concerning marriage of slaves when the partners were owned by different masters. For instance, the wife of a slave, as well as any children produced by his marriage, became the property of the husband's master. A married female slave could herself possess property, for the divorce regulations state that she may take her movables (presumably personal property) and small livestock, and —since she does not gain the status of a free woman by divorce—must return to her former master.[25] A child born after divorce must be offered first to her ex-husband's master, in a manner analogous to the presentation of the free divorced woman's child to her ex-husband. If the ex-husband's master refuses it, the child becomes the property of the master of its mother. An illegitimate child falls under the jurisdiction of the master of the mother's father or, if the mother's father is deceased, of her brother's master. It appears that decisions about unfree women and their children were in the hands of men to a greater extent than those about free women.

Dorian women, in contrast to Ionians, enjoyed many freedoms, and among Dorians the Spartans were the most liberated of all. The freedom of Spartan women seems to have been a result of the Dorian tradition with its communal social structure and separation of the sexes. But a comparison with Gortyn shows that Spartan women were unique in important details, including their marriage at a mature age and their exemption from women's traditional work. A chronological arrangement of the codes of Dorian Sparta and Gortyn and the code of Ionian Athens shows that the Spartan code, which antedated the Gortynian by a century or two, was the most favorable to women. The Athenian, codified only in the sixth century B.C., was the most restrictive, as we shall see in detail in Chapter IV.

### Ionian Women: Voices from the Grave

For Athenian women in the Dark Age and early Archaic period preceding the codification of their city's laws, the principal source of evidence is archaeological, especially the material from female burials and the depiction of women on pottery.[26] The survival and sometimes the excavation and reporting of such material is haphazard, and when the record is so uneven, the historian can more responsibly describe it than venture interpretations. However, where reasonable, I will infer from the dead to the living.

Sex roles that will be familiar to the modern reader were firmly established in the Dark Age in Athens. Both the living members of the family who supplied the dead with gifts for the grave and the craftsmen who fashioned the grave furnishings were concerned that the contents of the grave and the grave-marker itself be appropriate to and indicative of the sex of the deceased. The sex was indicated in various ways. In the Protogeometric period (ca. 1000–900 B.C.), male and female burials in Attica were distinguished by the shape of the amphoras in which ashes were buried or which were used to mark graves. The burials of males were normally associated with neck-handled amphoras, those of females with belly-handled ones with horizontal handles placed at the point of the greatest diameter of the belly. The belly-handled shape may have been used for carrying water, a chore traditionally performed by women.[27] In the late tenth century B.C., shoulder-handled amphoras began to replace belly-handled ones for female burials, and became usual in the ninth century B.C. [Plates 2 and 3]

On Geometric vases—which span the Dark Age and the early Archaic period—human figures are depicted for the first time since the fall of Mycenae. The earliest such figure is of a female mourner on a pottery fragment found in the Ceramicus in Attica.[28] With respect to the shape of the vases, the tradition established in the Protogeometric period tends to prevail. A belly-handled amphora is used for four of six female burials from Attica in which *prothesis* (lying-in-state of a corpse) and *ekphora* (transporting a corpse to its grave) are depicted in the vase paintings. Because the figures are sketched in a simple silhouette, it is very difficult to judge the sex of the deceased at a glance. Therefore an attempt has been made to decode various iconographic features in order to determine the sex of the corpses portrayed on *prothesis* and *ekphora* vases. More male corpses than female are depicted on the amphoras so far studied. Judging from the shape of the vases, and the sex of the corpses portrayed, it appears that more vases with scenes of *prothesis* and *ekphora* were associated with burials of males than with those of females.

The sex of a deceased Athenian from this time can also be determined by the nature of the offerings placed within the graves. Unlike the Spartans, Athenian women continued to perform the household tasks that were described in the Homeric epics. Thus the graves of women contain such items as spindle whorls, certain types of jewelry, and cooking pots, while those of men were provided with items typifying warriors—spears, shield bosses, and drinking cups. In addition, openwork *kalathoi*—small models of baskets probably used for produce or wool—though rare, are found in women's graves, yet another indication of the continuity of their domestic roles.[29]

Besides depictions of Athenian women as corpses, they are also shown on the Geometric *prothesis* and *ekphora* vases in the traditional role of tending the dead. To kinswomen fell the responsibility of washing, anointing, and dressing the corpse in preparation for burial. They also served as the chief mourners—joined by both the slave women of the household and professional female mourners who were hired for funerals. On these vases women may occasionally be recognized by the depiction of breasts, but they are, on the whole, much more readily identifiable in their various attitudes of lamentation—the classic gestures of female grief with both hands raised, or performing the ritual funerary dances, or beating their heads and tearing their hair. Contemporaneous Attic Geometric vases from Ceramicus show mourning women lacerating their foreheads and cheeks until they are bloody. It would have been difficult to depict the women's singing of the dirge visually, but literary references as early as Homer describe the lamentation as ranging from a wordless keening to a formal antiphonal song.[30] By contrast, the males tend to be shown mourning in a more rigid and restrained manner, usually with a single hand raised to the head.

Female figures are also differentiated by long robes, in silhouette; and when males, as charioteers, begin to be shown in robes, the females are distinguished by being given long hatched skirts. At times, too, the female members of the family of the deceased are distinguished from the professional mourners by their different clothing, and a few females, who must be relatives, are shown seated with children on their laps.

Women's association with rituals concerning the dead is still customary in Greece. Women have always been freer than men to indulge in displays of emotion, and are therefore more impressive participants at funerals. The washing and dressing of the corpse has certain analogies to the caring for infants; the cycle of life takes us from the care of women and returns us to the care of women.

As a realistic consideration, kinswomen had the most cause to be deeply grieved at the death of their male relatives, for the lives of women lacking the protection of men were truly pitiful. Women's dependency on men, which was apparent in the legends of the Bronze Age, can be documented for the Dark Age as well. Indeed, many of the similes in Homeric epic are thought to date from this period rather than from the Bronze Age. One such description is of a widow balancing wool in a pair of scales in order to earn a miserable wage for her children. The poetry of the early Archaic period gives a similar picture of women attempting to support themselves. A female day-laborer, especially if burdened with a child, would find it difficult to obtain employment. Hesiod advises the farmer to hire a servant with no baby to nurse.[31] A hymn to Demeter, probably composed in the seventh century B.C., describes how a free elderly woman may seek employment as a child nurse or a domestic. She waits for prospective employers at the village well.[32] Such a woman might be offered temporary employment as a mourner. At the funerals of her own father, husband, and sons, she must have cried for herself as much as for the dead.

Not only the offerings to the dead but the skeletons themselves can be eloquent, since inhumation and cremation were practiced simultaneously. However, a very small number of these from the Dark Age have been analyzed to determine their sex and age at death. The reader may wonder at my temerity in drawing any conclusions at all from the paltry amount of material available. The fact that our Dark Age evidence is consistent with the demographic patterns found in later pre-industrial societies where there is fuller documentation justifies its inclusion here. J. Lawrence Angel has analyzed the skeletal remains of one group of twenty-two graves (nine infants, two children, four female adults, seven male adults) from a family burial plot within the Athenian Agora by the Tholos which dates from the last quarter of the eighth century to the second quarter of the seventh.[33] The years associated with childbearing were apparently hazardous for the women, since the ages of death of three of the female skeletons were determined at 16–, 18+, and 50+; those of the males that could be determined were 34, 43, 44, and 48.

While it would appear likely that the people enshrined in durable tombs and the users of well-made Geometric pottery were wealthy or held positions of prestige, more comparatively poor burials have been found than rich ones, but some of the more opulent burials were those of women. The two richest burials in the Agora family plot were those of the young women, although the skeleton of the eighteen-year-old shows that she was not a woman of leisure, for she flexed her feet often either in climbing steep hills (common to Athenian topography) or in squatting before a cooking fire. One of the wealthiest Geometric tombs thus far excavated in Athens also belonged to a woman.[34] After cremation, this woman's ashes were buried with the jewelry she had worn at her *prothesis*. In addition to the usual offerings, her tomb contained two ivory stamp seals and a model of a granary. I assume that it is unlikely that wealthy Athenian women were personally involved in commercial activities, although they did work around the house. Therefore the stamp seals and granary model may symbolize the affluence and economic activity of the woman's father and husband, or may refer to some items in the woman's dowry or to her job as guardian of the household store-chamber. It may also be suggested that rich burials of women are a vicarious display of the wealth of the husband, father, or son who buried them.

The male–female population ratio at this period is startling: the Agora burial plot by the Tholos shows almost twice as many male burials as female, and the study of *prothesis* and *ekphora* vases also shows more male burials than female. This imbalance could be explained away by speculating that more men were honored with prestigious burials than women. But Homer, who is probably relating a Bronze Age tradition, although he may be reflecting the Dark Age, states that Priam had fifty sons but only twelve daughters; Nausicaa is an only daughter with a number of brothers; Andromache mentions her seven brothers. We have also seen that some Greek colonies were founded by men alone, who were then compelled to find wives among the native population. No doubt population pressure on the mainland was a factor in colonization: a rise in fecundity coupled with a decrease in infant and juvenile mortality has been traced for this period.[35] An ecologically sound method of limiting population is the destruction of the reproducing members of the group, the females, and the most likely reason for sexual imbalance in a population is female infanticide.[36] While it cannot be proven beyond doubt that newborn females were selectively eliminated, the evidence seems to point that way. Whether the resulting scarcity of women produced more competition for them is not known. However, it would not be correct to infer that mature women were despised during the Dark Age, just because female infanticide was practiced.

The basic type of grave-marker in the Archaic period became the stele, a narrow tapering rhomboidal slab of stone frequently showing a profile of a standing figure. Females never appear alone on these monuments in Athens at this time, but occasionally a male warrior is accompanied by a small figure of a female who must be a relative.[37] In other parts of the Greek world, dead women are commemorated by these steles. These monuments were very expensive, so sumptuary legislation may be responsible for the absence of steles erected to women in Athens.[38]

Marble statues of maidens (*korai*) and youths (*kouroi*) are characteristic examples of large-scale, free-standing sculpture in the Archaic period. [Plates 4–6] Several of the *kouroi* but few of the *korai* were used as grave-markers. What purpose the *korai* served otherwise is still in question. Gisela Richter speculates that the *korē* represents "a beautiful girl in the service of the goddess," since many were dedicated to various goddesses.[39]

Apparently, the earliest *korē* was dedicated about 660 B.C. to Artemis by a woman, Nikandre, who identifies herself by adding the names of her father, brother, and husband. But this is an exception; most *korai* are dedicated to goddesses by men. There was no difference between the dedications made by women and by men, nor by dedicators of different social classes who, in the case of Athenian women, run the range from a washerwoman to a magistrate's wife. The former may have used her dedicatory inscription as an advertisement of her profession, the latter as an announcement of her own and her husband's prosperity.[40]

The figures of *korai* and *kouroi* are derived from Egyptian prototypes of standing draped statues of males and females. The Greek adaption shows nude males while the females remain draped. Some *korai* are dressed in the Dorian *peplos,* which reveals the body, but most wear the heavier Ionian costume, concealing the figure with its multiple folds of cloth. Despite the drapery, the girls' buttocks are often voluptuously delineated, paralleling the representations of boys.[41] In the homosexual context of Greek antiquity, buttocks, not breasts, were the most attractive feature of a female figure. Long dark hair with a flower tucked in it was also admired, as we learn from the poetry of Archilochus and Semonides, and long curls are found on both *kouroi* and *korai.*[42] The marble was painted, and adorned with real earrings, bracelets, and necklaces. It seems reasonable that the *korē* should be represented fully clothed since she was to serve such modest goddesses as Artemis, Athena, and Hera, who are themselves always shown dressed. Due to her confining garments, the *korē* throughout her history stands with one foot slightly advanced, while the *kouros* figure developed into the male nude capable of a variety of poses. Owing to the solid columnar immobility of the heavily draped *korē* and to the practice of living women of carrying burdens on their heads, the female figure is occasionally employed instead of a column to support roofs. The supporting female statue, called a caryatid, was used in the Archaic treasuries of Siphnus and Cnidus at Delphi long before the well-known Classical caryatids of the Erechtheum in Athens. [Plate 7]

## The Women of Lyric Poetry

The Archaic period was an age of individualism in poetry. Attitudes toward women ran the full range from echoes of the misogyny discerned in Hesiod's description of Pandora (see p. 2) to the love of women expressed by both male and female poets.

Hesiod's hostility toward women was part of a general bitterness produced by the poet's feeling that he was living in an age of social and economic injustice. Beset by poverty, Hesiod considered a woman a necessity, but an economic liability whose vices resembled those of the first woman, Pandora:

> Who shuns wedlock and women's troubling deeds—
> And will not marry—comes to dire old age
> With none to nurse him, despite ample means;
> So, once he dies, his distant kinfolk split
> His substance. He who opts for wedlock's fate,
> And gets a wife who's good and fit of mind,
> Pits good against misfortune all his life.
> But he who gets one of the baneful sort,
> Lives with endless sorrow in his breast,
> Of heart and soul—this is a fatal ill! [43]

He advised:

Do not let a woman with a sexy rump deceive you with wheedling and coaxing words; she is after your barn. The man who trusts a woman trusts deceivers.

Bring home a wife when you are of the right age, not much under thirty nor much more—this is the right age for marriage. Let your wife have been grown up four years, and marry her in the fifth. Marry a maiden, so that you can teach her careful ways, and especially marry one who lives near you; but examine everything around and see that your marriage will not be a joke to your neighbors. For a man wins nothing better than a good wife, and, again, nothing worse than a bad one. [44]

The hostility of Hesiod is reiterated by Semonides, a poet-philosopher of the seventh century B.C., and by Phocylides in the sixth century B.C., who both compare women to species of livestock. Only one—the woman who is compared to a bee—is praiseworthy. The bee was notable not only for its industrious nature but for its asexual manner of reproduction.[45] Hence the virtuous wife must not display any interest in sex, for she might otherwise be led to commit adultery and make her cuckolded husband the laughingstock of his neighbors. Moreover, aside from pride, there was a practical reason for wanting a frigid wife. Hesiod tells us that only one son was desirable, although Semonides speaks of a number of children. A wife without a proclivity to sex would be more likely to bear a limited number of children. It is notable too that the woman with a small rump was not considered desirable, owing, no doubt, to the practice of anal intercourse which was also a useful method of contraception.

The great satire on women written approximately seven hundred years later by the Roman Juvenal was anticipated by the catalogue of women's vices by Semonides of Amorgos:

## ON WOMEN

From the beginning the god made the mind of woman
A thing apart. One he made from the long-haired sow;
While she wallows in the mud and rolls about on the ground,
Everything at home lies in a mess.
And she doesn't take baths but sits about
In the shit in dirty clothes and gets fatter and fatter.
The god made another one from the evil fox,
A woman crafty in all matters—she doesn't miss a thing,
Bad or good. The things she says are sometimes good
And just as often bad. Her mood is constantly shifting.
The next one was made from a dog, nimble, a bitch like its mother,
And she wants to be in on everything that's said or done.
Scampering about and nosing into everything,
She yaps it out even if there's no one to listen.
Her husband can't stop her with threats,
Not if he flies into a rage and knocks her teeth out with a rock,
Not if he speaks to her sweetly when they happen to be sitting among
    friends.
No, she stubbornly maintains her unmanageable ways.
Another one the Olympian gods fashioned from the dust of the earth,

And gave her to man: the simple-minded type. This kind of woman
Can't distinguish between good and bad. The only thing she understands
    how to do
Is eat. Not even if the gods have sent a bitter winter storm
Does she have the sense (though she's freezing) to drag a chair close to the
    fire.
Another is from the sea, and she has two kinds of dispositions;
One day she's full of laughter and good spirits,
And a friend who came to visit would remark of her:
"There's not a better or a fairer woman than this
In the whole of the human race!"
Another day she's completely unbearable—you can't even look at her
Or come near her, but at such times she rages terribly,
Snarling like a bitch over her pups;
Unfriendly and out of temper with everyone,
No less with her friends than with her enemies.
Just as the sea itself is often smooth and calm
And safe—a great delight to sailors
In the summer season; but it often rages
And swells up with deeply resounding waves.
It's this that such a kind of woman is most like
In her temperament; for the sea's nature is changeable.
Another woman is from the stumbling and obstinate donkey,
Who only with difficulty and with the use of threats
Is compelled to agree to the perfectly acceptable things
She had resisted. Otherwise in a corner of the house
She sits munching away all night long, and all day long she sits munching at
    the hearth.
Even so she'll welcome any male friend
Who comes around with sex on his mind.
Another kind of woman is the wretched, miserable tribe that comes from the
    weasel.
As far as she is concerned, there is nothing lovely or pleasant
Or delightful or desirable in her.
She's wild over love-making in bed,
But her husband wants to vomit when he comes near her.
She's always stealing and making trouble for the neighbors,
And she often filches the sacrificial offerings from the altars.
Another woman is born of the delicate, long-maned mare,
Who maneuvers her way around the slavish and troublesome housework,
And wouldn't put a finger to the mill, or so much as lift
The sieve, or sweep the dirt out of the house
Or go into the kitchen, for fear she'll get dirty.

She introduces her husband to the pinch of poverty.
Every day she takes a bath at least twice,
Sometimes three times, and anoints herself with fragrant oil.
She always wears her hair long and flowing,
Its deep richness highlighted with flowers.
And so such a woman is a thing of beauty for others to look upon,
But she's only a burden to her husband
Unless he happens to be a tyrant or a prince,
The kind whose heart is delighted by such things.
Another one is from the monkey. In this case Zeus has outdone himself
In giving husbands the worst kind of evil.
She has the ugliest face imaginable; and such a woman
Is the laughingstock throughout the town for everyone.
Her body moves awkwardly all the way up to its short neck;
She hardly has an ass and her legs are skinny. What a poor wretch is the
    husband
Who has to put his arms around such a mess!
Like a monkey she knows all kinds of tricks
And routines, and she doesn't mind being laughed at.
Not that there's anything that she can do well—no, it's this
That concerns and occupies her all day long:
How can she accomplish the greatest amount of harm.
Another woman is from the bee; the man who gets her is fortunate.
To her alone no blame is attached,
But life flourishes and prospers under her care.
She grows old cherishing a husband who cherishes her,
After she has borne to him a lovely and distinguished group of children.
Among all women her excellence shines forth,
And a godlike grace is shed about her.
She does not take pleasure in sitting among the women
When they are discussing sex.
Such women are granted to husbands as a special favor from Zeus,
For they are the best of all and exceptionally wise.
These are all the various tribes of women that exist now
And remain among men by the devising of Zeus.
For Zeus designed this as the greatest of all evils:
Women. Even if in some way they seem to be a help,
To their husbands especially they are a source of evil.
For there is no one who manages to spend a whole day
In contentment if he has a wife,
Nor will he find himself able to speedily thrust famine out of the house,
Who is a hateful, malicious god to have as a houseguest.
But whenever a man seems to be especially content at home,

Thanks either to good fortune from the gods or to his good relations with the
    rest
Of mankind, she'll find fault somewhere and stir up a dispute.
For whosoever wife she is, she won't receive graciously
Into the house a friend who comes to visit.
And you know, the very one who appears to be most moderate and prudent
Actually turns out to be most outrageous and shameful.
And when her husband is still in shock from finding out about her, the
Neighbors are having a good laugh because even he made a mistake in his
    choice.
For each man likes to regale others with stories of praise about his own wife,
While at the same time finding fault with any other man's wife.
We don't realize that we all share the same fate.
For Zeus designed this as the greatest of all evils
And bound us to it in unbreakable fetters.
Therefore Hades welcomes into his realm
Men who have fought together for the sake of a woman.[46]

On the other hand, the lyric poems of the female writers of the
Archaic Age give us the happiest picture of women in Greek literature. Nine of these poets were later considered to be the best of their
age, but some are little more than names to us; others are known
through a few fragments of their poetry, which survive because they
were praised and quoted in later Classical literature. None of the
women poets came from Athens. What is known of their lives is
generally unreliable, since it is based on anecdotes and biographies
written long after their deaths, which assume their poetry was au-
tobiographical. Thus we are told that Corinna defeated Pindar five
times in competition, and he in exasperation called her a sow;
Pausanias said that she owed her victory in part to her extraordinary
good looks.[47] Somewhat inconsistent with her own supposed competition with Pindar is Corinna's criticism of her teacher Myrtis, a
woman who was said to have been the teacher of Pindar as well:

> Even I find fault with Myrtis
> Of the sweet clear voice.
> Although she was a woman poet,
> Yet she challenged Pindar.[48]

Both Corinna and Pindar were Boeotian poets, but her work does not
bear comparison to his. Pindar's is international, and little con-

cerned with women except to note that they all hope to have a husband or son who is a victorious athlete.[49] Corinna's poetry is parochial in language and subject matter.

Sappho, the most admired of all female Greek poets, was said to have a following of students. The authority of the classical scholar Ulrich von Wilamowitz-Moellendorff enshrined the theory that Sappho was the leader of a cult of young girls chastely worshiping Aphrodite and studying a curriculum suitable for nice young ladies.[50] There is little support for this theory either in her poetry or in the ancient literary gossip. Sappho's poems are often addressed to women, and they show a passionate involvement comparable to that found in the works of her contemporary male poets addressed to women and men:

> He seems to me just like the gods,
> That man who sits opposite you
> And, while close to you, listens to
> You sweetly speaking
> And laughing with love—things which cause
> The heart in my breast to tremble.
> For whenever I look at you,
> I can speak no more.
> My tongue freezes silent and stiff,
> Light flame trickles under my skin,
> I no longer see with my eyes,
> My ears hear whirring,
> Cold sweat covers me, shivering takes
> Me complete captive, I become
> More green than the grass, near to death
> To myself I seem.[51]

Sappho's poetry can be compared to the love poetry of numerous males who found young women attractive, though not necessarily to the exclusion of homosexual interests. The following work was written by Alcman, a male poet of Sparta, in the mid-seventh century B.C.:

> . . . with limb-loosening desire, and more softly
> Than sleep or death she glances,
> Nor is she sweet in vain.
> Astymeloisa does not reply to me.

> But holding a garland,
> Like a star shooting through
> The blazing firmament
> Or a golden sprig or soft down . . .[52]

Many modern scholars have vehemently denied that Sappho's sentiments occasioned overt erotic activity. The Greeks certainly realized that Sappho wrote about the sexual activities of women. Few fragments survive from this portion of her work: on one papyrus fragment the first five letters of *olisbos* (leather phallus) may be read with near certainty. Part of another poem preserved on parchment relates: ". . . on a soft bed you satisfied your desire." "You" in Greek can be masculine or feminine, but Sappho is not known to have written erotic poems to men.[53] In Greek literature generally, references to the women of Lesbos connoted unusually intense eroticism, both homosexual and heterosexual. Anacreon, writing in the generation after Sappho, complained that the girl from Lesbos whom he desired "gapes after some other woman." [54] The homosexual reputation of Lesbian women was the theme of Lucian's fifth "Dialogue of the Courtesans," written in the second century A.D. On the other hand, in Athenian comedy the verbs *lesbiazein* and *lesbizein* ("to play the Lesbian") and other references to the women of Lesbos connote enthusiasm for all sorts of sexual experiences and "whorish behavior." [55]

If her poems do have biographical elements, Sappho could well have been bisexual, like aristocratic Greek males, for although she did not address erotic poetry to men, she was married and had a daughter:

> I have a lovely child, whose form is like
> Gold flowers, my heart's one pleasure, Cleis,
> For whom I'd not give all Lydia, nor fair . . .[56]

She was born into an aristocratic family in 612 B.C. on the island of Lesbos, which she was forced to leave for a time when the tyrant Pittacus came to power. That Sappho did not live a secluded life is testified to by her political poems as well as by her indignation when her extravagant brother made himself ridiculous by buying a famous courtesan at a high price and setting her free.[57] The stories that Sappho committed suicide by leaping from the Leucadian Rock for the love of a sailor and that she was small and ugly were probably invented in later antiquity to show that she would have preferred male lovers to female, if she could have attracted them.[58]

As a poet, she was inventive, using new poetic structures and meters, but she was a self-conscious artist too, often addressing herself. Although so little of her poetry survives, the power of her writing is great enough to show that she merits the praise she earned from antiquity, when Plato called her the tenth Muse,[59] to the present.

In contrast to the personal poetry of the aristocratic Sappho, there are some songs surviving that were performed by choirs of maidens and women. Judging from the extant fragments and remarks of ancient authors, these songs ran the full range from the informal folksongs of spinners and weavers to performances by professionals at festivals.

Apart from dirges, already mentioned, there were maiden songs, *partheneia,* which were formal choral hymns sung by unmarried girls to the accompaniment of the flute. A large fragment of one of these maiden songs, written by the poet Alcman in Sparta, has been preserved.[60] This song mentions a number of myths and cult practices, but I am interested here in the personal references in it. The choir names most of the girls in it, and singles out some for special praise. Girls are compared to the sun, their hair to gold, their ankles are lovely, and they run swiftly like fillies. They say of their leader, "Hagesichora exhausts me." We may choose to interpret this phrase as "exhausts me" with praising her, or with trying to win at a festival, or sexually and emotionally. The last interpretation is supported by our knowledge that erotic attachments between older women and young girls were encouraged at Sparta.[61] It is likely that in the female atmosphere of the girls' choir lesbian relationships flourished.

The most important factor, both at Sparta and at Lesbos, in fostering female homoerotic attachments was that women in both societies were highly valued. They were admired and loved by both men and women. Personal beauty was cultivated by women at both Lesbos and Sparta. Lesbos was one of the places where beauty contests for women were held,[62] and the poem of Alcman gives some attributes considered desirable in young women. In addition, the talents of accomplished women like Sappho and Hagesichora must have made them attractive to people of both sexes. Women did not, as has been suggested, turn to other women in desperation, due to men's disparagement of them. Rather, it appears that they could love other women in milieux where the entire society cherished women, educated them comparably to men of their class, and allowed them to carry over into maturity the attachments they had formed in the all-female social and educational context of youth.

The women poets were not unique, for their works allude to groups of women involved in literary pursuits. Sappho mentioned other women poets in Lesbos, and Corinna addressed some of her lyrics to "white-robed Boeotian women." In Rhodes, the philosopher Cleobulus in the sixth century B.C. advocated that girls be educated, and his daughter, Cleobuline, in imitation of her father, was able to compose riddles in verse.[63] As far as can be determined, the educated women of Archaic Greece were all members of the upper class. Unlike some men of the Archaic period, they did not write poetry because they were lame, or angry at political or social issues. Rather, the poetry of the women is the product of leisurely contemplation. It is interesting that there are no traces of literary activity among Athenian women. The city whose men would be responsible for the most notable artistic creations in Classical Greece produced no female artists.

# IV

## WOMEN AND THE
## CITY OF ATHENS

IN THE sixth century B.C. the Athenian lawgiver Solon institution-
alized the distinction between good women and whores. He
abolished all forms of self-sale and sale of children into slavery
except one: the right of the male guardian to sell an unmarried
woman who had lost her virginity. As part of his extensive legislation
covering many aspects of Athenian life, Solon regulated the walks,
the feasts, the mourning, the trousseaux, and the food and drink of
citizen women. He is also said to have established state-owned brothels
staffed by slaves, and thus to have made Athens attractive to foreigners who wanted to make money, including craftsmen, merchants,
and prostitutes. In the Classical period, Solon's laws continued to
exert tremendous influence over the lives of Athenian women.

I would attribute this legislation neither to misogyny nor to
Solon's homosexuality. These regulations, which seem at first glance
antifeminist, are actually aimed at eliminating strife among men and
strengthening the newly created democracy. Women are a perennial
source of friction among men. Solon's solution to this problem was
to keep them out of sight and to limit their influence. Furthermore,
much of this legislation—including the limitation on ostentatious
funerals (for which large numbers of women would be employed as
paid mourners) and the regulation of feasts, trousseaux, and food
and drink—was sumptuary in nature and intended to curb the power
of the aristocracy in Athens of the late Archaic period.

## The Dispute over Status

Whether Solon's regulations improved the status of citizen women or detracted from it is debatable. Clearly, as members of the citizen class, they advanced over those people living in Athens who were not considered citizens. Yet their advance was predicated on the status loss of lower-class women: the slaves who staffed the brothels. And the status of citizen women and men relative to each other poses still another question, which scholars tend to answer with excessive subjectivity.

While there is general agreement that politically and legally the condition of a woman in Classical Athens was one of inferiority, the question of her social status has generated a major controversy and has become the focus of most recent studies of Athenian women.[1] Opinions range from one extreme to the other. Some scholars hold that women were despised and kept in Oriental seclusion, while others contend that they were respected and enjoyed freedom comparable to that of most women throughout the centuries—we may add: "at least before the advent of the women's movement." Still others think that women were kept secluded, but in that seclusion were esteemed and ruled the house.

The first position is succinctly stated by F. A. Wright in a book published in 1923 and obviously influenced by the wave of feminism which culminated in the passage of the Nineteenth Amendment. This book was reissued in 1969 and now appears quaint in its blatant polemicism:

> The fact is—and it is well to state it plainly—that the Greek world perished from one main cause, a low ideal of womanhood and a degradation of women which found expression both in literature and in social life. The position of women and the position of slaves—for the two classes went together—were the canker-spots which, left un- healed, brought about the decay first of Athens and then of Greece.[2]

In reaction to those who considered the life of an Athenian woman little better than that of a harem slave, other scholars asserted that despite her formal handicaps the Athenian woman was neither despised nor secluded. Most modern treatments taking this position go back to the radical essay of A. W. Gomme published in

1925.[3] The many advocates of Gomme's position include Moses Hadas and H. D. F. Kitto.[4] These scholars, no less than Wright, were the victims of their own times and social backgrounds. Inspired by their admiration for the Athenians, they were reluctant to believe that the Athenians might not have treated their wives the way cultivated gentlemen in the twentieth century treat theirs. Furthermore, they had no inkling that many wives of such cultivated gentlemen were bitterly dissatisfied with their lot.

Two contemporary scholars who subscribe to neither of these extremes of opinion are Victor Ehrenberg and W. K. Lacey.[5] For example, they call attention to a life spent mostly inside a dark, unsanitary house and to women's lack of access to the educational values of Athenian life. Ehrenberg believes that women did not attend the theater. But Lacey points out that the Athenians were extremely protective of their women, and seclusion may be viewed as the handmaiden of protection.

The wide divergence of scholarly opinion is puzzling, and cannot be attributed to sexist bias—for male partiality can be detected on both sides of the argument, and Lacey is the only one who is aware of modern concepts of women's emancipation.[6] The principal reason for the two viewpoints lies in the genre of the evidence consulted. Gomme and his followers, relying predominantly, or exclusively, on the evidence from Classical tragedy, and believing that the heroines were modeled directly on Athenian women of the fifth century B.C., determine that women were respected and not secluded. Lacey, who explicitly rejects the testimony of tragedy as not representative of normal people in a normal family, and Ehrenberg, who accepts only Euripides, while finding Sophocles and Aeschylus less close to reality, paint a sorrier picture of the position of women.

Lacey and Ehrenberg rely heavily upon the Attic orators, while the majority of the followers of Gomme, in contrast, scarcely cite them. Hadas gives the reason that speeches are too polemical and present a one-sided, abnormal picture. The evidence from comedy is less decisive, and is cited in support of both positions.

The preceding brief survey has demonstrated that the question of the social status of women is part of a larger dispute concerning the appropriate source of evidence for women's life in Athens. The critical factor appears to be the heroines of Aeschylus and Sophocles. The scholars who consider Antigone and Electra, for example, as "real" evidence for women of the fifth century B.C. will believe that the status of women was high. On the other hand, evidence from orators and other prose writers points usually to a low status, while comedy and Euripides give ambiguous testimony. The scholars surveyed do not give equal weight to all available evidence, but deliberately exclude or explain away the literature not supporting their positions. Moreover, archaeological evidence is not widely used; Ehrenberg even cautions against trusting isolated pieces of material evidence.

I feel that the issue of status is in itself misleading, and that the broad range of scholarly opinion results from treating women as an undifferentiated mass. It is also blurred by the unconscious tendency to view the ancient world in terms of modern values. Unless both the sphere of action and the class of women in that sphere are defined, the discussions about status will continue to fail to come to a consensus. The archaeological evidence from Athens of the Dark Age and Archaic period examined in Chapter III showed rigid distinctions between male and female roles, but that was all it showed. The Athenians of the Classical period continued to hold rigid expectations of proper behavior according to sex, but, because there is more material available, we can see that they also applied different standards to different economic and social classes of women and men, according to the categories of citizens, resident foreigners (metics), and slaves. Behavior appropriate to one group of women detracted from the status of another group, and this distinction was confirmed by the laws attributed to Solon.

Political roles in Classical Athens must be considered in terms of duties rather than rights. Obligations to family and state were the strongest compulsion in the lives of citizens, both male and female. The principal duty of citizen women toward the *polis* was the production of legitimate heirs to the *oikoi*, or families, whose aggregate comprised the citizenry. Every generation the members of the *oikoi* were charged with the perpetuation of the cults of their ancestors as well as the maintenance of the lines of descent. In effect, the interest of the state coincided with the interest of the family in seeing that individual families did not die out.

## Epiklēroi

Women as well as men could serve the state in preserving the independence of the *oikoi*. In families in which a son was lacking, the daughters were responsible for perpetuating the *oikos*. In such a family the daughter was regarded as "attached to the family property"; hence her name *epiklēros*. The family property went with her to her husband, and thence to their child. This arrangement shows that although males were preferred to females, succession at Athens was not strictly agnatic in the sense that only males were legally able to inherit, although the *epiklēros* never truly owned her father's property. It was the duty or privilege of the nearest male kinsman to marry the heiress. The order of succession to the hand of the heiress was the same order in which the male kinsmen would have succeeded to the father's estate if there had not been any heiress at all, i.e., brothers of the deceased, then sons of brothers of the deceased; there is some ambiguity as to whether the estate—and the hand of the heiress—then went to sons of the sisters of the deceased or to grandsons of brothers of the deceased. The disparity in the ages of the resulting married couple was not a factor, as long as they were capable of reproduction.

The bizarre ramifications of the epiklerate are too numerous to be fully investigated here.[7] An heiress might have already been married at her father's death, and not necessarily to the nearest male kin. Whether the next-of-kin had the right to dissolve the marriage of a married heiress is debatable. The consensus of scholarly opinion is that the marriage could be dissolved only if it had not produced a son, for if the *epiklēros* had a son her property was destined for him. However, this has not been satisfactorily proven.

The amount of wealth that accompanied the heiress was the significant factor in attracting the next-of-kin. A wealthy heiress generated lively competition. We know of at least two men who divorced their wives in order to marry heiresses, both providing for the remarriage of their ex-wives.[8] Andocides, in his speech "On the Mysteries" in 400 B.C., alleged that the serious charge of profaning the Eleusinian Mysteries was framed against him in order to divert him from claiming the hand of a rich heiress. A poorer heiress may have inherited nothing more than her father's debts. The state obliged the next-of-kin to marry her himself, or to provide her with a dowry sufficient to attract a husband.[9]

The stipulations regarding Athenian heiresses appear much harsher than those at Sparta and Gortyn (see pp. 40–41). In Sparta only unmarried girls were subject to the laws concerning heiresses,[10] and in Gortyn an heiress could free herself of the obligation to marry by relinquishing part of her inheritance. But if it is at all valid to comment on the Athenian treatment of the heiress, it is reasonable to point out that the regulation that seems cruel and mercenary in the case of the wealthy heiress is protective and charitable in the case of the poor woman, who without the attraction of a dowry would remain husbandless and pitiful. A brief statement by Aristotle implies that the regulations for resident foreigners (metics) in the matter of inheritance and heiresses were similar to those for citizens, inasmuch as he stated that legal actions concerning estates and heiresses which the archon (a chief magistrate) initiates in the case of citizens are similarly introduced by the polemarch (a magistrate with jurisdiction over actions involving persons who are not Athenian citizens) in the case of metics.[11]

## Dowry, Marriage, and Divorce

As a logical consequence of the woman's duty to Athens, marriage and motherhood were considered the primary goals of every female citizen. The death of a young girl often elicited lamentations specifically over her failure to fulfill her intended role as a wife. Epitaphs express this feeling, and some vases of the shape used to transport water for a prenuptial bath mark the graves of girls who died unwed. The dead maiden is portrayed dressed as a bride on these memorial *loutrophoroi* vases.

Citizen women were perpetually under the guardianship of a man, usually the father or, if he were dead, the male next-of-kin. Upon marriage a woman passed into the guardianship of her husband in most matters, with the important limitation that her father, or whoever else had given her in marriage, retained the right to dissolve the marriage.[12] If the husband predeceased the wife, the guardianship of her dowry and perhaps of her person passed to her sons if they were of age, or to their guardians. If a widow had no children, she would return to the power of her original guardian or his heirs. A widow was protected by the archon, who could prosecute offenders in her behalf.

Responsible fathers in Classical Athens did not raise female babies unless they foresaw a proper marriage for them at maturity. The initial consideration of the father was financial. Custom dictated that a dowry commensurate with the father's economic status be provided for a woman's maintenance. Vase paintings representing women seated on clothing chests allude to the dowries possessed by brides.[13] A father would not raise more girls than he could provide with dowries, and larger dowries tended to attract wealthier and more desirable suitors. In cases where the father had not shown proper foresight or had suffered reverses, dowries were contributed from other sources. The wealthy frequently dowered their poorer relatives. We are told without further explanation that the law required that dowries be provided for poor girls of even passably attractive appearance, and a few times Athens provided dowries for daughters of men who had served the state.[14] Lack of a dowry gave a hostile orator a chance to assert that no legal marriage had taken place, or gave self-righteous husbands an opportunity to boast that they had been compassionate enough to marry without the promise of a dowry.[15] The marriage of the dowryless Elpinice to Callias was exceptional, for he was very wealthy and could overlook the dowry in his desire for a marriage alliance with a poor branch of the noble family of Philaidae. There may have been women of citizen origin who lacked dowries or guardians to arrange marriages for them, and who were thus compelled to become concubines, but our evidence for this group of women is meager.[16] In addition to her dowry, a bride had a small trousseau, limited by Solon to three dresses and some other paraphernalia of little value.[17] The trousseau was usually not included in the dowry, but would customarily remain with her as her personal property at the conclusion of a marriage.[18]

The Athenians were protective of their women. A woman's dowry was to remain intact throughout her lifetime and to be used for her support; neither her father, nor her guardian, nor her husband, nor the woman herself could legally dispose of it. Upon marriage, the dowry passed from the guardianship of the father to that of the groom. The groom could use the principal but was required to maintain his wife from the income of her dowry, computed at 18 per cent annually. Upon divorce, the husband was required to return the dowry to his ex-wife's guardian, or pay interest at 18 per cent. Thus her support would continue to be provided for, and, with her dowry intact, she would be eligible for remarriage. A widow, especially if she had increased her property through inheritance from her late husband, would also be an attractive candidate for remarriage.[19]

A betrothal was contracted between the guardian of the bride and the groom or, if the latter was still young, the guardian of the groom. Marriage arrangements were made by men on the basis of economic and political considerations, and girls were always obliged to marry the men their male relatives selected for them. The bride and groom may have never set eyes upon one another, but there were many marriages between first cousins or other relatives, who presumably would have seen each other at such family ceremonies as funerals.[20] Marriage to relatives was attractive especially among the wealthier families in democratic Athens, when inroads were constantly made against the fortunes of the wealthy: such marriages provided a way of consolidating the resources of the family, facilitated agreement between parties who knew and trusted each other, gave relatives preferential access to brides, and forestalled enforcement of the law of the epiklerate.

The purpose of marriage was procreation, within the limits of the economic resources of the family. Before the groom joined her on their wedding day, the bride ate a fruit with many seeds, symbolizing fertility.[21] The birth of a child, especially a son, was considered a fulfillment of the goal of the marriage.[22]

A girl was ideally first married at fourteen to a man of about thirty.[23] The necessity that the bride be a virgin, coupled with the ancient belief that young girls were lustful, made an early marriage desirable.[24] The husband who married at thirty could well be dead at forty-five, having begotten two or three children within the marriage and leaving his wife a candidate for remarriage. Late marriage of men in Athens can be attributed to their duty to serve as soldiers for ten years, but it appears also to have been an adaptation to the low proportion of females in the population. A young widow could serve as wife in a number of serial marriages. Since marriage was the preferable condition for women, and men were protective of their women, a dying husband, like a divorcing husband, might arrange a future marriage for his wife.[25]

Divorce was easily attainable. either by mutual consent or through action on behalf of either one of the spouses. and there was no stigma attached.[26] When the divorce was initiated by the husband, he was required merely to send the wife from his house. When the wife wished a divorce. she needed the intercession of her father or some other male citizen to bring the case before the archon. There are only three cases known from the Classical period where an Athenian divorce proceeded from the wife's side. Two are from the fourth century. and were negotiated exclusively among men. The third case was remarkable in that a woman attempted to obtain a divorce on her own initiative. During the stress of the Peloponnesian War. Hipparete attempted to divorce Alcibiades. She left her husband's house and moved in with her brother Callias. She then set off to register her divorce with the archon, evidently unaccompanied by her brother, for at the tribunal she was seized by Alcibiades and forcibly carried back to his house.[27]

Since children were produced to perpetuate the father's house, they were the property of their father, and remained in his house when marriages were dissolved through death and probably also in cases of divorce. The divorcée or widow was thus entirely free to remarry and to bear children to a new husband.[28]

## The Propagation of Citizens

The parentage determined the eligibility of children for citizenship—not an unusual criterion, save for the ambiguity of Athenian attitudes toward the value of the maternal contribution to the foetus. For instance, Apollo, in Aeschylus' *Eumenides,* presented in 458 B.C., states that the mother contributes to conception in a passive way as a receptacle for the father's seed:

> I shall explain this—and speak quite bluntly, so note.
> She who is called the mother is not her offspring's
> Parent, but nurse to the newly sown embryo.
> The male—who mounts—begets. The female, a stranger,
> Guards a stranger's child if no god bring it harm.
> I shall present you evidence that proves my point.
> There may be a father, and no mother. Nearby
> Stands my witness, the child of Olympian Zeus
> Who was not nourished in the dark depths of a womb,
> Yet such a child as no goddess could ever bear.[29]

These statements are understandable in view of the fact that the mammalian ovum was unknown; hence a woman's contribution to a baby was not fully understood. This is why an agricultural society would use a metaphor such as "sowing" for sexual intercourse: the (visible) male semen was held to be the seed, sown in what appeared to them to be a fertile field—but merely a field. However, this view is contradicted by the contemporary Athenian law which forbade marriage between siblings who had come from a single mother, while children of the same father but different mothers were permitted to marry. A further inconsistency is found in the regulations we have already discussed concerning the *epiklēros,* which encouraged a close degree of inbreeding within the paternal line.

We have instances from the late Archaic and early Classical periods of some of the leading citizens—among them Megacles and Miltiades—being married to foreign women while their children by them were considered to be citizens. The influence of powerful fathers-in-law was desirable from the standpoint of the ruling classes, but not so in terms of Athenian notions of democracy. Yet not until the legislation of Pericles in 451–50 B.C. was it necessary that the mother of citizens be a citizen herself. This law was prompted by the realization that the number of citizens was too greatly increased.[30] This same law was later relaxed, at a point in Athenian history when the population had dwindled and it was necessary to increase the number of citizens.

Pericles, in the funeral oration he delivered after only one year of the Peloponnesian War, exhorted married women to bear more children.[31] The shortage of males became more critical as the war continued. The proportion of women in the city was increased by the departure of a large expeditionary force, consisting of 4,000 hoplites, 300 cavalry, and 100 triremes to Sicily in 415 B.C. Moreover, the occupation of Decelea in 411 B.C. forced the Athenians to fight throughout the year, rather than, as previously, only in the summer. Evidence of the continuing shortage of men can be found in the arming of slaves and in the abnormal deployment of knights for the naval battle of Arginusae.[32]

One effect on women was that fewer potential husbands were available. This concern is voiced in 411 B.C. in *Lysistrata.*[33] The corollary to the dearth of husbands naturally would have been a decrease in the number of legitimate sons born. The diminution would have been intolerable, in a state engaged in a lengthy war. Therefore, owing to the lack of husbands, and the need to increase the population, the Athenians stretched the concept of legitimacy. As Diogenes Laertius states: "For they say the Athenians, because of the scarcity of men, wished to increase the population, and passed a vote that a man might marry one Athenian woman and have children by another." This practice, then, explains the stories that Cal-

lias, son of Hipponicus (see p. 81), and Socrates and Euripides each
had two wives, and that Myrto was the mother of the two sons of
Socrates who were still children in 399 B.C.[34] Though bigamy was not
normally tolerated in Athens, temporary bigamy was a necessary
and expedient response to the high wartime mortality rate of males,
the excess number of women, and the need to replenish the
population.[35]

In these three known cases of bigamy, all the wives were Athenian citizens. However, since the chief requirement of the citizenship
law had been Athenian parentage on both sides, and citizenship had
not been predicated on actual marriage, the relaxation of this law
may imply that foreign women were now permitted to be mothers of
Athenian citizens. In other words, what was new in this period was
not so much the fact of legal bigamy—although it is important that
such legalization entitled the children of the second wife to inherit
from their father—but rather that the situation of Athens before 451
B.C. was restored, and Athenian men could marry foreign women
and have children who would enjoy the privileges of citizenship.

Some Athenian men may well have preferred foreign women to
Athenians. One of the more abominable crimes of the Thirty Tyrants (404–403 B.C.) was that they were responsible for the spinsterhood of Athenian daughters.[36] They accomplished this, no doubt, by
executing many eligible men who were their political adversaries;
and, by continuing to countenance the relaxation of the citizenship
law, they were not forcing the surviving men to marry Athenian
brides. When the democrats deposed the Thirty in 403 B.C., the
citizenship law was reimposed, making Athenian women desirable
marriage partners if only because they were once again the sole
means of producing children who could be legitimate heirs. (The
children produced by the mixed unions preceding the reimposition
of the law continued to be considered citizens.) [37]

Many a play of New Comedy ends happily with the recognition
that a young woman of unknown parentage who is about to become
a concubine is truly an Athenian citizen and can marry her lover.
Foreign women residing in Athens were tempted to pretend they
were citizens in order to obtain the security and advantages of
marriage to male citizens. The celebrated speech *Against Neaira*,
attributed to Demosthenes, is the prosecution, probably in 340 B.C.,
of a woman who had practiced prostitution as a foreign slave in
Corinth, with several notable and wealthy men among her clients.

When freed, she lived in Athens, with the children who had been
born to her in slavery, as the legitimate wife of an Athenian citizen. It
is indicative of the invisibility acquired by the ex-slave prostitute
upon becoming a respectable Athenian wife that her husband in
turn was able to pass off her daughter (born in slavery) as a citizen,
giving her twice in marriage to citizens, one of whom was no less a
personage than the King Archon, a high religious magistrate.

## Biology of Motherhood and Demographic Speculations

The average age of menarche, as well as the age of a woman's
first marriage, was fourteen.[38] J. Lawrence Angel's studies of skeletal
remains indicate that the average adult longevity in Classical Greece
was 45.0 years for males and 36.2 for females.[39] Other sorts of studies
give lower figures for both sexes, but all agree that females
predeceased males by an average of five to ten years.[40] Without the
intervention of war—which would selectively affect the mortality of
males—the sex difference in longevity alone would be responsible for
a large ratio of men to women in the population. According to
Angel, the interval between childbirths was approximately four
years. Allowing for two years of adolescent sterility after menarche,
if the typical female died at 36.2, she would have borne five or six
children. Angel's examination of female skeletal remains shows an
average of 4.6 births per woman, with 1.6 juvenile deaths, resulting
in 3 survivors per female. According to these calculations, the
Athenian population would have increased each generation, and
indeed Aristotle stated that Pericles' citizenship law was enacted
because of the large number of citizens.

What mechanisms did Pericles use to contain the growth of the
population? What proportion of the citizenry was male, what
proportion female? How many young men died on the battlefields
and were buried en masse or cremated, thus depriving us of the
opportunity to analyze their skeletons or read their tombstones?
Since there is no way of definitely ascertaining the demography of
Classical Athens, what follows is an attempt to reconstruct a puzzle
with many of the pieces missing.

Homosexuality, anal intercourse, recourse to prostitutes and
slaves or dislike of women, and the preference for a sexually inactive
wife continued to be adaptations for population control. There is

little specific information for the Classical period on female contraceptive techniques, but it may be assumed that certain time-honored methods were employed.[41] Abortion was practiced, although those who took the Hippocratic Oath promised never to administer abortifacients. Aristotle distinguished between abortion before and after the foetus felt sensation and had life, by stating that the former was sanctionable but the latter was not.[42]

Cemeteries bear witness to the high rate of infant mortality. The natural mortality of infants in Classical Athens was so high as to preclude the wholesale practice of infanticide.[43] Nevertheless, I think that it was practiced to some extent, for it was necessary in order to limit the population in peacetime, and that more female infants were disposed of than male. We also hear little of twins in Classical Greece and can deduce that usually only one of a pair was raised. Since a baby was not a member of the family until the father made a ceremonial declaration to that effect, the distinction between exposure of the newborn and late abortion was blurred. Theoretically, in order to perpetuate each *oikos* it was necessary that each family contribute at most one daughter to the supply of eligible brides. Through remarriage—which occurred not infrequently during the fifth and fourth centuries B.C., and is well documented for the upper classes—a woman could produce heirs for more than one family, and an unmarried man who lacked a son could adopt one to perpetuate his *oikos*. Girls were rarely adopted. The adoption of a niece by the wealthy Hagnias in 396 B.C. may have been a result of the dearth of young men and the surfeit of unmarried women following the disastrous events of the second half of the Peloponnesian War.[44]

It was necessary to have only one male heir. However, for insurance, a family probably would raise more than one son. There was less compulsion for a family to raise more than a single daughter, although some did raise a number of daughters. Extra males did not threaten to increase the population permanently, for many men were killed in war or could migrate to colonies.

After Pericles' citizenship law discouraged marriage to foreigners, if my demographic speculations are correct, there was not a sufficient number of citizen brides for those who survived through whom additional families could be engendered. The citizenship law may have been reimposed because, even in the brief time when it was not in force, a sufficient number of citizen children had been produced and the war was subsiding. The quotation from Diogenes Laertius (above, p. 66) and Aristotle's statement that the imposition of the citizenship law by Pericles was motivated by the growth in the citizen population show that the Athenians understood that the simplest means of controlling the growth of the population was by increasing or decreasing the number of females who could produce citizen children.[45] The increase was effected by the relaxation of the citizenship law, the decrease by female infanticide and the reimposition of the citizenship law. In normal times, when citizen men outnumbered citizen women, there were not enough brides for each man to be able to marry.[46] In unusual periods—for example, during the last quarter of the fifth century B.C., when the male population had been depleted by the many years of war and by the loss of a huge contingent of soldiers in Sicily—some men had legitimate relationships with more than one woman.[47]

It must be recognized that ancient literary sources may merely take note of the children who mattered most: that is, the boys. But a casual survey definitely gives the impression of a preponderance of male children among well-known Athenians. Socrates had three sons, Pericles two legitimate sons and another by Aspasia. Plato had two brothers, one sister, and one half-brother. A study of the propertied and influential families listed in Johannes Kirchner's classical work, *Prosopographica Attica*, shows that, of 346 families, 271 had more sons than daughters and that the ratio of boys to girls is roughly five to one.[48] These statistics have some significance but cannot be taken at immediate face value, since Herodotus reported that Cleomenes died childless, leaving only a daughter,[49] and in modern Greece, when a peasant with three sons and two daughters is asked how many children he has, he is likely to answer, "three." We may also observe an oversight in Herodotus' report that before the battle of Salamis, the Athenians asked the rest of the Greek fleet for protection so that they might evacuate their children and women from Attica; but upon arriving in their city the Athenians overlooked the women and actually made a proclamation that each man should save his children and slaves.[50]

## Women at Work

By the late fifth century B.C., owing to the need for the safety afforded by city walls, urban living replaced farming for many Athenians. Thus, when one compares Sparta to Athens, it is necessary to remember that the former never comprised more than a settlement of villages, while Athens was one of the largest Greek cities.[51] The effect of urbanization upon women was to have their activities moved indoors, and to make their labor less visible and hence less valued.

Urban living created a strong demarcation between the activities of men of the upper and lower classes, as well as between those of men and women. Men were free to engage in politics, intellectual and military training, athletics, and the sort of business approved for gentlemen. Some tasks were regarded as banausic and demeaning, befitting slaves rather than citizens. Naturally, a male citizen who needed income was unable to maintain the ideal and was forced to labor in banausic employment. Women of the upper class, excluded from the activities of the males, supervised and—when they wished —pursued many of the same tasks deemed appropriate to slaves.[52] Since the work was despised, so was the worker. Women's work was productive, but because it was the same as slaves' work, it was not highly valued in the ideology of Classical Athens. The intimacy of the discussions between heroines and choruses of female slaves in tragedy and the depictions of mistress and slave on tombstones imply a bond between slave and free, for they spent much time together and their lives were not dissimilar.[53]

Yet the hostility engendered by women of the leisured class who did not work, but sat at home as idle parasites, is apparent in Xenophon's report of a conversation between Socrates and Aristarchus.[54] Aristarchus complains that, due to political turmoil following the establishment of oligarchy, fourteen of his female relatives have moved into his house for protection and he cannot afford to maintain them. Socrates suggests that they be put to work; Aristarchus counters that they are freeborn ladies, not accustomed to working. Socrates convinces Aristarchus that labor is not demeaning and that the women themselves would be happier if employed productively. The women are put to spinning and weaving—skills they had learned as part of a gentlewoman's education, in order to be able to supervise slaves, but which they had never expected to be compelled to use for monetary gain. The result is an improvement in the dispositions of the women, as well as in the attitude of the man of the house toward them. We are led to understand that he kept them at these jobs permanently, and made a profit too. We should keep in mind that Socrates' suggestions for the amelioration of Athenian life were acceptable only to his own small circle, and that his disciple Xenophon was a theoretician, wealthy, and an exile. However, the problems with which Socrates concerned himself were widespread, and had been noted even in the Archaic period in the poetry of Hesiod and Semonides.

Women of all social classes worked mainly indoors or near the house in order to guard it. They concerned themselves with the care of young children, the nursing of sick slaves, the fabrication of clothing, and the preparation of food. The preparation of ordinary food was considered exclusively women's work. During the siege of Plataea, when the city was evacuated, one hundred and ten women were left behind to cook for the four hundred men remaining to defend the city.[55]

The tasks enumerated by Homer for mortal women and goddesses are the same tasks pursued by women in Athens four hundred years later. The only technological advance facilitating women's work that can be detected in urban Athens was the improvement of the water supply in the late sixth century B.C. Transporting water in a pitcher balanced on the head was a female occupation. Because fetching water involved social mingling, gossip at the fountain, and possible flirtations, slave girls were usually sent on this errand.[56]

Women did not go to market for food, and even now they do not do so in rural villages in Greece.[57] The feeling that purchase or exchange was a financial transaction too complex for women, as well as the wish to protect women from the eyes of strangers and from intimate dealings with shopkeepers, contributed to classifying marketing as a man's occupation.

Wealthier women were distinguished by exercising a managerial role, rather than performing all the domestic work themselves. Xenophon wrote a treatise elevating household management to the status of a science. According to the *Oeconomicus,* the wise husband will teach this science to his young bride. The husband and wife are to have a partnership, he performing the outdoor work, including bringing food and wool and other commodities, she supervising the transformation of the raw materials into a finished product. The good wife, according to Xenophon, has a favorable relationship with her slaves, but even more onerous duties than they, since she bears the responsibility of caring for the household's possessions. The Socratic principle that knowledge is virtue is given practical application. The wife who masters the science of economics has so greatly improved herself that Socrates pays her the ultimate compliment: he says that she displays "a masculine mind." [58]

Poorer women, even citizens, went out to work, most of them pursuing occupations that were an extension of women's work in the home. Women were employed as washerwomen, as woolworkers, and in other clothing industries. They also worked as vendors, selling food or what they had spun or woven at home. Some women sold garlands they had braided. Women were also employed as nurses of children and midwives. One woman is depicted on a vase as a vase painter, but it is impossible to determine from such a portrayal whether she was a citizen.[59]

An important source for our knowledge of the occupations pursued by women is the dedications that freedwomen made to Athena when they were released from obligations to their former owners.[60] It was customary to offer a silver cup valued at one hundred drachmas, and lists of the dedicators, with their origins and occupations, survive. The respectable occupations available to these freedwomen are not noticeably more numerous or diverse than those open to citizens.

Although some prostitutes acquired a transitory wealth, few women became rich by working.[61] A few metic women did engage in large-scale financial transactions, but it was very unusual for a citizen woman to do so. Women could not buy or sell land. Athenian law restricted women and minors to contracts valued at less than a *medimnus* of barley (a *medimnus* could sustain a normal family for six days).

In the fifth and fourth centuries, Athenian women could acquire property through their dowries, or by gift, or by inheritance as sisters, cousins, nieces, and aunts, though probably not as mothers. Some women were acutely aware of financial matters, but their property was nevertheless managed by male guardians.[62] The Athenian provisions are in stark contrast to those of Sparta and Gortyn, which gave women real control over their property.

*Education*

Direct participation in the affairs of government—including holding public office, voting, and serving as jurors and as soldiers —was possible only for male citizens. The advanced education of a boy concentrated on the art of rhetoric, with the aim of delivering persuasive speeches at public meetings and winning a fine reputation among men. Physical education was also stressed in order to provide the state with strong soldiers. The qualities admired in girls were the opposite from those desired in boys: silence, submissiveness, and abstinence from men's pleasures.[63] The statesman Pericles, in his funeral oration delivered in 430 B.C., advised the widows of fallen soldiers that the greatest glory would accrue to the woman who was least talked about by men, whether in complimentary or scandalous terms.[64] Since citizen girls were not to look forward to the public careers that brought status to men, it was sufficient for them to be instructed in domestic arts by their mothers. While her male contemporary was living in his parents' house and developing mental and physical skills, the adolescent girl was already married and had young children. Thus the discrepancy in the educational levels of men and women, added to the huge age differential between bride and groom, resulted in feelings of condescension and paternalism on the part of the husband, and a marriage characterized by a lack of friendship in the modern sense between husband and wife.

Athenian law of all periods tended to regard the wife as a veritable child, having the legal status of a minor in comparison to her husband. Although males came of age at eighteen, females never did; the childbearing wife was really a child herself. That the husband would rule over the wife and children was considered natural by Aristotle. He deduced that the friendship between husband and wife was "unequal" and that the connubial relationship was based on utility, in contrast to the equitable relationships between men which are the basis of social and political organization. Man and wife need each other, Aristotle admitted, but their relationship was as a benefactor to beneficiary.[65] Aristotle was describing the patriarchal family of Classical Athens, but his influence was widespread and enduring.

## Religion

Religion was the major sphere of public life in which women participated, although it is necessary to remember that at Athens cult was subordinate to and an integral part of the state, and the state, as we have seen, was in the hands of men. Since it would be impossible to survey here all the Athenian cults in which women played a role, we shall examine only three, and these in a limited way: the cult of the Olympian goddess Athena, the Mysteries of Demeter and Korē at Eleusis, and the exclusively female celebration of the Thesmophoria.[66]

Athena Polias was the patron goddess of Athens, and the priestess of Athena Polias was a person of great importance and some influence. The priestesshood was hereditary in the noble family of the Eteoboutadae. Herodotus gives two early indications of the political use of the prestige of the priestess on behalf of democratic factions.[67] In 508 B.C., when the Spartan King Cleomenes attempted to meddle in Athenian politics by opposing the popular reformer Cleisthenes and approached the shrine of Athena, the priestess reminded him that it was not lawful for Dorians (*sc.* foreigners) to enter. Again, the priestess supported the decision to evacuate Athens before the battle of Salamis in 480 B.C. by reporting that the sacred snake of Athena had already departed from the Acropolis. Inscriptions and dedications honoring the priestesses of Athena are common, especially from the Hellenistic and Roman periods, and some of their names are inscribed on seats in the theater of Dionysus.[68] Women and men participated in the Panathenaea, a festival celebrated annually on the birthday of Athena, and quadrennially with greater magnificence. From the religious viewpoint, the essential feature of the festival was the sacrificial offering of animals. Preceding the sacrifice was a procession that conducted the sacrificial victims to the altar. The Parthenon frieze depicts women in this procession mingling with men. Of particular note are the young girls, called *kanēphoroi,* who carried sacred baskets in the procession. The *kanēphoroi* were virgins selected from noble families. Their virginity was a potent factor in securing the propitious use of the sacred offerings and sacrificial instruments carried in their baskets. To prevent a candidate from participating in this event was to cast aspersions on her reputation. High on the list of women around whom—as passive and unwitting objects of insults to be avenged—the course of history has turned is the sister of Harmodius. The sons of the tyrant Pisistratus first invited her to be a basket-bearer and then rejected her, claiming she was unsuitable. This insult to his sister provoked Harmodius and his friend Aristogiton to the act of assassination in 514 B.C., an act that earned them reputations as the liberators of Athens.[69]

Every fourth year at the Greater Panathenaea a new *peplos* (robe) was manufactured to be worn by an ancient image of Athena.[70] The weaving of the cloth was begun by two of the *arrēphoroi,* who were girls between the ages of seven and eleven, chosen from noble families by the King Archon to perform a variety of religious functions for a year. Other women continued the weaving and embroidering of the *peplos.* For the Panathenaic procession the *peplos* was spread like a sail above a ship on wheels. The Parthenon frieze depicts the presentation of the *peplos* to Athena.

Lesser and Greater Mysteries were celebrated annually at Eleusis in honor of Demeter and her daughter Korē (Persephone).[71] [Plate 8] The rituals in earliest times were connected with the death and rebirth of grain and developed into an allegory of human immortality. The Eleusinian Mysteries survived as the most revered Greek cult until the end of paganism. Yet little is known for certain about the Mysteries, and there is scarcely any indication of the reason for their popularity.

Originally a private family cult of the noble Eumolpidae, the Mysteries came under the control of the Athenian state before 600 B.C. The chief priest, the *hierophantēs,* most exalted of all Athenian priests, was a Eumolpid and held office for life. There were additional male officials, among whom the *dadouchos,* or torchbearer, was next in importance after the *hierophantēs.* He was assisted by a priestess called the *dadouchousa.* Other female celebrants included two priestesses known as *hierophantides,* also Eumolpidae, who held office for life and who could be married. One *hierophantis* served Demeter, the other Korē, and both were the main assistants of the *hierophantēs.* A group of priestesses *panageis* (sacrosanct), also known as *melissae* (bees), lived together in segregated dwellings and had no contact with men. The name "bees" probably alludes to the asexuality associated with these insects (p. 49). The function of these priestesses is unknown.

Rivaling the *hierophantēs* in prestige was the chief priestess of Demeter. She came from the family of either the Phileidae or the Eumolpidae. The priestess of Demeter, like the *hierophantēs*, was paid an obol (a small coin) daily by everyone being initiated into the Lesser or Greater Mysteries. The priestess was eponymous—that is, at Eleusis events were dated by the name of the priestess and her successive years in office.[72]

All women, men, children, and slaves of Greek speech, untainted by homicide, were eligible for initiation into the Mysteries. The preliminary rites included a bath of purification, fasting, sacrifices, and the drinking of the *kykeōn*, a barley potion. Only female initiates participated in the *kernophoria*, the bearing of the sacred vessels, which was one of the preliminary ceremonies. The initiates also watched women perform sacred dances, in commemoration of the time when the women of Eleusis danced in honor of Demeter. Included in the ritual were recitation, the revelation of sacred objects, and a dramatic performance probably showing the sorrow of Demeter at the abduction of Korē and her subsequent joy at her daughter's return. The priestess of Demeter played the roles of both Demeter and Korē.[73] In view of the multiple manifestations of the mother goddess and son-consort dyad throughout antiquity, especially in the Middle East, one may well be astounded at the appeal that a unique religion centering on a mother and daughter held for Athenians.

Another festival honoring Demeter, but strictly reserved for women, was the Thesmophoria.[74] Unlike the Eleusinian Mysteries, the Thesmophoria never developed into more than an agrarian festival, but it was noted for preserving its ancient rituals without alteration. At Athens the celebration took place at the autumn sowing in order to ensure the growth of the seed grain by means of fertility magic. The precise nature of the rites and the days on which they were enacted are much disputed, but the following interpretation seems plausible.

The Thesmophoria was celebrated for three days. The first day was titled *kathodos* (going down) and *anodos* (rising up). Pigs, which were animals sacred to Demeter, had been thrown into subterranean caves early in the summer, probably at the festival of Demeter and Korē known as the Scirophoria. On the first day of the Thesmophoria, women went down into the caves and recovered the remains of the pigs, which they mixed with seed grain and placed on altars.

The second day was titled *nēsteia* (fasting). The women fasted sitting on the ground, mimicking Demeter's behavior at the loss of her daughter. On the third day, *kalligeneia* (fair birth), the remains of the pigs and seed grain were scattered in the fields.

Only free women of unblemished reputation were permitted to participate in the Thesmophoria.[75] They were chaste for three days in preparation for the festival and continued to abstain during the course of it. Yet they indulged in the foul language and obscenities characteristic of fertility rituals. The women chose their own officials from among themselves.[76] Men were involved only to the extent that, if they were wealthy, they were compelled to bear the expense of the festival as a liturgy or tax in behalf of their wives.[77]

The existence of exclusively women's festivals has been variously explained. One hypothesis is that women's cults were survivals from a matriarchal period when all religion was in the hands of women. Another explanation notes that women in early societies were in charge of gardening, and hence involved in fertility cults. Regardless of the social structure, women's connection with birth and fertility is obvious, and it is not difficult to understand the urge to apply women's influence to the crops.

A comparison between Archaic and Classical Athens gives the impression that women were forced into obscurity in the latter period. Certainly there are no stories of respectable women in the fifth century B.C. to compare with those surrounding the members of Pisistratus' court. It may be suggested, on the basis of comparisons between Archaic and Classical Athens and between Athenian and Spartan or Roman society, that some women—at least those of the upper class—flourished in an aristocratic society, while none fared as well under the democracy. The curbing of the aristocrats by the democracy of the fifth century B.C. entailed the repression of all women, but leaned especially heavily on the aristocrats who had the time and the means to make and enjoy displays of wealth. It may also be suggested that after the class stratification that separated individual men according to such criteria as noble descent and wealth was eliminated, the ensuing ideal of equality among male citizens was intolerable. The will to dominate was such that they then had to separate themselves as a group and claim to be superior to all nonmembers: foreigners, slaves, and women.

# V

## PRIVATE LIFE IN
## CLASSICAL ATHENS

SOCRATES' BLUNT dismissal of his wife Xanthippe from his deathbed and his desire to die among his male companions is a dramatic, if exaggerated, indication of the emotional gulf between husband and wife.[1] The distance between husbands and wives extended to other spheres. Athenian men and women lived separate lives, and most of our information is about men's lives. It is almost easier to describe the activities of men and then simply say women did not do most of these things.

### The Seclusion of Women

The separation of the sexes was spatially emphasized While men spent most of their day in public areas such as the marketplace and the gymnasium, respectable women remained at home. In contrast to the admired public buildings, mostly frequented by men, the residential quarters of Classical Athens were dark, squalid, and unsanitary.[2]

Women stayed home not only because their work did not allow them much chance to get out but because of the influence of public opinion. Many families were likely to own at least one female slave,[3] but even a woman with slaves was tied down by the demands of her household, husband, and infants.[4] [Plate 9] Wealthier women were most likely to stay home and send their slaves on errands. But poor women, lacking slaves, could not be kept in seclusion,[5] and in fact women found pleasure in the company of other women, for they gossiped while fetching water, washing clothes, and borrowing utensils.

Women of all economic classes went out for festivals and funerals. The close association of women and mourning noted for earlier periods (see p. 43) continued in Classical Athens. In an effort to promote democratization, Solonian legislation had curtailed the participation of women in funerals, for mourning by large numbers of women had been a means for ostentatious families to parade their wealth. The *prothesis* (lying-in-state) formerly held in the courtyard was to take place indoors. Only women over sixty years of age or within the degree of children of cousins were permitted to enter the room of the deceased and to accompany the dead when the corpse was carried to the tomb, following the men in the funeral procession.[6] Xanthippe's visit to Socrates on the day he was to die was not warmly received, but Socrates' behavior was unusual. When some men were condemned to death by the notorious Thirty, they summoned their sisters, mothers, wives, or other female relatives to see them in prison.[7]

Whether women attended dramatic performances has been much disputed. It seems likely that they did, but the contrary can be maintained with plausibility.[8] Dramatic festivals evolved from the worship of Dionysus, and all the roles were acted by male actors; but, as Euripides' *Bacchae* demonstrates, women were highly enthusiastic participants in the cult of this god. On the other hand, women who did not have slaves to tend their babies were probably not able to attend a full day's performance, or even to see one play. What is interesting about this controversy is that, numerous though they probably were over the years, the women, absent or present, were not noticed by our ancient authorities.

The separation of the sexes was expressed in private architecture by the provision of separate quarters for men and women.[9] Women usually inhabited the more remote rooms, away from the street and from the public areas of the house. If the house had two stories, the wife along with female slaves lived upstairs. The sexes were separated to restrain the household slaves from breeding without the master's permission.[10]

There are, however, some hints that the usual standards of decorum were broached during the second half of the Peloponnesian War. Andocides describes an infamous *ménage à trois* consisting of Callias and two citizen women, one who was his legitimate wife, and the second his wife's mother who became his concubine and eventually bore a son to him.[11] The second example is that of Hipparete, the wife of Alcibiades, who does appear to have acted with extraordinary independence when she left his house in order to obtain a divorce.

Another well-born woman whose behavior was unusual was Agariste, the wife of Alcmaeonides. She was one of three witnesses who gave evidence that Alcibiades celebrated the Mysteries in the house of Charmides.[12] That she witnessed this celebration at night and publicly identified several participants is remarkable in view of the constraints on women in times of peace.

Free women were usually secluded so that they could not be seen by men who were not close relatives. An orator could maintain that some women were even too modest to be seen by men who were relatives, and for a strange man to intrude upon free women in the house of another man was tantamount to a criminal act.[13] In the first quarter of the fourth century B.C., a husband who murdered his wife's seducer gave a vivid picture of his living arrangements:

> Athenians, when I decided to marry, and brought a wife to my house, for a while I was inclined not to bother her, but neither was she to be too free to do as she wished. I watched her as much as was possible, and took my duty as a husband seriously. But when my son was born, I began to trust her, and put all my possessions in her hands, presuming that this was the greatest proof of intimacy.
>
> In the beginning, Athenians, she was the best of all wives. She was clever, economical, and kept everything neat in the house. But then my mother died; and her death was the cause of all my troubles. For when my wife attended her funeral, she was seen by this man, and, as time passed, he seduced her. He looked out for our slave who goes to market and, making propositions, he corrupted her.
>
> Now first, gentlemen, I must tell you that I have a small two-story house, with the women's quarters upstairs, the men's downstairs, each having equal space.
>
> When our son was born, his mother nursed him; but in order that she might avoid the risk of climbing downstairs each time she had to clean the baby, I used to live upstairs and the women below. And so it became quite customary for my wife to go downstairs often and sleep with the child, so that she could give him the breast and keep him from crying.

This was the situation for a long time, and I never became suspicious, but I was so simple-minded that I believed my own was the chastest wife in the city.

Time passed, gentlemen; I came home unexpectedly from the country, and after dinner my son began crying and fretting. Actually, the slave was annoying him on purpose to make him do this, for the man was in the house—as I found out later.

I told my wife to go and give the baby the breast, to stop his crying. At first she refused, as though glad to see me home again after my long absence. Then I became angry and told her to go.

"Oh, yes," she said, "so that you can have a try at the little slave girl here. You dragged her about before, when you were drunk!"

I laughed. She got up, went out of the room, closed the door, pretending it was a joke, and turned the key in the lock. I, thinking nothing about it, nor having the slightest suspicion, was glad to go to sleep after my journey from the country.

Toward dawn she returned and unlocked the door. I asked her why the doors had been creaking during the night. She said that the lamp beside the baby had gone out and she had gone to get a light at the neighbor's.

I was silent, and thought it really was so. But it did seem to me, gentlemen, that she had put makeup on her face, despite her brother's death less than thirty days before. Even so, I said nothing about what she did. I just left, without a word.[14]

The speaker, Euphiletus, is defending himself against a charge of premeditated homicide, because he and his friends slew Eratosthenes when he caught his wife in bed with him.

The speech raises a number of suspicions about the motives of Euphiletus. After his wife had given birth to a son, the purpose of their marriage was fulfilled. Euphiletus very carefully points out that his wife's indiscretion began after the child was born, and therefore there can be no doubt about the legitimacy of his son. He moved upstairs and probably was cavorting with the slave girl. He says that his wife accused him of this, and we may consider the charge to be true, or wonder why the mother rather than the slave was cleaning the baby in the middle of the night. Euphiletus may have been able to retain his wife's dowry for his son as a penalty for her adultery, although this is not certain. It would seem, however, that if a cuckolded husband had to surrender the dowry, then he would be penalized for a crime not committed by him; if an adulterous wife was sent back to her relatives without her dowry, they would be penalized for not having brought her up properly. Euphiletus was a person of moderate wealth. He admits that his house is small; he has only one female slave and does not employ a wetnurse. Even so, he maintains separate living quarters for husband and wife, although the wife sometimes sleeps in her husband's room. (His claim that he did not bother his wife much at first probably is a euphemism for not making sexual demands on her.)

The clothing of respectable women also served to conceal them from the eyes of strange men. Women's clothing was, by modern standards, simple.[15] The material used in Classical times by respectable women was usually wool or linen, but prostitutes wore saffron-dyed material of gauzelike transparency. The style of dress was either Ionian or Dorian. A *himation,* or shawl, was worn with either style and could be drawn over the head as a hood. Since the Ionic *chiton* was confining, it tended to be the garment worn in public, and a shorter tunic was worn around the house and as a nightdress and petticoat. There was a large variety of sandals and slipprs. Sandals with thongs between the toes were worn, as well as sandals with straps bound around the lower leg as far as the knee. Some women wore shoes with platform soles to increase their height.[16]

Vase paintings show women bathing themselves and attending to various parts of their toilette. They removed their pubic hair by singeing and plucking.[17] Cosmetics were used by housewives as well as by prostitutes. A white complexion was considered attractive, since it proved that a woman was wealthy enough not to go out in the sun. Powder of white lead was commonly used for this, and when women went outdoors they protected themselves from the sun with a parasol. Rouge was used on the cheeks.

Although dress was simple, jewelry and hairdos could be complicated. Women wore their hair loose, surmounted by a coronet or headband, or up in a chignon or net. False curls seem to have been used sometimes. Slaves' hair, however, was usually cropped. Some of the exquisite jewelry can still be admired, since it was preserved along with the bronze mirrors and containers for cosmetics in the graves of the women with whom they were buried.

Some women are portrayed on their tombstones choosing jewelry from a chest proffered by a slave, or adorning themselves with the aid of a mirror. [Plates 10 and 11] In Chapter III we noted the lack of Archaic tombstones commemorating women in Attica, and ventured to guess that their absence was stimulated by sumptuary laws in force in the sixth century B.C. Since the dress and activities of women are frequently an index to the wealth of their husbands, we are not surprised to find in the burials of women an indication of the family's status and the paraphernalia appropriate to a leisured class.

## *The Physical Condition of Women*

The study of Geometric cemeteries suggested that female deaths increased during the childbearing years (see p. 45). Childbirth was difficult. Medea announced that she would prefer to stand in the front line of battle three times than to give birth to one child.[18] Many women made offerings in gratitude to Eileithyia, goddess of childbirth. The robes of women who died in childbirth were dedicated to Artemis at Brauron,[19] since she was patroness of the life cycle of women—and there are several Classical relief sculptures apparently of women who died in childbirth.[20] Beginning in Classical times and continuing through the Roman period, women outnumber men as donors to Asclepius, the god of health.[21]

Mothers and midwives normally assisted women in childbirth.[22] There were male physicians, but some examples drawn from Hippocrates' *Aphorisms* do not indicate that their ministry was notably beneficial:

30.   Acute illnesses are fatal to pregnant women.

31.   Miscarriage follows blood-letting in pregnant women, especially if the foetus is large.

32.   If a woman vomits blood, this stops with the onset of menstruation.

41.   To determine whether a woman is pregnant, give her a drink of hydromel on retiring when she has not had supper. If she suffers from colic in the stomach she is pregnant; if not, she is not pregnant.

42.   A pregnant woman has a good complexion if the child is male; a poor complexion if the child is female.

43.   If a pregnant woman has erysipelas of the womb, she will die.

48.   A male foetus leans to the right, a female to the left.

49.   When a drug that produces sneezing is used to expel the afterbirth, stop up the mouth and nose.

Motherhood at an early age. combined with a life spent indoors. was disadvantageous to the health of the Athenian woman. More children were born in the first half of the twenty-year reproductive period than in the second half. making the period from approximately sixteen to twenty-six years old the most hazardous. It is interesting to recall here Plutarch's approbation of the Spartan custom of having girls marry at eighteen. since they are then in a better physical condition to bear children. although he preferred earlier marriages for other reasons. Xenophon. Plato. and Aristotle all believed that Spartan customs concerning women were more wholesome. Xenophon praised the Spartans for nourishing their girls as well as their boys. for it was unusual among the Greeks to do so.[23] This differentiation in nourishment could exist even for suckling newborns. The "mothers' rations" awarded to Ionian women in 489 B.C. in Persepolis were exactly twice as much wine, beer, and grain for women who had given birth to boys as for those who had borne girls.[24]

Xenophon also approved of the Spartan custom of encouraging women to exercise so that they could maintain a good physical condition for motherhood. The well-developed physiques of Spartan women caused comment among the Athenian housewives in the comedy *Lysistrata*,[25] although it may be suggested that performing household chores, especially moving back and forth before the loom, offered an Athenian woman ample opportunity for strenuous exercise.

In the *Republic,* Plato prescribed physical exercise for women and stated that females should become parents for the first time at twenty and males at thirty. Later, in the *Laws,* he reduced the age minimum for females to any time between sixteen and twenty.[26]

Aristotle suggested that pregnant women be forced to exercise by passing a law that they must take a daily walk to worship the divinities presiding over childbirth. He also noted that it was undesirable for the very young to produce offspring, since more of the babies were likely to be female, and the mothers endured a more difficult labor and were more likely to die in childbirth. He suggested that the optimum age for marriage was eighteen for women, thirty-seven for men.[27]

Many women did survive the childbearing years, though the fact that there is less information about menopause than about menarche implies that fewer women underwent this experience. The age of menopause was typically from forty to fifty.[28] Solon's Funeral Law, permitting women over sixty who were not close relatives to visit corpses, demonstrates that some women attained old age.[29] There were some old men as well, although as a group the elderly formed but a small percentage of the total population.

## Sexuality

The sexual behavior of citizen women was regulated by laws—mostly those attributed to Solon, who was himself a homosexual.[30] The guardian of an unmarried woman caught *in flagrante delicto* had the right to sell her into slavery. I do not know of any case where this sale actually occurred, whether because the severity of the penalty was a deterrent, or because the father was reluctant to make the scandal in his family public. Since the aim of marriage between citizens was the production of legitimate children, adultery was a public offense because it could result in the introduction of a child unrelated to the husband—and possibly the offspring of a non-Athenian—into the husband's house and kinship-group cults and onto the rolls of Athenian citizens. Both parties were severely punished, but, despite the penalties, cases of adultery are recorded.

Whether adultery came about through rape or seduction, the male was considered the legally guilty or active party, the woman passive. The husband of a raped or adulterous woman was legally compelled to divorce her. The accused woman had no opportunity to proclaim her innocence, though, with difficulty, her guardian might do so in her behalf. A woman thus condemned was not allowed to participate in public ceremonies, nor to wear jewelry, and the most severe deprivation was probably that she would be a social outcast and never find another husband.

The penalties for the male caught in adultery with a citizen woman are indicative of the Athenian attitude toward their households and their women. The penalty for rape was less than for seduction. Seduction was considered a more heinous crime than rape, for it implies a relationship over a period of time during which the seducer wins the affection of the woman and access to the possessions of her husband's household. In a city where only men and male children belonged to families in any permanent sense, but where women were easily transferred from their fathers' families to those of successive husbands, men were readily suspicious of the loyalty of women to the families in which they found themselves. Therefore, the aggrieved husband had the right but not the obligation to kill the seducer. The rapist gained the enmity of the woman, and thus posed less of a threat to the husband. The penalty for rape was a monetary fine.

Interestingly, Athenian law governing sexual behavior was not limited to what one must not do, but also concerned itself with what one should do. Thus the husband of an heiress was to consort with her three times a month. While this suggests that the main purpose of their union was to produce an heir, Plutarch adds another dimension to the relationship when he says that any husband ought to show affection to a good wife three times a month because the result will be a reduction in marital tensions.[31]

Intercourse thrice monthly was deemed sufficient sexual attention for "good" citizen wives; many wives surely had fewer opportunities. As we have seen, the social segregation of the sexes in Classical Athens and the legal stipulations regarding connubial relations could make sex between husband and wife an obligatory act—fulfilled by procreation—rather than an intimate emotional encounter. In *Lysistrata*, it is true that husbands are brought to their knees by sheer sexual starvation, but this does not contradict the assertion that connubial intercourse was devoid of any concept of spiritual union. If the husband was not away on a military campaign, or enjoying the company of his fellows in homosexual relations, or consorting with prostitutes, he was likely, if he had fathered the requisite number of children, to sleep in separate quarters or with his female slaves, rather than risk his wife's abortion or infanticide. Thus, we may assume that the sexual experience of the majority of Athenian citizen women was not satisfying.

In view of the severe penalties, adultery was not a comfortable or wise alternative for either men or women, and, taking all factors into consideration, the Athenian atmosphere was not conducive to homoerotic relationships between women. Therefore, masturbation seems to have been viewed as an acceptable outlet for women's sexual appetites. [Plate 12] Some vase paintings depict phallic instruments being used by women for self-stimulation, and references are made to such devices by the respectable wives in *Lysistrata:*

LYSISTRATA: This is something I've been tossing about many sleepless nights.

CALONICE: It must be getting thin if you've been wearing it down.[32]

In this sex-starved climate, resort to onanism among women would be almost expected. Though Plato invented a fable—attributing the story to Aristophanes—in which he purported to explain the natural origin of female homosexuality,[33] we have no solid evidence of lesbian relationships actually occurring among citizen women. However, we should not take arguments *ex silentio* in matters of ancient history as valid; our sources may simply have not been interested in describing sexual activities other than those of men.

We may, however, weigh the likelihood of lesbianism among the respectable women of Athens against the absence of two important factors present in the societies of Sparta and Mytilene in Lesbos, where we know with some certainty that female homosexuality existed. In Athens, unlike the other cities, women did not generally find high esteem in the eyes of other women; and adolescent Athenian women were not educated in the kind of all-female setting common to Sparta and Lesbos. As we have seen, Athenian women were not only cut off at a very early age from contacts with males, including their husbands, but were most often secluded in the home—away from relations with any women other than their mother and sisters, or their female slaves.

We do know, on the other hand, that prostitutes in Athens enjoyed not only a full range of heterosexual diversions, but homosexual relations as well—again, on the basis of vase paintings showing phallic devices designed for simultaneous use by two women. But the gap between respectable women and prostitutes was so wide that we cannot begin to infer from one group to the other; rather, we must consider the latter a case unto themselves.

## Prostitutes

Prostitution flourished in Greece as early as the Archaic period. Large cities, especially those on the coast visited by sailors, supported vast numbers of prostitutes. As we mentioned earlier, one of the means for making Athens an attractive city on the mainland was the establishment of state-owned brothels to be staffed by slave women.[34]

Not only slaves were prostitutes. Like any slave, a prostitute could be granted her freedom by her owner, or could arrange to buy her own freedom by contracting a loan from a benefit club sometimes composed of past clients. She would repay the loan from her earnings as a free prostitute.[35] In this way many freedwomen and free noncitizen women permanently domiciled in Athens practiced the profession. They had to be registered and were subject to a special tax. Those at the top of this social scale were called *hetairai,* or "companions to men." Many of these, in addition to physical beauty, had had intellectual training and possessed artistic talents, attributes that made them more entertaining companions to Athenian men at parties than their legitimate wives. It is no accident that the most famous woman in fifth-century Athens was the foreign-born Aspasia, who started as a *hetaira* and ended as a madam, and in the course of her life lived with Pericles, the political leader of Athens. Aristophanes jokingly claimed that due to her influence Pericles started the Peloponnesian War.[36] Plutarch was much kinder, and added:

> Sources claim that Aspasia was highly valued by Pericles because she was clever and politically astute. After all, Socrates sometimes visited her, bringing along his pupils, and his close friends took their wives to listen to her—although she ran an establishment which was neither orderly nor respectable, seeing that she educated a group of young female companions to become courtesans. Aeschines says that Lysicles the sheep-dealer, a man lowly born and humble of nature, became the most important man of Athens by living with Aspasia after the death of Pericles. Consequently there is a good deal of truth contained in the *Menexenus* of Plato (even if the first part is written with tongue in cheek) when it states that she had the reputation of associating with many Athenians as a teacher of rhetoric. Nevertheless, it appears as if Pericles' affection toward Aspasia was chiefly erotic in its nature. For his legal wife was a close relative of his who had previously been wed to Hipponicus and bore to him Callias, "the Wealthy"; while married to Pericles she bore him Xanthippus and Paralus. Later, as they found living together to be unsatisfactory, with her consent he married her to another man, and he himself took Aspasia and cherished her deeply. The story goes that he would kiss her warmly both when he left for the marketplace and when he returned home each day.

In comedies she is referred to as the new Omphale, and Deianira, and Hera. Cratinus openly called her a whore in the following passage:
"As his Hera, Sodomy bore Aspasia,
    A shameless whore."
Moreover, it appears likely that she bore him a bastard son, because Eupolis, in the *Demes*, depicts him as inquiring:
"Does my bastard son live?"
To which Myronides replies:
"Yes, and he would have been a man long ago,
    Had he not been afraid of the harlot's evil." [37]

Modern scholarship contradicts some of Plutarch's assertions. It seems likely that the liaison of Pericles and Aspasia began at least five years after he divorced his wife. She bore one son to Pericles and one to Pericles' successor Lysicles.[38]

In Plato's *Menexenus,* to be sure not a serious work, we learn that Aspasia composed the funeral oration referred to above (p. 74). The oration includes recommendations for the strict conduct of citizen women, and in the *Menexenus* Aspasia is shown to make much of women's ability to bear and nurse babies.[39] These opinions seem unsuitable in the mouth of an educated and liberated woman such as Aspasia, but it is necessary to remember that she made the recommendations for the wives of citizens, not for women like herself.

Married Athenian men were allowed to copulate with prostitutes. Of course, female slaves were also available to their masters or their masters' friends for sexual purposes.[40] We hear little about the objections of their wives, although Euphiletus' wife bantered her husband about his intimacy with their slave. However, when Alcibiades flaunted his freedom to consort with prostitutes by bringing them into his house, his wife walked out and attempted to get a divorce. She had a very large dowry (ten talents at marriage and ten at the birth of a son) which Alcibiades would have been forced to return if the divorce had been granted. Therefore, when Hipparete attempted to register her divorce with the archon, Alcibiades picked her up bodily and brought her home through the marketplace, with no one daring to oppose him. She continued to live with him until her death not long after.[41] When Alcibiades himself died in exile and dishonor, a faithful courtesan, Timandra, took care of his funeral.

Men were unlikely to marry before the age of thirty, and un-married men had no opportunities for heterosexual activity except with prostitutes and slaves. Since there seem to have been fewer women than men in the general population at this time, shared women, or prostitutes, were a solution. Some men lived with con-cubines in a more or less permanent union. When a man lived with a concubine, she was considered his sexual property in much the same way as a legitimate wife. The rape or seduction of a concubine drew the same penalties as offenses committed against a legitimate wife. The important difference between legitimate marriage and less for-mal unions was that, after the citizenship law of 451–450 B.C., the children of concubines could not be considered citizens and there were also problems about their ability to inherit.

Prostitutes were notoriously mercenary. They were the only women in Athens who exercised independent control over con-siderable amounts of money. From the time of Rhodopis, the Egyptian courtesan freed by Sappho's brother, prostitutes were credited with using their money in extraordinary ways. Rhodopis was reputed to have supplied the funds to build a pyramid. He-rodotus discounts this story, but describes the expensive dedication that he believed she made at Delphi.[42] This was the first of many Greek stories of lavish prostitutes.

Rhodopis and Aspasia were unusually successful. In the absence of male protectors, the careers of prostitutes were hazardous. Neaira, it is true, managed to raise three children, but it seems likely that prostitutes practiced infanticide to a greater extent than citizen wives. Prostitutes may have preferred daughters to sons so that they might succeed them in the profession. They also bought young slave girls or collected the female newborns exposed by others.[43] They trained the girls in their trade, and kept them in brothels to ensure an income for themselves when they were past their prime.

Though the life of the Athenian woman looks bleak from a modern vantage point, especially in contrast to the opportunities available to the Athenian man, we are in no position to judge whether most women were discontented and unhappy. Citizen women were cared for and protected by law, and they had the satisfaction of knowing that their children would be citizens. Through the institution of the dowry, most women enjoyed eco-nomic security throughout their lives, and widows and old women were specifically protected by law.[44] Comedy, although full of misogyny, also reveals mutual affection in marriage. Women's opinions had some influence, for the prosecutor of Neaira reminds the jury that they will be compelled to answer to their wives, daughters, and mothers if they acquit her.[45] Although there were slaves in the household, when a wife was away from the house she was sorely missed because children and household needed her attention.[46] Funerary reliefs show the sorrow of the entire household—husband, children, and slaves—at the death of a wife. The following is an epitaph of the fourth or third century B.C., from Piraeus, the port of Athens:

> Chaerestrate lies in this tomb. When she was alive
> her husband loved her. When she died he lamented.[47]

Although to a modern woman, the role of neither *hetaira* nor secluded housewife appears attractive, it is tempting for us to idealize the former and to pity the latter.[48] The *hetaira* had access to the intellectual life of Athens, which we nowadays treasure, and a popular courtesan who was not a slave had the freedom to be with whoever pleased her.[49] Admittedly our sources are biased, but the fact that we know of some courtesans who attempted to live as respectable wives, while we know of no citizen wives who wished to be courtesans, should make us reconsider the question of which was the preferable role in Classical Athens—companion or wife.

# VI

## IMAGES OF WOMEN
## IN THE LITERATURE OF
## CLASSICAL ATHENS

*Women in Tragedy versus Real Women*

IF RESPECTABLE Athenian women were secluded and silent, how are
we to account for the forceful heroines of tragedy and comedy? And
why does the theme of strife between woman and man pervade
Classical drama? Before proceeding to complex explanations which
are directly concerned with women, it is necessary to repeat the
truism that the dramatists examined multiple aspects of man's relationship to the universe and to society; accordingly, their examination of another basic relationship—that between man and woman—is
not extraordinary. It is rather the apparent discrepancy between
women in the actual society and the heroines on the stage that
demands investigation. Several hypotheses have been formulated in
an attempt to explain the conflict between fact and fiction.

Many plots of tragedy are derived from myths of the Bronze Age
preserved by epic poets. As we have observed, the royal women of
epic were powerful, not merely within their own homes but in an
external political sense. To the Athenian audience familiar with the
works of Homer, not even an iconoclast like Euripides could have
presented a silent and repressed Helen or Clytemnestra. Likewise,
the Theban epic cycle showed the mutual fratricide of the sons of
Oedipus. The surviving members of the family were known to be
Antigone and Ismene. Sophocles could not have presented these
sisters as boys. In short, some myths that provided the plots of

Classical tragedies described the deeds of strong women, and the Classical dramatist could not totally change these facts.

Those who believe in the historical existence of Bronze Age matriarchy also propose an answer to our questions: the male-female polarity discernible in Bronze Age myths can be explained by referring to an actual conflict between a native pre-Hellenic matriarchal society and the patriarchy introduced by conquering invaders.

The Bronze Age origin of these myths does not explain why Athenian tragic poets, living at least seven hundred years later in a patriarchal society, not only found these stories congenial but accentuated the power of their heroines. For example, in the *Odyssey* Aegisthus is the chief villain in the murder of Agamemnon, but in the tragedies of Aeschylus a shift was made to highlight Clytemnestra as the prime mover in the conspiracy. Electra, the daughter of Clytemnestra, is a colorless figure in mythology, and in the *Odyssey* Orestes alone avenges his father; but two dramatists elevated Electra and created whole plays around her and her dilemma. Similarly, Sophocles is thought to have been responsible for the story of the conflict between Creon and Antigone. Homer, it is true, showed how Calypso and Circe could unman even the hero Odysseus, who more easily survived other ordeals, but these two were immortal females. The mortal women in epic, however vital, are not equivalent in impact to tragic heroines, nor is their power such as to produce the male-female conflicts that tragedy poses in a pervasive and demanding way.

A number of scholars find a direct relationship between real women living in Classical Athens and the heroines of tragedy.[1] They reason that the tragic poets found their models not in the Bronze Age but among the real women known to them. From this theory they deduce that real women were neither secluded nor repressed in Classical times. They use as evidence, for example, the fact that tragic heroines spent much time conversing out-of-doors without worrying about being seen. This argument lacks cogency, since the scenes of tragedy are primarily out-of-doors and female characters could scarcely be portrayed if they had to be kept indoors. The proponents of this argument question how dramatists could have become so familiar with feminine psychology if they never had a chance to be with women. They ignore the fact that playwrights were familiar with their female relatives, as well as with the numerous resident aliens and poor citizen women who did move freely about the city. At least one group of women—the wives of citizens with adequate means—probably was secluded.

It is not legitimate for scholars to make judgments about the lives of real women solely on the basis of information gleaned from tragedy. When an idea expressed in tragedy is supported by other genres of ancient sources, then only is it clearly applicable to real life. Ismene's statement that the proper role of women is not to fight with men[2] can be said to reflect real life, since it agrees with information derived from Classical oratory and from comedy. But when Clytemnestra murders her husband, or Medea her sons, or when Antigone takes credit for an act of civil disobedience, we cannot say that these actions have much to do with the lives of real women in Classical Athens, although isolated precedents in Herodotus could be cited for passionate, aggressive women (including a barbarian queen who contrived the murder of her husband with his successor; another who opposed men in battle; and a third who cut off the breasts, nose, ears, lips, and tongue of her rival's mother).[3] However, as images of women in Classical literature written by men, heroines such as Clytemnestra, Medea, and Antigone are valid subjects for contemplation.

Retrospective psychoanalysis has been used to analyze the experience of young boys in Classical Athens, and thus to explain the mature dramatist's depiction of strong heroines. According to the sociologist Philip Slater, the Athenian boy spent his early formative years primarily in the company of his mother and female slaves.[4] The father passed the day away from home, leaving the son with no one to defend him from the mother. The relationship between mother and son was marked by ambiguity and contradiction. The secluded woman nursed a repressed hostility against her elderly, inconsiderate, and mobile husband. In the absence of her husband, the mother substituted the son, alternately pouring forth her venom and doting on him. She demanded that he be successful and lived vicariously through him. The emotionally powerful mother impressed herself upon the imagination of the young boy, becoming the seed, as it were, which developed into the dominant female characters of the mature playwright's mind. The Classical dramatist tended to choose those myths of the Bronze Age that were most fascinating to him, since they explored certain conflicts that existed within his own personality. The "repressed mother" explanation works in inverse

ratio to the power of the heroines produced by the son: the more
repressed his mother was and the more ambivalent her behavior, the
more dreadful were the heroines portrayed by the dramatist-son.

Slater's theory is an interesting attempt to answer a difficult
question. Some readers may abhor the interpretation of classical
antiquity by means of psychoanalytic approaches. But since the
myths of the past illuminate the present, it appears valid to examine
them with the critical tools of the present. Still, there are problems
with Slater's analysis, just as there were with the more traditional
ones. First, although adult Athenians lived sex-segregated lives, it is
far from certain that fathers were distant from children. Inferences
from the modern "commuting father" have too much influenced
Slater's view of antiquity. In fact, comedy shows a closeness between
fathers and children: children could accompany fathers when they
were invited out, and a father claimed to have nursed a baby and
bought toys for him.[5] Second, the reader would have to accept
Slater's premise that women constrained in a patriarchal society
would harbor rage, whether or not they themselves were aware of it.
As noted in the preceding chapter, the epitaphs of women assumed
that their lives were satisfactory, although this evidence may be
somewhat discounted since the inscriptions were selected by the
surviving members of the family, most probably male. But even
today many believe that women can find happiness in the role of
homemaker, particularly when traditional expectations are being
fulfilled. Thus Athenian women may well have lacked the internal
conflict of, say, Roman women, who were plagued with the frustra-
tions arising from relative freedom which confronted them with the
realm of men, but tantalizingly kept its trophies just beyond their
grasp. Is it more reasonable to suggest from a modern viewpoint that
the boredom of tasks like constant weaving must have driven Athenian women to insanity, or, in contrast, to call attention to the
satisfaction women may have felt at jobs well done?

I am not convinced that we can learn much about the Athenian
mother from Slater, but his work is useful for the analysis of the
male playwright's creative imagination. For explanations of
the powerful women in tragedy, we must look to the poets, and
to other men who judged the plays and selected what they thought
best. The mythology about women is created by men and, in a
culture dominated by men, it may have little to do with flesh-
and-blood women. This is not to deny that the creative imagination

of the playwright was surely shaped by some women he knew. But it was also molded by the entire milieu of fifth-century Athens, where separation of the sexes as adults bred fear of the unfamiliar; and finally by the heritage of his literary past, including not only epic but Archaic poetry, with its misogynistic element.

Misogyny was born of fear of women. It spawned the ideology of male superiority. But this was ideology, not statement of fact; as such, it could not be confirmed, but was open to constant doubt. Male status was not immutable. Myths of matriarchies and Amazon societies showed female dominance. Three of the eleven extant comedies of Aristophanes show women in successful opposition to men. A secluded wife like Phaedra may yearn for adultery; a wife like Creusa may have borne an illegitimate son before her current marriage; a good wife like Deianira can murder her husband. These were the nightmares of the victors: that some day the vanquished would arise and treat their ex-masters as they themselves had been treated.

Most important, in the period between Homer and the tragedians, the city-state, with established codes of behavior, had evolved, and the place of women as well as of other disenfranchised groups in the newly organized society was an uncomfortable one. Many tragedies show women in rebellion against the established norms of society. As the *Oresteia* of Aeschylus makes clear, a city-state such as Athens flourished only through the breaking of familial or blood bonds and the subordination of the patriarchal family within the patriarchal state. But women were in conflict with this political principle, for their interests were private and family-related. Thus, drama often shows them acting out of the women's quarters, and concerned with children, husbands, fathers, brothers, and religions deemed more primitive and family-oriented than the Olympian, which was the support of the state. This is the point at which the image of the heroine on the stage coincides with the reality of Athenian women.

## Masculine and Feminine Roles in Tragedy

The proper behavior of women and men is explored in many tragedies. This is not to say that it is the primary theme of any tragedy. Aeschylus' *Agamemnon* is about the workings of justice, but the discussion of this tragedy in these pages will set aside the principal idea and focus on the secondary theme of sex roles and antagonisms.

Womanly behavior was characterized then, as now, by submissiveness and modesty. Ismene in *Antigone,* Chrysothemis in the plays dealing with the family of Agamemnon, Tecmessa in *Ajax,* Deianira in *Trachinian Women,* and the female choruses in tragedy act the role of "normal" women. Because of the limitations of "normal" female behavior, heroines who act outside the stereotype are sometimes said to be "masculine." Again, it is not a compliment to a woman to be classified as masculine. Aristotle judged it inappropriate for a female character to be portrayed as manly or clever.[6]

Heroines, like heroes, are not normal people. While in a repressively patriarchal culture, most women—like Ismene—submit docilely, some heroines—like Clytemnestra, Antigone, and Hecuba—adopt the characteristics of the dominant sex to achieve their goals. The psychoanalyst A. Adler termed the phenomenon "masculine protest."[7] In *Agamemnon,* the first play of the *Oresteia* trilogy, Aeschylus shows Clytemnestra with political power, planning complex strategies involving the relaying of signal beacons from Troy, outwitting her husband in persuading him to tread upon a purple carpet, and finally planning and perpetrating his murder. Unrepentant, she flaunts her sexual freedom by announcing that the death of Cassandra has brought an added relish of pleasure to her, and that her situation will be secure as long as her lover Aegisthus lights the fire on her hearth (1435–36, 1446–47). The double entendre is especially shocking because a woman traditionally lit the fire on her father's or husband's hearth.

Thus the chorus of old men of Argos considers that her ways are masculine and reminds her that she is a woman, addressing her as "my lady" (351). When it quizzes her as though she were a silly child, she answers with a brilliant, complex speech displaying her knowledge of geography (268–316; cf. 483–87). To a chorus slow to digest the fact that she has murdered Agamemnon, Clytemnestra impatiently retorts, "You are examining me as if I were a foolish woman" (1401). The chorus continues to meditate upon the fact that their king has been killed by a woman (1453–54). Had Aegisthus himself performed the murder, as he was reputed to have done in the *Odyssey,* the chorus would better have accepted it. The old men find the reversal of sex roles in Clytemnestra and Aegisthus monstrous (1633-35; 1643-45).

In the *Eumenides*, which was the final play of the *Oresteia*, Aeschylus restores masculine and feminine to their proper spheres. Orestes, who chose to murder his mother in vengeance for her murder of his father, is defended by Apollo and Athena. The power of the uncanny, monstrous female spirits of vengeance (formerly called "Erinyes" or "Furies") is tempered and subordinated to the rule of the patriarchal Olympians. Henceforth, as Eumenides, or fair-minded spirits, they will have a proper place in the affections of civilized people.

The portrayal of the masculine woman as heroine was fully developed in Sophocles' *Antigone*. The play opens with the daughters of Oedipus lamenting the laws established by the tyrant Creon. Their brother Polyneices lies dead, but Creon has forbidden that the corpse be buried, as punishment for the dead man's treachery against his native land. While Antigone urges that they perform the burial rites, her sister Ismene seizes upon the excuse that they are not men: "We were born women, showing that we were not meant to fight with men" (61-62). She uses the frequently significant verb *phyō*, implying that it is by nature *(physis)* rather than by man-made convention that women do not attempt to rival men.

Creon, a domineering ruler, reveals particular hostility in his relations with the opposite sex. His prejudices are patriarchal. He cannot understand his son Haemon's love for Antigone, but refers to a wife as a "field to plow" (569). The sentiments of Apollo in Aeschylus' *Eumenides* (657-61; see p. 65) must be recalled here: since the male seed is all-important, any female will suffice. Apollo's idea is restated by Orestes in Euripides' *Orestes*.[8] Simone de Beauvoir, in *The Second Sex*, traced the phallus/plow-woman/furrow as a common symbol of patriarchal authority and subjugation of woman.[9] Moreover, as modern feminists have pointed out, the repressive male cannot conceive of an equal division of power between the sexes, but fears that women, if permitted, would be repressive in turn. So Creon, the domineering male, is constantly anxious about being bested by a woman and warns his son against such a humiliation (484, 525, 740, 746, 756).

On the other hand, Ismene—perhaps because she stayed at

Thebes while Antigone shared the exile of her father—has been indoctrinated into the beliefs of patriarchal society: men are born to rule, and women to obey. Antigone bitterly rejects her sister's notion of the natural behavior of women. Polynices is buried secretly, and Creon, the guard, and the chorus all suppose that only a man could have been responsible (248, 319, 375). Thereupon forced to confess to Creon that she has in fact buried her brother, Antigone refers to herself with a pronoun in the masculine gender (464). Creon, in turn, perceives her masculinity and refers to Antigone by a masculine pronoun and participle (479, 496). He resolves to punish her, declaring, "I am not a man, she is the man if she shall have this success without penalty" (484–85). (Similarly, Herodotus notes that Queen Artemisia, who participated in Xerxes' expedition against Greece, was considered masculine, and that the Athenians were so indignant that a woman should be in arms against them that for her capture alone they offered a financial reward.) [10]

Feeling, then, that in daring to flout his commands Antigone has acted as a man—for a true woman would be incapable of opposition—Creon, when he declares sentence upon the sisters, asserts that "they must now be women." However, he continues to refer to them in the masculine gender (579–80). The repeated use of a masculine adjective to modify a feminine noun is noteworthy, because in classical Greek, adjectives regularly agree with the gender of the modified noun (the masculine gender may be used in reference to a woman when a general statement is made).[11]

We may note the male orientation of the Greek language, in which general human truths, though conceived as referring specifically to women, can be cast in the masculine gender. Perhaps this grammatical explanation will suffice when the change in gender is sporadic. However, the masculine gender used to refer to a female in specific rather than general statements—a rare occurrence in Greek—occurs with significant frequency in *Antigone*. It is, I believe, a device used by the playwright in characterizing the heroine who has become a masculine sort of woman. In her penultimate speech, Antigone explains her willingness to die for the sake of a brother, though not for a husband or child.

> For had I been a mother, or if my husband had died, I would never have taken on this task against the city's will. In view of what law do I say this? If my husband were dead I might find another, and another

child from him if I lost a son. But with my mother and father hidden
in the grave, no other brother could ever bloom for me. (905-12)

Herodotus also relates a story about a woman who, when offered the
life of a husband, a son, or a brother, chooses a brother for the same
reason as Antigone.[12]

A number of Sophoclean scholars have judged the speech spur-
ious, or pronounced the sentiments unworthy of the heroine.[13] They
consider the choice of a brother over a child bizarre. And yet, in the
context of Classical Athens, Antigone's choice is reasonable.
Mothers could not have been as attached to children as the ideal
mother is nowadays. The natural mortality of young children would
seem to discourage the formation of strong mother-child bonds. In
addition, patriarchal authority asserted that the child belonged to
the father, not the mother. He decided whether a child should be
reared, and he kept the child upon dissolution of a marriage, while
the woman returned to the guardianship of her father or, if he were
dead, her brother. Thus the brother-sister bond was very precious.

The preference for the brother is also characteristic of the masculine woman, who may reject the traditional role of wife and
mother as a result of being inhibited by external forces from displaying cherishing or nurturing qualities.[14] The masculine woman
often allies herself with the male members of her family. In this
context we may note Antigone's firm and repeated denunciations of
her sister (538-39, 543, 546-47, 549). She also judges her mother
harshly, blaming her for the "reckless guilt of the marriage bed,"
while the chorus, seeing only her father's disposition in her, calls her
"cruel child of a cruel father" (862, 471-72). Her disregard of her
sister is so complete that she actually refers to herself as the sole
survivor of the house of Oedipus (941).[15]

In the end, Antigone reverts to a traditional female role. She
laments that she dies a virgin, unwed and childless (917-18), and
commits suicide after being entombed alive by Creon. In classical
mythology, suicide is a feminine and somewhat cowardly mode of
death. Ajax, like Deianira, Jocasta, and Creon's wife Eurydice, had
killed himself because he could not live with unbearable knowledge.
Haemon, like Phaedra, Alcestis, Laodamia, Dido, Evadne, and Hero, kills himself for love, justifying Creon's earlier concern over his
"womanish" tendencies. Of all tragic heroines, Antigone was the
most capable of learning through suffering and achieving a tragic

vision comparable to that of Oedipus. Her death erased that possibility.

The fate of Haemon illustrates the destructive quality of love. The chorus gives voice to this idea:

> Love, invincible love, who keeps vigil on the soft cheek of a young girl, you roam over the sea and among homes in wild places, no one can escape you, neither man nor god, and the one who has you is possessed by madness. You bend the minds of the just to wrong, so here you have stirred up this quarrel of son and father. The love-kindling light in the eyes of the fair bride conquers. (781–96) [16]

*Antigone* is a complex and puzzling play. According to Athenian law, Creon was Antigone's guardian, since he was her nearest male relative.[17] As such, he was responsible for her crime in the eyes of the state, and his punishing her was both a private and public act. He was also the nearest male relative of his dead nephews, and he, not Antigone, was responsible for their burial. Creon put what he deemed to be the interests of the state before his personal obligations.

The differences between Creon and Antigone are traditional distinctions between the sexes. According to Freud, "Women spread around them their conservative influence. . . . Women represent the interests of the family and sexual life; the work of civilization has become more and more men's business." [18] The civilizing inventions of men are listed by the chorus of *Antigone:* sailing, navigation, plowing, hunting, fishing, domesticating animals, verbal communication, building houses, and the creation of laws and government (332–64). These were mainly masculine activities.

The Greeks assumed that men were bearers of culture. For example, according to myth, Cadmus brought the alphabet to Greece; Triptolemus—albeit prompted by the goddess Demeter—brought the use of the plow; while Daedalus was credited with the scissors, the saw, and other inventions. The specific achievements of women—which were probably in the realm of clothing manufacture, food preparation, gardening, and basketmaking, and the introduction of olive culture by Athena—do not appear in Sophocles' list, nor in a similar list in Aeschylus' *Prometheus Bound.*[19]

Creon's lack of insight into the necessity of the duality of male and female led to the death of Antigone and to his own annihilation as well. Creon's wife died cursing him. Moreover, in a society where sons were expected to display filial obedience, Haemon chose Antigone over his father and his choice was not held against him. His death was not a punishment for disobedience. *Antigone* and many other tragedies show the effect of overvaluation of the so-called masculine qualities (control, subjugation, culture, excessive cerebration) at the expense of the so-called feminine aspects of life (instinct, love, family ties) which destroys men like Creon. The ideal, we can only assume—since Sophocles formulates no solution—was a harmonization of masculine and feminine values, with the former controlling the latter.[20]

## Euripides' Women: A New Song

> Streams of holy rivers run backward, and universal custom is overturned. Men have deceitful thoughts; no longer are their oaths steadfast. My reputation shall change, my manner of life have good report. Esteem shall come to the female sex. No longer will malicious rumor fasten upon women. The Muses of ancient poets will cease to sing of my unfaithfulness. Apollo, god of song, did not grant us the divine power of the lyre. Otherwise I would have sung an answer to the male sex.[21]

Thus sang the female chorus of Euripides' *Medea* in 431 B.C. Were they directly reflecting the attitude of the poet? Noting the absence of female tragedians, did Euripides turn his gift of poetry to compositions in behalf of women? Of all the images of women in classical literature, those created by Euripides pose the greatest dilemma to the modern commentator.

Among ancient critics, Euripides was the only tragedian to acquire a reputation for misogyny. In the comedy *Thesmophoriazusae*, by his contemporary Aristophanes, an assembly of women accuse Euripides of slandering the sex by characterizing women as whores and adultresses:

> By the gods, it's not out of any self-seeking
> That I rise to address you, O women. It's that
> I've been disturbed and annoyed for quite some time now
> When I see our reputations getting dirtied
> By Euripides, son of a produce-salesgirl,

And our ears filled with all sorts of disgusting things!
With what disgusting charges has he *not* smeared us?
Where hasn't he defamed us? Any place you find
Audiences, or tragedies, or choruses
We're called sex fiends, pushovers for a handsome male,
Heavy drinkers, betrayers, babbling-mouthed gossips,
Rotten to the core, the bane of men's existence.
And so they come straight home from these performances
Eyeing us suspiciously, and go search at once
For lovers we might hide about the premises.
We can't do anything we used to do before.
This guy's put terrible ideas in the heads of
Our menfolk. If any woman should start weaving
A wreath—this proves she's got a lover. If she drops
Anything while meandering about the house,
It's *Cherchez l'homme!* "For whom did the pitcher crack up?
It must have been for that Corinthian stranger!"
If a girl's tired out, then her brother remarks:
"I don't like the color of that girl's complexion."
If a woman just wants to procure a baby
Since she lacks one of her own, no deals in secret!
For now the men hover at the edge of our beds.
And to all the old men who used to wed young girls
He's told slanderous tales, so that no old man wants
To try matrimony. You remember that line:
"An old bridegroom marries a tyrant, not a wife." (383–413)

If he cuts up Phaedra,
Why should *we* worry? He's neglected to tell how
A woman flung her stole in front of her husband
For scrutiny under the light, while dispatching
The lover she's hidden—not a word about that!
And a woman I know claimed that her delivery
Lasted ten whole days—till she'd purchased a baby!
While her husband raced to buy labor-speeding drugs
An old crone brought her an infant, stuffed in a pot,
Its mouth stuffed with honeycomb so it wouldn't cry.
When this baby-carrier gave the signal, she yelled,
"Out, husband, out I say! I think the little one's
Coming" (the baby was kicking the *pot's* belly)!
So he runs out, delighted; she in turn pulls out
What had plugged up the infant's mouth—and he hollers!
The dirty old woman who'd brought in the baby

Dashes out to the husband, all smiles, and announces,
"You've fathered a lion—he's your spitting image
In all of his features including his small prick
Which looks just like yours, puckered as a honeycomb."
Why, don't we do such naughty things? By Artemis
We do. Then why get angry at Euripides?
We're accused of far less than what we've really done! (497–519) [22]

Since the borderline between levity and seriousness in Aristophanes' comedies is ambiguous, and the world is often topsy-turvy,
in antiquity, as now, it has been difficult to decide whether he truly
thought Euripides was a misogynist or the opposite. Influenced by
Aristophanes, many biographical sketches written about Euripides
after his death presented him as a misogynist and repeated the
insulting charge that his mother was a vegetable-monger. According
to Aulus Gellius, writing in the mid-second century A.D.:

Euripides is said to have had a strong antipathy toward nearly all
women, either shunning their society due to his natural inclination, or
because he had two wives simultaneously—since that was legal according to an Athenian decree—and they had made marriage
abominable to him.[23]

The ancient biographies of Euripides are unreliable, since they do
not hesitate to cull material from the author's creations and apply it
indiscriminately to his life. Therefore inconsistent with Gellius is the
anecdote reported by Athenaeus at the end of the second century
A.D.:

The poet Euripides was fond of women. Hieronymus, at any rate, in
*Historical Commentaries,* says, "When someone said to Sophocles
that Euripides was a woman-hater in his tragedies, Sophocles said,
'When he is in bed, certainly he is a woman-lover." [24]

In addition to the pronouncements of ancient critics, the plays
themselves provide evidence of misogyny, although one ought not
attribute to a playwright the remarks of his characters. Apparently
obvious sources are the anti-female pronouncements scattered
through the tragedies. In Euripidean tragedy, misogynists like Hippolytus and Orestes (in *Orestes),* masochists like Andromache, aggressive women like Medea and Phaedra, and sympathetic female

choruses are equally capable of misogynistic remarks. In these statements women are usually lumped together as a nameless group, defined simply as the "female sex," in a manner rarely applied to males. These statements are platitudes, familiar to women even today, but are so arresting by their stark hostility that it is easy to overlook how few they are in the context of Euripides' extant work.

Some of the abbreviated platitudes are: "Women are the best devisers of evil." [25] "Women are a source of sorrow." [26] Others point out that if their sex life is satisfactory, women are completely happy;[27] clever women are dangerous;[28] stepmothers are always malicious;[29] upper-class women were the first to practice adultery;[30] and women use magical charms and potions with evil intentions.[31] The longest and best-known tirade against women was delivered by Hippolytus:

> O Zeus, why, as a fraudulent evil for men,
> Have you brought women into the light of the sun?
> For if you wished to engender the mortal race,
> There was no need for women as source of supply,
> But in your shrines mortal men could have offered up
> Either gold or iron or heavy weight of bronze
> To purchase their breed of offspring, each paid in sons
> According to his own gift's worth, and in their homes
> They could live without women, entirely free.
> Yet now to our homes we bring this primal evil,
> And—without a choice—drain the wealth from our households.
> Woman is a great evil, and this makes it clear:
> The father who sires her and rears her must give her
> A dowry, to ship off and discard this evil.
> Then he who takes in his home this baneful creature
> Revels in heaping upon his most vile delight
> Lovely adornment, and struggles to buy her clothes,
> Poor, poor fellow, siphoning wealth from his household.
> He cannot escape his fate: gaining good in-laws
> Brings joy to him—and preserves a bitter marriage;
> But an excellent wife with worthless male kinfolk
> Weights him down with good luck *and* misfortune alike.
> A nobody's simplest to marry, though worthless,
> A woman of guilelessness set up in the house.
> I hate clever women. May my home never house
> A woman more discerning than one ought to be.
> For Cypris more often produces wrongdoing

In clever females. An untalented woman
Through lack of intelligence stays clear of folly.
No servant should have to come close to a woman.
Instead they should live among dumb, savage creatures,
So they would have no humans whom they could talk to
And no one who'd respond to the things that they say.
But now evil women sit at home and plan evils—
Plots their servants execute when they go outside.
And so, evil woman, you've come, to propose that
I sleep with her whom my father alone may touch.
I'll wipe out your words with streams of running water,
Drenching my ears. How, tell me, might I be evil
When I feel impure from even hearing such things?
Be certain my piety protects me, woman.
If my oaths to the gods hadn't caught me off guard,
I would not have refrained from telling my father.
But now, while Theseus is out of the country,
I'll depart from this house—and keep my mouth silent.
Returning when my father does, I shall witness
How you and your mistress manage to confront him.
I'll have firsthand knowledge of your effrontery.
Go to hell, I'll never have my fill of hating
Women, not if I'm said to talk without ceasing.
For women are also unceasingly wicked.
Either someone should teach them to be sensible,
Or let me trample them underfoot forever.[32]

I can scarcely believe that so subtle a dramatist as Euripides, who called into question traditional Athenian beliefs and prejudices surrounding foreigners, war, and the Olympian gods, would have intended his audience simply to accept the misogynistic maxims. Rather, he uses the extreme vantage point of misogyny as a means of examining popular beliefs about women. On the other hand, Euripides does not present a brief for women's rights. Not only is Greek tragedy not a convenient vehicle for propaganda, but the playwright saw too many contradictions in life to be able to espouse a single cause. Euripides is questioning rather than dogmatic. Judgments about his presentation of heroines vary, some critics believing he is sympathetic, some antipathetic.

My subjective estimate of Euripides is favorable. I do not think it misogynistic to present women as strong, assertive, successful, and sexually demanding even if they are also selfish or villainous. Other feminists share my opinion, and British suffragists used to recite speeches from Euripides at their meetings. Yet, it is fair to add that conventional critics—who far outnumber feminists—judge that Medea and Phaedra disgrace the entire female sex, and label Euripides a misogynist for drawing our attention to these murderesses. The controversy that the doctrines of women's liberation invariably arouse among women is analogous to the dilemma posed by subjective judgments of Euripides. For every feminist who insists that women have the same capabilities (whether for good or for evil) as men, but that they have been socialized into their present passivity, there have been countless conservatives denying that women are what the feminists claim they are.

Many women perpetrate villainous deeds in Euripidean tragedy. However, old myths are paraded not to illustrate that the female sex is evil, but rather to induce the audience to question the traditional judgment on these women. Euripides counters the ideas expressed in the misogynistic platitudes by portraying individual women and their reasons for their actions. The crime of Clytemnestra had tainted the entire female sex ever since Agamemnon's judgment of her in the *Odyssey*.[33] Euripides reiterates the accusations but adds a strong defense for Clytemnestra in her speech to her daughter Electra:

> Tyndareus placed me in your father's care,
> So that neither I nor my offspring would perish.
> Yet he promised my child marriage to Achilles
> And left our household, taking her off to Aulis,
> Where the ships anchored, stretched her out above the flames,
> Then slit the white throat of my Iphigenia.
> Had it been to save our state from being captured,
> Preserve our homes, or protect our other children,
> One death averting many, I'd be forgiving.
> But because Helen proved lustful, and her husband
> Didn't know how to punish his wife's seducer,
> For the sake of these people he destroyed my child.
> In this I was wronged, but for this I would never
> Have behaved like a savage, nor slain my husband,
> But he returned to me with a crazed, god-filled girl,
> And took her into our bed—so the two of us,
> Both of us brides, were lodged in the very same house.[34]

Elsewhere, Phaedra ponders the moral impotence of humanity, not specifically of the "weaker sex," noting that people may know what virtue is, but not achieve it.[35]

Helen was reviled in every classical tragedy where her name was mentioned, including those by Euripides.[36] Yet Euripides also wrote an entire play, *Helen,* using the myth that she was not at Troy at all but imprisoned in Egypt, remaining chaste throughout the Trojan War.

Self-sacrifice or martyrdom is the standard way for a woman to achieve renown among men; self-assertion earns a woman an evil reputation. But in Euripides this formula is not so simple. Medea and Hecuba are lavishly provoked. They refuse to be passive, and take a terrible revenge on their tormentors. Medea murders her own children and destroys her husband's new bride and father-in-law with a magic potion. Hecuba kills the two children of her son's murderer and blinds their father. The desire for revenge is un-feminine,[37] as had been noted for Sophocles' Antigone; Hecuba is often referred to with masculine adjectives.[38] Her vengeance is considered so ghastly that she ends up metamorphosed into a barking bitch. Medea escapes, but since she clearly had loved her children, one can imagine her perpetual anguish. When I compare Euripidean to Sophoclean heroines, I prefer Euripides' Medea and Hecuba, for they are successful. Deianira, in Sophocles' *Trachinian Women,* naïvely mixes a potion intended to restore her husband's affection for her; instead, the potion tortures and kills him. Antigone courageously and singlemindedly defends her ideals, and is willing to die for them, but her last words dwell not upon her achievements but lament that she dies unwed. Medea and Hecuba are too strong to regret their decisions.

Euripides shows us a number of self-sacrificing heroines who win praise from the traditionally minded. But it seems to me that the playwright does not totally approve of them. Among self-denying young women, Iphigenia is willing to submit to the sacrificial knife, arguing that in wartime "it is better that one man live to see the light of day than ten thousand women." [39] Similarly, Polyxena wins the praise of soldiers for the noble way she endures being sacrificed to the ghost of Achilles.[40] Evadne kills herself because she cannot live without her husband,[41] and Helen is expected to do the same if she learned of her husband's death.[42] Alcestis died to prove her love for her husband, and thereby won honor for all women, but her father-in-law suggests that she is foolish.[43] Euripides structures these plays so as to leave us doubtful whether the men for whom the women sacrificed themselves were worth it.

The double standard in sexual morality is implicit in many of the myths Euripides chose as the basis of his plots. He is the first author we know of to look at this topic from both the woman's and the man's point of view. Many husbands are adulterous. Enslaved after the fall of Troy, Andromache laments:

> Dearest Hector, I, for your sake, even joined with you in loving, if Aphrodite made you stumble. I often offered my breast to your bastards so as not to exhibit any bitterness to you.[44]

Some wives, notably Medea and Clytemnestra, reacted with overt hostility to their rivals and husbands. Hermione, on the other hand, reasoned that the legitimate wife was in a better position regarding money, the household, and the status of her children and that it was better to have an unfaithful husband than to be unwed.[45] Euripides appears to question the patriarchal axiom that husbands may be polygamous, while wives must remain monogamous, when he shows us Phaedra committing suicide because she merely thought about adultery and points out that women suspected of sexual irregularities are gossiped about, while men are not.[46] Euripides does not advocate that women should have the same sexual freedom as men, but rather suggests that it is better for all concerned if the husband is as monogamous as the wife.

Even when they are not essential to the plot, the horrors of patriarchy compose a background of unremitting female misery. Grotesque marriages or illicit liaisons humiliating or unbearable to women abound in Euripides. Andromache is forced to share the bed of her husband's murderer. Cassandra becomes the concubine of Agamemnon, destroyer of her family and city. Hermione marries Orestes, who had threatened to kill her. Clytemnestra marries Agamemnon, the murderer of her son and first husband. Phaedra is married to the hero who seduced her sister and conquered her country. Alcestis returns from the dead to "remarry" the husband who let her die in his stead.[47]

Euripides shows us women victimized by patriarchy in almost every possible way. A girl needs both her virginity and a dowry to attract a husband.[48] Women are raped and bear illegitimate children whom they must discard. The women are blamed, while the men who raped them are not.[49] When marriages prove unfruitful, wives are inevitably guilty.[50] Despite the grimness of marriage, spinsterhood is worse.[51]

Women as mothers always arouse sympathy in Euripides. All his women love their children and fight fiercely in their behalf.[52] Even Medea never stopped loving her children, although she murdered them to spite Jason. Women glory especially in being the mothers of sons, and the lamentation of mothers over sons killed in war is a standard feature in Euripides' antiwar plays.[53] Yet in patriarchal society the father is the more precious parent. The suffering of the children of Heracles in the absence of a father is the basic plot of the *Heracleidae*. Mothers whose husbands are dead refer to their children as "orphans." [54] Alcestis, when she chooses death, includes in her calculations that her children need a father more than a mother, but expresses some doubt whether he loves them as much as she does.[55]

In subtle ways Euripides reveals an intimacy with women's daily lives remarkable among classical Greek authors. He knows that upon returning from a party a husband quickly falls asleep, but a wife needs time to prepare for bed. The chorus of Trojan women relates that, on the night Troy was taken, "My husband lay asleep. . . . But I was arranging my hair in a net looking into the bottomless gleam of the golden mirror, preparing for bed." [56] Euripides recognizes that childbirth is a painful ordeal, that daughters are best helped by their mothers on these occasions, and that after giving birth women are disheveled and haggard.[57]

Although the dramatic date is the Bronze Age, the comments of various characters on questions of female etiquette in Euripidean tragedy anachronistically agree with the conventions of Classical Athens: women, especially unmarried ones, should remain indoors;[58] they should not adorn themselves nor go outdoors while their husbands are away, nor should they converse with men in public;[59] out of doors a woman should wear a veil;[60] she should not look at a man in the face, not even her husband.[61]

In the post-Classical period Euripides enjoyed greater popularity than the other tragic poets. His influence can perhaps be detected even among the early Christians who idealized the dying virgin as the most valuable of martyrs, and among whom—in a manner not dissimilar to Euripides' Bacchantes—women spread the worship of a revolutionary cult which challenged established religion.

The women of Sophocles and Aeschylus have a heroic dimension which says little about women in Classical Athens. The women of Euripides are scaled down closer to real life, and in this respect the tragic poetry of Euripides approaches comedy.

## Women in Aristophanes

Aristophanes is an appropriate bridge between Euripides and Plato, for he criticizes the radical views of both on women. The three authors touch on a number of the same topics, including women's sexual desires and the marriage relationship. Before proceeding, let the reader be duly cautioned that women were by no means the only victims of Aristophanic invective and ridicule—the comic poet was a critic and teacher of the entire society. It is also necessary to remember Aristotle's axiom that comedy presents people as worse than they really are, and that the literary genre itself demands obscenity, which is sometimes distinctly unfunny to a modern reader.

The three comedies in which women play the largest part are *Lysistrata* and *Thesmophoriazusae,* both produced in 411 B.C., and *Ecclesiazusae,* produced in 391 B.C.[62] These three plays reveal a range of attitudes toward women from misogyny to sympathy, and probably reflect, with the distortion to be expected in comedy, the feelings of the Athenian audience.

All the conceptions about women which are scattered through Aristophanes' other comedies are concentrated in *Lysistrata.* The play was performed in the twentieth year of the bloody Peloponnesian War. Many rational solutions to the political problems of Greece had been tried, without success. Aristophanes, in *The Birds,* produced in 414 B.C., had even imagined a peaceful commonwealth in the sky. In *Lysistrata,* he turned to another fantastically absurd solution: a sex strike on the part of the women of Greece. The women, led by the Athenian Lysistrata and aided by the Spartan Lampito, withdraw to the fortified Athenian Acropolis. A few ribald scenes with panting, sex-starved men show that the tactic works. The women achieve their objective. Peace is declared between the warring Greek states, and husbands go home with their wives. The superficial elements of the plot thus appear complimentary to women: they have succeeded where men had failed.

Feminists may disagree over the granting or withholding of sex as a weapon against men, and classicists familiar with the bisexuality of the Athenians ponder the effectiveness of a sex strike.[63] More fundamentally, we can consider whether Aristophanes presents an attractive picture of women in his comedies. My impression is that Aristophanes was no more favorably disposed toward women than the ordinary Athenian.

The heroine, Lysistrata, is intelligent and successful, but she admits that her knowledge is derived from listening to her father and other older men talking. She is the vehicle of some of the most misogynistic jibes in the play, informing the audience that women are never on time and prefer drinking wine and sexual intercourse to all other forms of activity. She also feels the body of Lampito and contributes to the lewd appraisals of the physical attractions of the women who join the strike. Lysistrata exhibits hatred of the femininity in herself, but since she's a woman, we are ready to assume that her opinions about women must be correct.

Elements of *Lysistrata* reappear in other plays. Praxagora, the heroine of *Ecclesiazusae*, resembles Lysistrata, although her personality is less clearly defined. Praxagora admits that she acquired her skill in public speaking from listening to men. She is also highly critical of other women whose intelligence is not capable of carrying out the strategies she formulates for them.[64] In contrast to the sympathy between women which can be detected in Euripides, women in Aristophanes exhibit little loyalty to other women. Younger women are spiteful to older women when competing for a young man. Wives despise and envy prostitutes.[65]

The bibulousness and lust of women are common occasions for laughter in Aristophanes. It is illuminating to compare Euripides' treatment of the same themes. In the *Bacchae*, the tragic poet shows why women, confined to the loom and spindle, welcome the orgiastic release promised by the wine god. Likewise, in Euripides' depiction of Phaedra it is evident that he understands a woman's struggle against ungovernable erotic impulses. Aristophanes merely points to these vices as inherent weaknesses of women.

In *Lysistrata*, men are also lustful, but their urges are better governed than those of the women. The men in Aristophanes prefer heterosexual relationships. They enjoy looking at the unclothed female body of Peace at the end of *Lysistrata,* and sexual desire for their wives ultimately compels husbands to abandon warfare. Yet, during the strike by wives, Aristophanes offers alternatives to men: homosexuals and female prostitutes, who were not invited by the wives to participate in the strike. In contrast to the men, the women are deprived of sexual relationships and break their oaths by sneaking off the Acropolis to return to their homes. The sex strike causes greater deprivation to women than to men, and can even be viewed as a strike against women. Sex-starved though they are, the women do not consider turning to other women for homoerotic gratification, nor does it occur to them to employ any of the famous male prostitutes of Athens, the youthful slaves reserved for the pleasures of men.

Women as well as men are viewed as gluttons. One reason for their objection to war is that their favorite gourmet treats, including a particular variety of eel, are difficult to obtain (336). On the other hand, the alimentary system particularly of men is referred to in numerous scatological jokes.

Aristophanes is probably most unkind in his depictions of older women. The vices detected in all women are particularly grotesque in old hags. They are nymphomaniacs, but their objects of desire are younger men.[66] They are drunken and lewd.

In Aristophanes, women's clothing can function as a symbol of degradation. Although it is fair to note that the exchange of clothing between husbands and wives in *Ecclesiazusae* merely disgruntles the men, Lysistrata suggests that a magistrate be dressed in women's attire to humiliate him. We are reminded of Euripides' portrayal of Pentheus in the *Bacchae.* Pentheus also felt discomforted by masquerading as a woman, but Euripides shows him as an unsympathetic character.

Expressions of compassion are rare in Aristophanes. Yet he records the anguish war can cause to women because of their family relationships. Mothers lose sons, and girls must abandon the prospect of marriage. Aristophanes was a firm believer in the nuclear family. He disliked Euripides' heroines for sabotaging their families by adultery and the introduction of suppositious children into the house, and he criticized utopian schemes that abolished the family.[67]

## Utopian Literature

The introduction of monogamous marriage was considered a civilizing step in the progress of humanity. According to a myth known only through post-Classical sources, the Athenians attributed this institution to their legendary first king, Cecrops. During his reign, when Athena and Poseidon contested the patronage of Athens, the women, who were more numerous, voted for Athena while the men voted for Poseidon. In revenge, the men took away the vote from women and declared that no longer would children be known by their mother's name. Formerly, sexual intercourse had been promiscuous, and children did not know their fathers. Hence, marriage was instituted by men as a punishment for women, simultaneous with the loss of women's political equality and sexual freedom.[68]

The utopian literature of the Classical period recommended a return to what were thought to be some of the primitive features of Athenian society. In terms of women's lives, these would include the elimination of monogamous marriage and known paternity of children, and the opportunity to play a role in public affairs and enjoy sexual freedom. In utopian literature, women approached closer to equality than they did in any other genre of ancient literature or in real life In the utopian community of Phaeacia described in the *Odyssey* (6–8), the status of the sexes was more equal than anywhere else in the Homeric epic. The major extant utopian works of the Classical period containing explicit provisions for women are the *Republic* and the *Laws* of Plato.[69] Aristotle also mentions some features of the utopias envisioned by other ancient authors.

Greek utopias, rather than being thoroughly equalitarian, are invariably stratified by classes. In the *Republic*, Plato included women among the ruling elite. His provisions for the highest class of women, the guardians, provide an index for the philosopher's beliefs about the potentialities of women. Within the guardian class there was additional stratification, with the males as a whole forming a higher class than the females. There was no equality between the sexes in Utopia, but Plato admitted that the greater physical strength of the male was the only important distinction for social capacity. The female guardians, of course, ruled over both males and females of the lower classes. Thus some women, at least, were superior to many men.

The higher status of women in Utopia was suggested neither for the particular benefit of real women nor out of sympathy with their plight. Rather, certain proposals which happened to affect women were made for the purpose of eliminating civil strife. Private property was a major source of contention. The philosopher Phaleas of Chalcedon foresaw marriages between wealthy and poor and suggested that wealth be equalized by having the rich give dowries but not receive them, and the poor receive dowries but not give them.[70] Plato went further in his *Republic* and totally abolished the possession of private property for his highest stratum of citizens.

The elimination of private property meant that no man needed a legitimate heir of known parentage. Thus, Utopia could eliminate sexual monopoly over women, which was recognized as a major source of friction among men. Herodotus had reported that the Agathyrsi practiced promiscuous intercourse so that they could all act like brothers and kinfolk and not treat each other with envy and hatred.[71] In the *Republic* the necessity for monogamous marriage among the guardians was eradicated. Plato proposed that women and children in the guardian class be the common property of the males, and went to great lengths to elaborate the means whereby parents were not to recognize their biological offspring. He proposed that the female guardians of marriageable age be held as a community of wives, never mentioning the community of husbands that would have inevitably existed simultaneously in the absence of monogamous marriage. Thus it is clear that the sharing of wives must be viewed as another aspect of the elimination of all private property. The wives are, in fact, referred to by the legal term for jointly held property: *koina.*[72]

Like other irrational appetites which could not be totally eliminated from Utopia, sexual desire was subject to strict regulation and matings were controlled. Criticizing ideas similar to those expressed in the *Republic,* Aristophanes showed women demanding sexual satisfaction, especially old women demanding that young men first have intercourse with them before proceeding to the younger, more attractive women.[73] Nevertheless, in the *Republic,* the inclinations of the female guardians are not taken into consideration, but the males' are: Plato established as a work incentive more frequent intercourse with the women.

The notions that rivalry for wives could foster ill feeling among men and that heterosexual intercourse could be a reward give still another dimension to the question of the sexual desirability of respectable women in the Athens that Plato knew. Sharing of wives and children—in other words, the abolition of the private family and the *oikos* system—would promote good feeling among men. The community of wives became a standard feature of utopian philosophy and was found in the ideal societies envisioned in the Hellenistic period by the Stoics Zeno and Chrysippus, by Diogenes the Cynic, and by Iambulus.[74]

Prostitution was eliminated from Utopia, either explicitly or implicitly. In the *Ecclesiazusae*, the women banned prostitutes.[75] Plato specifically outlaws Corinthian *hetairai*—for these women connoted a luxurious, degenerate community. He does not mention other prostitutes, but it is difficult to imagine where they might be useful in the top stratum of his *Republic*. In the paradise proposed by Crates the Cynic of the late third or second century B.C., there was a community of women and children similar to Plato's, and prostitutes were specifically eliminated.[76]

In the *Republic* Plato stated that males and females were similar in nature, and that the only significant distinction between the sexes was that the male begets and the female bears children. Since the sexes were similar in all respects except physical strength, they were assigned similar duties. Because Plato had great faith in education, he prescribed the same curriculum for guardians of both sexes to prepare them for their duties. He also relieved guardian women from the biological burdens accompanying motherhood, by providing for the assistance of nurses.

Many of Plato's ideas derived from an idealized view of Spartan women. Like Spartans, the female guardians pursued a program of physical fitness, waited until adulthood to bear children, could bear legitimate children to more than one man with the proviso that he be a member of the approved social class, and moved freely in public. Plato went even further than the Spartans in prescribing that women strip for exercise and in delaying the age of childbearing to twenty, rather than the Spartan norm of eighteen.

In view of the limited lives of Athenian women and the misogyny of classical literature, the provisions for the female guardians in the *Republic* are remarkable. Plato's critique of marriage and the nuclear family, coupled with his provisions for an androgynous life style accessible through equal education and state-supported child care, foreshadows the ideas of modern radical feminists such as Shulamith Firestone and Simone de Beauvoir. And the elimination of private property in the *Republic* brings to mind the Marxist doctrine that the accumulation of wealth and the monogamous marriage led to the subjection of women.[77] Yet Plato's philosophy was not undiluted feminism.[78] He did not believe that women were, on the whole, equal to men, although some women were potentially superior to some men. He also repeatedly classified women with children, perhaps because, in his own city of Athens, the wives often were only fourteen years old.

In his later work, the *Laws,* Plato described a less utopian but more feasible community than he had in the *Republic*. The result was a compromise between the idealism of the *Republic* and the reality of Athenian life. The differences in the provisions for women begin with the notion in the *Laws* that there are important distinctions between the sexes beyond their reproductive roles. In the *Laws,* Plato reinforced traditional sex roles, making females obedient, modest, temperate, and gentle, and males competitive and aggressive. The education of girls was similar to that of boys, but the emphasis was different. For example, a program of physical fitness was prescribed for both sexes, but girls were not required to participate in the more martial and competitive activities (8. 834D). Married women were to exercise clothed (8. 833D), rather than nude as in the *Republic*. While in the *Republic* women who showed an inclination could be employed as warriors, in the *Laws* women served only after their childbearing years and then only in emergencies (7. 814). The sexes were distinct even in music: modest songs were appropriate to women, noble and manly music to men (7. 802E).

In the *Laws* women were more limited by their biological functions. Monogamous marriage was mandatory. The age of marriage for girls was between sixteen and twenty, for men between thirty and thirty-five (6. 785B–C). A ten-year period of procreation followed (6. 784B). Only after childbearing were women free to serve the community in other capacities. Older women were employed in prestigious ways, but ones that reinforced traditional sex roles. They supervised the administration of marriage laws, the family, human reproduction, and the rearing of young children. They were free to have intercourse with whoever pleased them, but were not to produce children nor draw attention to these post-marital affairs (6. 784E-785A).

The interest in the role of women which we have detected in Euripides, Aristophanes, and Plato can be analyzed in relation to a relaxation of traditional patterns of living during the Peloponnesian War (431-404 B.C.). Profound civic disturbances as well as simple warfare are described by Thucydides.

Due to the conditions of ancient warfare, more men than women were killed and the female-male population ratio rose accordingly. In Athens, this increase was aggravated by the departure of a large expedition for Sicily in 415 B.C., plus the Spartan occupation of Decelea in 411 B.C., which forced the Athenians to fight throughout the year rather than, as previously, only in the summer. We assume that many Athenian women were forced to abandon their seclusion and perform tasks formerly reserved for men.

Some may have abandoned their decorum as well. However, Thucydides, the dominant historical source for the period, has little to say specifically about women, but the comedies of Aristophanes dating from the second half of the war show that the profound disturbances in traditional morality throughout the cities of Greece had their disruptive effect upon women and family life. The unusual behavior of Hipparete, of the second wife of Callias, and of Agariste (see p. 81) was surely the result of the turmoil of war.

We are reminded of the freedom enjoyed by Spartan women while their husbands were away at war for long periods of time, and see here an anticipation of the liberty to be gained by Roman women in similar circumstances. However, in Athens the period of men's absence was relatively brief, and we cannot detect any permanent change in the political, legal, or economic status of women of the Classical Age after the Peloponnesian War.[79] Yet a revaluation of women's position in society was under way in some intellectual circles,[80] and there was a perceptible change in the depiction of the female figure in the visual arts which can best be discussed in the context of the Hellenistic Age.

# VII

## HELLENISTIC WOMEN

THE HELLENISTIC world was dramatically different from that of the preceding period. Loss of political autonomy on the part of the city-states wrought a change in men's political relationships to their societies and to each other. These changes, in turn, affected women's position in the family and in society. The effect on any individual woman depended largely on her social class and the area of the world in which she lived.

The amount of information available on Hellenistic women is surprisingly large, especially in comparison with the dearth of material on Greek women in earlier periods.[1] The abundance of information about the royal women of Greek descent during the Hellenistic era can be attributed both to the impact these memorable women had on ancient authors and to the fact that they involved themselves in the political activities of men—which are, after all, the concern of most historians. The experience of women of lesser status can also be found in public records, as some freeborn women gained more influence in political and economic affairs, besides expanding their options with regard to marriage, public roles, education, and the conduct of their private lives. Finally, the experience of women—from slaves and courtesans to queens—has been preserved in the cultural artifacts of the period. Close scrutiny of the representation of women in sculpture, vase painting, New Comedy, and other art forms yields much insight into their sexual experiences as well as into the nature of their everyday lives. The commentary of philosophers—for the most part urging the retention of traditional female roles—reveals that women's position altered as society changed during this period.

## Wives and Mothers of the Macedonian Conquerors

Macedonia, located in the wilds of northern Greece, was ruled by kings. The conquest of the rest of Greece by Philip II, who acceded to the throne of Macedon in 359 B.C., brought an end to the independence of the city-states. The further imposition of Macedonian power on the East by Philip's son, Alexander, ultimately resulted—after fifty years of war among his successors—in the establishment of dynasties of Macedonians: the Antigonids in Greece, the Ptolemies in Egypt, and the Seleucids in Asia Minor. The competition for power among these rulers concerns us here only insofar as the women of their courts were affected. Scholars usually define the Hellenistic period as the three centuries between the death of Alexander in 323 B.C. and the Roman settlement of Egypt in 30 B.C., but our time span will be more flexible.

Among Macedonian ruling families, the relationship between mother and son could be much stronger and more significant than that between husband and wife. Many Macedonian kings indulged in both formal and informal polygamy, and because they often chose not to confer most-favored status on one of their wives—thereby making clear as well which of their sons was the designated successor to the throne—they fostered a climate of intrigue and struggle for power within their courts which could end in their own death at the hands of a power-hungry mother plotting on behalf of her son. The stories that have come down to us portray the Macedonian queens as ambitious, shrewd, and, in many instances, ruthless. The common elements of the tales relate the elimination —often by poison—of political antagonists and rival queens and their progeny, the murder of the husband, and the queen's expectation that she will enjoy more power in the reign of her son than she did when her husband was on the throne. Clearly, these are women competing in a traditionally male arena, and using decidedly male tactics and weapons, in addition to poison, said to be a "woman's weapon."

Aside from Cleopatra VII, who will be discussed again later, the most powerful and illustrious of the Macedonian princesses were Olympias and Arsinoë II. Olympias is famous as the mother of Alexander the Great. At the court of her husband, Philip II, Olympias struggled against rival wives, mistresses, and their children to assure Alexander's succession to the throne of Macedonia. Though she ultimately suffered defeat and exile, she was clearly a woman of genius and determination. Plutarch has given us even more enticing evidence of her unique qualities:

> Once a serpent was seen stretched out next to the body of Olympias as she slept, and this, more than anything else, they say, abated the ardor of Philip's passion for her. Accordingly, he no longer came often to sleep next to her, either because he feared some spells and charms might be put on him by her or thought she had intercourse with some superior being. But there is another story about these matters: All the women of this region were addicted to Orphic rites and the orgies of Dionysus from extreme antiquity. ... Olympias, who affected these divine inspirations more enthusiastically than other women, and performed them in more barbaric fashion, would provide the revelers with large tame snakes which often would crawl out from the ivy and the mystic winnowing baskets and wind themselves around the wands and garlands of the women, thus terrifying the men.[2]

The psychological impact that such a mother must have had on Alexander has long been a subject of historical speculation.

Alexander was proclaimed king after the murder of Philip in 336 B.C. The murder was blamed on Olympias, probably unjustly (she was in exile at the time), although she had much to gain when her twenty-year-old son succeeded his father. Two years later, Alexander set out on his conquest of the Persian Empire. While Alexander was absent on campaign, Olympias presided over the court of Macedonia. She competed for power with Antipater, whom Alexander had left at home as viceroy. Politically, Alexander supported Antipater, but he never ceased to be personally devoted to his mother.

Although the pattern of alliances of strong mothers and sons was repeated time and again (it was echoed in the behavior of the Roman empresses, though, unlike the Romans, the Macedonian princesses were not commonly accused of aimless sexual licentiousness but of using sex to further their political ambitions), women were also used in passive roles by Hellenistic kings in ways that paralleled those employed by the Greek tyrants of the Archaic Age. The marriages of Macedonian princesses, for example, were often arranged by their male guardians to cement alliances between men: the guardian and the husband. These dynastic marriages were dissolved when new alliances appeared politically more attractive. However, the unilateral rejection of a queen by the husband in favor of another could result in violence, and once the disfavored bride's father or guardian became involved, marriage alliances often produced international entanglements. One of the many unfortunate marriages was that of Berenice and Antiochus.

In 253 B.C. Ptolemy II of Egypt arranged a diplomatic marriage between his daughter Berenice and the Seleucid Antiochus II. Imitating the ostentatious tyrants of the Archaic Age, Ptolemy gave his daughter so lavish a dowry that she was nicknamed "Phernophoros" (dowry-bringer). Antiochus repudiated his former wife and halfsister Laodice, but later, apparently through personal preference, he returned to live with Laodice without formally divorcing Berenice. Ptolemy II had given his daughter in marriage with the expectation that the bridegroom would repudiate earlier wives and their children in favor of the new wife, and, most important of all, he expected that the offspring of his daughter would inherit the throne. The bridegrooms, as was mentioned earlier, in order to avoid offending the families of earlier wives and for personal reasons as well, did not always make decisive pronouncements of who was the most important wife and whose child would inherit the throne.[3]

Laodice, like Olympias before her, was driven to desperate measures on behalf of her sons. She took the opportunity to poison Antiochus, and had Berenice and her baby murdered in order to assure the succession of Seleucus, the elder of her two sons by Antiochus. Berenice's brother, Ptolemy III, then king of Egypt, arrived with troops too late to save his sister, but avenged her and exploited the situation by precipitating the Third Syrian War (246–241 B.C.).[4]

The Ptolemies, as the sad story of Berenice demonstrates, readily arranged dynastic marriages for their women. But four of the first eight Ptolemies married their sisters.[5] The marriage of full sister and brother had never been encouraged among Greeks or Macedonians, who regarded it as incestuous, but it had been a local Egyptian custom of the royal family, to whom the Ptolemies wished to appear as successors.[6] Moreover, brother–sister marriage eliminated foreign influences from the court. The first marriage of full brother and sister among the Ptolemies was that of Ptolemy II and Arsinoë II, who were both officially worshiped as divine during their lifetimes, reviving another traditional Egyptian custom which was also followed by their successors.[7]

Arsinoë ruled with her brother for approximately five years, until her death in 270 B.C. As was customary in Macedonian courts, she inaugurated her reign by accusing all her rivals of treason and having them eliminated. She was the first Egyptian queen whose portrait was shown with her husband's on coins, and Theocritus and Callimachus celebrated her in poetry. The period when Arsinoë joined her brother in the government was characterized by a dramatic improvement in the military and political affairs of Egypt; Arsinoë herself was responsible for the expansion of Egyptian sea power.[8] Though some historians condemn her for unbridled ambition, most agree that she surpassed her brother in talent for governing Egypt.

Olympias and Arsinoë are only two in a long line of queens of Greek extraction leading up to the famous Cleopatra. In 51 B.C., at the age of seventeen, Cleopatra VII and her brother Ptolemy XIII, then ten years old, inherited the throne of Egypt. A feud between the two heirs was settled with the assistance of Julius Caesar, who left Cleopatra on the throne with her younger brother Ptolemy XIV. In 47 B.C., Cleopatra bore a son whom she named Caesarion, since she claimed Caesar as the father. Caesar invited her to Rome, where she lived as his mistress for the two years until his assassination. After returning to Egypt, she eliminated all potential rivals to the throne, in the fashion of Hellenistic monarchs, by arranging for the deaths of her brother-consort and her sister Arsinoë. Cleopatra's relationship with Marc Antony compels us to consider her more fully in the next chapter. Nevertheless, the phenomenon of Cleopatra must be set firmly in the context of Ptolemaic queens, shrewd, able, and ambitious. She was not a courtesan, an exotic plaything for Roman generals. Rather, Cleopatra's liaisons with the Romans must be considered to have been, from her viewpoint, legitimate dynastic alliances with promises of the greatest possible success and profit to the queen and to Egypt.

No Hellenistic queen had political power solely by virtue of birth, except when she was destined to marry her brother. Only in Egypt, during the decline of the Ptolemies, did a daughter (Berenice

III), or a sister (Cleopatra VII) with her brother (Ptolemy XIII), succeed to the throne. But many women wielded power as wives or mothers, especially of weak kings, and as regents for young sons or absent husbands, or through the dynamism of personal ambition. The competent women visible in Hellenistic courts were one of the positive influences of this period toward increasing the prestige of nonroyal but upper-class women.

## Growing Competence in Public Realms

The status of the Hellenistic queen becomes intelligible against the background of the status of other women in Greek cities and interacts with it. The less-restricted movement of queens in spheres of activity formerly reserved for men set a style that was emulated by some wealthy and aristocratic women. The legal and economic responsibilities of women increased, but political gains were more illusory. The apparent formal expansion of women's competence may be attributable to the fact that for the Hellenistic period there exist data from many different areas inhabited by Greeks, while our view of women's position in Classical Greece is monopolized by the situation at Athens and the implication that, on the whole, Sparta was exceptional because of a unique social system. In other words, we may hypothesize that non-Athenian women even outside Sparta may have been less restricted before the Hellenistic period, but this cannot be documented.

As living queens were being celebrated by poets and receiving numerous public honors, so public decrees honoring women were published in the Greek world in the Hellenistic period, and increased in frequency under Roman rule.[9] Priestesses and women performing religious services received the most numerous honors, as they had even in Classical Athens. In the second century B.C. lengthy decrees were passed for Archippe by the assembly of Cyme in Asia Minor, detailing her generosity, including the amount she had spent on wining and dining the entire population.[10] Even in Athens, Pericles' idea that women should not be spoken of, either for praise or blame, no longer prevailed. With aristocratic ostentation, fathers of girls who spun wool and embroidered the *peplos* of Athena had decrees passed honoring their daughters' service.[11] The names of many girls of noble families are listed.

Women were also the beneficiaries of the more generous granting (for diplomatic, economic, and cultural reasons) of citizenship and political rights by Greek cities that was a characteristic phenomenon in this cosmopolitan period. A few women obtained awards of political rights or held public office. Some were awarded honorary citizenship and the rights of proxeny (privileges granted to foreigners) by foreign cities in gratitude for services performed.[12] In 218 B.C. Aristodama, a poetess of Smyrna, was granted honorary citizenship by the Aetolians of Lamia in Thessaly because her poetry had praised the Aetolian people and their ancestors.[13] An inscription records the existence of a female archon (magistrate) in Histria in the second century B.C.[14] In the first century B.C. another female magistrate, Phile of Priene, became the first woman to construct a reservoir and aqueduct.[15] It is very likely that she was made a magistrate because she promised to contribute to the public works out of her private funds. Here we have one of the main reasons for the increased importance of women: the acquisition and use of economic power.

These women were exceptional, and most others continued to be excluded from participation in government. But since, at least from our viewpoint, under the domination of Hellenistic monarchs the implications of citizenship and its privileges were less far-reaching for men than they had been in the independent city-states of the Classical world, on the one hand the gap in privileges between men and women was much narrowed, and on the other, the men—rather than attempting to hoard them—became more ready to share with women the less-valued privileges they had.

Although the increase in the political involvement of nonroyal Greek women was slight, a slow evolution in legal status, particularly in private law, can be traced. This change can be seen more in the areas newly Hellenized through Macedonian conquest than in the old cities of the Greek mainland. In this milieu of the deracinated Greek, lacking the traditional safeguards of the *polis*, a Greek woman might not have easy recourse to the protection of her male guardians, and hence she required both an ability to safeguard herself and an increased legal capacity to act on her own behalf.

Papyrus documents from Egypt provide abundant evidence in the field of private law, but the assumption must not be made that Hellenistic law was uniform, nor that Egyptian practices apply to other areas.[16] It is necessary to distinguish between laws governing Greek women living in Egypt and laws for native Egyptians, which, although not sufficiently studied, appear less stringent. Greek women, when they acted within the traditional conventions of Greek law, continued to need a guardian; Egyptian women did not. A guardian was required when a Greek woman made a public declaration or incurred a contractual obligation concerning persons or property. Examples of these contracts are countless. Documents show women as purchasers, sellers, lessors, lessees, borrowers, lenders; women were as liable as men for the various taxes that attached to these commercial activities. Women also had the right to receive and make legacies, acting with their guardians, and they usually named their husbands and children as heirs.[17]

Greek women in Egypt were nevertheless permitted to act without a guardian in some situations. A woman was permitted to write a petition to the government or police on her own behalf, since this involved neither contractual obligation nor undue publicity. In these petitions, some women exploit the notion that they are members of the weaker sex, without male defenders: one asks for special consideration as "a needy defenseless woman"; another says she is obviously deserving of pity because she is a "working woman"; a third asks to be relieved of the obligation to cultivate state land, citing earlier decisions where women were granted exemptions solely on the basis of their sex, and adds that she is "childless and incapable of providing even for myself."[18] Widows or mothers of illegitimate children could give their daughters in marriage and apprentice their sons. In at least one case we know of, a widow had the right to expose a posthumous infant after obtaining the permission of her former mother-in-law.[19]

The expansion of married women's rights can be seen in a marriage contract of 311 B.C. between a Greek man and woman living in Egypt:

> In the 7th year of the reign of Alexander, son of Alexander, the 14th year of Ptolemy's administration as satrap, in the month Dius.
> Contract of marriage of Heraclides and Demetria.
> Heraclides takes as his lawful wife Demetria of Cos from her father Leptines of Cos and her mother Philotis. He is free; she is free. She brings with her to the marriage clothing and ornaments valued at 1000 drachmas. Heraclides shall supply to Demetria all that is suitable for a freeborn wife. We shall live together in whatever place seems best to Leptines and Heraclides, deciding together.
> If Demetria is caught in fraudulent machinations to the disgrace

of her husband Heraclides. she shall forfeit all that she has brought with her. But Heraclides shall prove whatever he charges against Demetria before three men whom they both approve. It shall not be lawful for Heraclides to bring home another woman for himself in such a way as to inflict contumely on Demetria, nor to have children by another woman, nor to indulge in fraudulent machinations against Demetria on any pretext. If Heraclides is caught doing any of these things, and Demetria proves it before three men whom they both approve, Heraclides shall return to Demetria the dowry of 1000 drachmas which she brought, and also forfeit 1000 drachmas of the silver coinage of [Ptolemy bearing a portrait head of] Alexander. Demetria and those helping Demetria shall have the right to exact payment from Heraclides and from his property on both land and sea, as if by a legal judgment.

This contract shall be valid in every respect. wherever Heraclides may produce it against Demetria, or Demetria and those helping Demetria to exact payment may produce it against Heraclides, as though the agreement had been made in that place.

Heraclides and Demetria shall each have the right to keep a copy of the contract in their own custody, and to produce it against one another. Witnesses.[20]

The most striking features of this agreement are the recognition of two codes of marital behavior—one for the husband. another for the wife—and the stipulation that both codes are subject to interpretation by the couple's social peers. The moral element explicit in the phrases "disgrace of her husband" and "contumely on Demetria" should be noted: social and moral rights and obligations are recognized in both partners. The husband's potential indiscretions are elaborated, while the wife's are modestly veiled. In the Hellenistic context, the contractual obligations may be interpreted as: no extramarital sex at all for the wife; casual adultery, especially with slave girls or prostitutes, permitted to the husband; no second quasi-legitimate domestic establishment by the husband with another woman whose presence would be odious to Demetria and whose children could have claims on his estate.

The definition of the marital offense by the judgment of the couple's circle and the use of property to exact stipulated damages as punishment are both quite commendable legal ideas. A notional fund is established, consisting of the value of the wife's dowry and an equivalent sum contributed by the husband. The contract provides that if transgression of the moral code is proved to the satisfaction of the three arbitrators, the fund is to become the property of the wronged party by way of damages to that party and punishment for the transgressor.

The document makes no provision for inheritance or for the division of communal property in case of divorce. No doubt explicit stipulations were not needed because a pattern pertaining to such topics was already established in the Greek colony at Elephantine.

The mother's participation in the giving of her daughter in marriage is unusual. The bride does not sever ties with her family, for there is the possibility of continuing interference by the bride's father in determining where the couple will live, and the references to "those helping Demetria" probably envision the aid of her father and other relatives in extracting justice from her husband. Justice consists in obtaining the notional fund, for one purpose of marriage contracts is the protection of property.

As the Hellenistic era progressed, the role of the bride's father diminished. It was common for a father to give a daughter in marriage in his role of formal guardian, but some contracts were made simply between a woman and man agreeing to share a common life.[21] The right of the married daughter to self-determination against paternal authority began to be asserted. According to Athenian, Roman, and Egyptian law, a father was permitted to dissolve his daughter's marriage against her will. However, later, in Roman Egypt, under Egyptian law, the authority of the father over a married daughter was curtailed by judicial rulings stating that the wishes of the woman were the determining factor. If she wished to remain married, she could do so.[22]

Divorce is foreseen in numerous marriage contracts, allowing husband and wife equal opportunity to repudiate each other. Deeds of divorce are also found. The most important provision is for the return of the dowry. Children were to be maintained by the father, although they did not necessarily reside with him. Maintenance by the father was fair, since communal property usually remained with him. A marriage contract of 92 B.C. that discusses the protection of communal property during the duration of the marriage makes it clear that a wife usually suffers financially upon the dissolution of a marriage, for she receives no portion of the shared property but simply the return of her dowry.[23] This document also defines the sexual behavior required of the husband rather specifically, so as to include not bringing in a second wife, not keeping a concubine or a boy lover, and not having children by another woman nor living in another house apart from the wife.

Gains in economic responsibility outstripped women's legal competence during this period. Not only in Egypt but in other areas of the Greek world respectable women were participating more actively in economic affairs. Greek women exercised control over slaves, for they are common among the manumittors named in inscriptions. There are 123 women among the 491 manumittors listed at Delphi before 150 B.C. The records of land sales from Ceos and Tenos also list many women. There is good evidence for economic activity of women at Delos: married women, assisted by their guardians, borrowed money—suggesting that they rather than their husbands were responsible for their own debts—and wives of borrowers are recorded as "agreeing to" loans made by their husbands. At Amorgos, likewise, inscriptions show husbands making contracts concerning property with the explicit agreement of their wives.[24] Moreover, as we have observed above, a few women won public acclaim for generous contributions from their personal funds. Yet it must be acknowledged that even where male guardians are not specifically mentioned as participants in women's financial transactions, they are operating, at the very least, as some sort of legal fiction. Sparta was an exception, for there women employed their money as they wished, in spite of the occasional disapproval of male relatives.

Spartan women were a conspicuous group of wealthy females. The richest people in Hellenistic Sparta were the mother and grandmother of King Agis. Women owned two-fifths of the land, and they opposed economic reforms which would have redistributed the wealth of Sparta. Like wealthy men, they sometimes chose to exhibit race horses at the Olympic games in order to draw attention to themselves and their prosperity. Their names are recorded on inscriptions which they erected and on victor lists. Two Spartans (Cynisca and Euryleonis) and a courtesan (Bilistiche of Argos, who was the concubine of Ptolemy II) were the first women whose horses won at Olympia.[25]

In Athens, in contrast to some other parts of the Greek world, there was little, if any, economic or legal emancipation of citizen women. In fact, from 317 to 307 B.C., during the government of Demetrius of Phalerum, there was less freedom than in the Classical period. The legislation of Demetrius reflected the ethical ideas of Aristotle, who, as we have seen, believed that the deliberative part of woman's soul was impotent and needed supervision.[26] Demetrius established a board of "regulators of women" (*gynaikonomoi*), who censored women's conduct and also controlled the lavishness of dinner parties.[27] Aristotle observed that the supervision of women was suitable for states that have leisure and property, and was primarily directed at the regulation of upper-class extravagance, for the poor lacked slaves and were obliged to send their wives out on the errands of servants.[28] Wealthy and independent women, such as Spartans and prostitutes, might show off fortunes which were truly in their own hands, but the wife of a wealthy man, as I have suggested in my comments on Solon's sumptuary legislation, could be used as an emblem of her husband's prosperity. Hence the regulation of women in Athens, especially in association with restrictions on dinner parties, was actually a limitation of the extravagance of men.

## The Responses of Philosophers to Social Realities

Athens remained the center for philosophy—as it had been in the Classical period—and citizen women in Athens still were by and large exposed to nothing more intellectual than practical training in domestic matters.[29] At the opening of the Hellenistic Age, men continued to be attracted to the Peripatetic followers of Aristotle, who explained man's public role by analogy to his place in the individual family—a microcosm of the patriarchal city-state. Theophrastus, another disciple of Aristotle, theorized that more education would turn women into rather lazy, talkative busybodies.[30] Even the upper class, to which one would naturally look for an endorsement of schooling for women, did not educate its daughters.

Meanwhile, there flourished new philosophies offering guides to the individual in a world far larger than a city-state. Nevertheless, despite the changing world, Stoicism, by far the most popular of the Hellenistic philosophies, reinforced traditional roles for women.

This position may have been partially a response to the realization that a few respectable women—but a highly conspicuous few—were trespassing on male territory. The Neopythagoreans, a small sect obviously distressed by the economic, political, and social vicissitudes of the time, took comfort in formulating intricate and highly restrictive codes of conduct for women, thus to ensure for themselves some measure of harmony in a world that otherwise resisted their theorems. The only two schools of thought that theoretically advocated the emancipation of women—the nonconformist Epicureanism and Cynicism—gained few prominent adherents and had little impact on official attitudes toward women.

Zeno (335–263 B.C.), the founder of the Stoic school of philosophy, had envisioned a community of wives—similar to the sharing of women described in Plato's *Republic* (see p. 116)—but his followers abandoned utopian schemes and urged monogamous marriage on their adherents.[31] The Stoic doctrine of equality and brotherhood of man, while contributing to the breakdown of class distinctions, did not posit equality between the sexes. The Stoics joined the Peripatetics in recommending the familiar roles of wife and mother for women. Stoicism was adapted by the Romans, and, to a large extent, it was owing to Roman influence that marriage and the rearing of children were elevated to the level of moral, religious, and patriotic duty.

The practical direction of Stoicism was a response to a social need. Owing to men's reluctance to marry and the practice of exposing unwanted children, Greek cities were becoming underpopulated. Polybius, a historian of the second century B.C., attributed the tendency to celibacy and the reluctance to raise children to men's pretentiousness, greed, and laziness.[32] However, for some, the old incentives for marriage—which were essentially religious, economic, and political—had vanished. Men had once married out of religious duty to their ancestors, with the primary objectives of perpetuating family lines and maintaining family cults and tombs. But in the Hellenistic period, the values of the Classical period were losing their potency. Communal ideals were replaced by the goal of individual self-satisfaction. People drifted away from their lands. Some moved from their ancestral plots to the cities because of fear of attacks coming from constantly warring Hellenistic monarchs and later from the Romans. Some joined overseas colonies, effectively abandoning their family tombs. As was the case in the earlier period of colonization, the Dark Age, a wife and family were an encumbrance for a colonist, although some took them along.

The Hellenistic period was also marked by an increasing gap between the wealthy and the poor; many people lost their lands through poverty. The economic considerations determining marriage among the poor are elusive; the degree of poverty is the determining factor. On the one hand, it can be argued that a wife and children are a resource of free labor for a poor man; on the other, that there is an economic level below which a man may not hope to support a wife and family.

For men of all social classes—including the late fifth-century nobles Conon and Xenophon—there were new and more exciting careers. For the mercenary soldiers and adventurers who drifted about calling no city their own, sexual satisfaction was easy to find, and a concubine was less burdensome than a wife. The raising of children was a commitment with little appeal for a wanderer. His children would not be likely to be granted citizenship in a city that was not his father's native land. In this context, another traditional impetus to marriage among the upper class—political alliance—retained its validity only among the very few who ruled and contracted dynastic marriages. For the subjected multitudes, which now included the upper classes, political power could no longer be an incentive to marriage.

Confronted by the fluctuating mores of the Hellenistic period, the Neopythagoreans were concerned about the proper behavior of women and wrote several texts on the subject. Whether the authors of these writings lived at Rome, Alexandria, or elsewhere, and whether they wrote as early as the fourth century or as late as the first century B.C., are subjects of scholarly controversy. Pythagoras, the founder of a religious order at Croton in the late sixth century B. C., had had many women followers who were admitted on equal terms with men. Adherence to his doctrines required a rigorous discipline. The regulations specifically enjoined upon women are not extant, but they are likely to have included measures concerning abstinence or moderation, possibly in the realms of financial expenditures and sexual activity, if it is true that many husbands actually sent their wives to study with Pythagoras. Some Neopythagorean texts that do discuss the correct behavior of women are extant, and certain of these are attributed to female writers. The authors are at least as likely to have actually been male, but this cannot be conclusively proven. To "Theano" (the name of the wife or daughter of Pythagoras) were attributed Hellenistic texts giving rules for the proper behavior of women whose husbands were adulterous. "Melissa" wrote on the obligations of women, especially that of abstaining from luxury. "Perictione" was the name of Plato's mother, and it was claimed that she had been a disciple of Pythagoras. In the Hellenistic period several treatises were written purporting to be by Plato's mother; but the ascription was deliberately fraudulent; they were probably written by some later Perictione or by a Neopythagorean disciple who then attributed his or her work to some "Perictione." One such little-known treatise gives us a spectacularly early example of "advice to young ladies":

We must deem the harmonious woman to be one who is well endowed with wisdom and self-restraint. For her soul must be very wise indeed when it comes to virtue so that she will be just and courageous [*lit.* manly], while being sensible and beautified with self-sufficiency, despising empty opinion. For from these qualities fair deeds accrue to a woman for herself as well as for her husband, children, and home; and perchance even to a city, if in fact such a woman were to govern cities or peoples, as we see in the case of a legitimate monarchy. Surely, by controlling her desire and passion, a woman becomes devout and harmonious, resulting in her not becoming a prey to impious love affairs. Rather, she will be full of love for her husband and children and her entire household. For all those women who have a desire for extramarital relations [*lit.* alien beds] themselves become enemies of all the freedmen and domestics in the house. Such a woman contrives both falsehood and deceits for her husband and tells lies against everyone to him as well, so that she alone seems to excel in good will and in mastery over the household, though she revels in idleness. For from all these activities comes the ruination that jointly afflicts the woman as well as her husband. And so let these precepts be pronounced before the women of today. With regard to the sustenance and natural requirements of the body, it must be provided with a proper measure of clothing, bathing, anointing, hair-setting, and all those items of gold and precious stones that are used for adornment. For women who eat and drink all sorts of extravagant dishes and dress themselves sumptuously, wearing things that women are given to wearing, are decked out for seduction into all manner of vice, not only the bed but also the commission of other wrongful deeds. And so, a woman must merely satisfy her hunger and thirst, and if she is of the poorer class, her chill, if she has a cloak made of goatskin. To be consumers of goods from far-off lands or of items that cost a great amount of money or are highly esteemed is manifestly no small vice. And to wear dresses that are excessively styled and elaborately dyed with purple or some other color is a foolish indulgence in extravagance. For the body desires merely not to be cold or, for the sake of appearances, naked; but it needs nothing else. Men's opinion runs ignorantly after inanities and oddities. So that a woman will neither cover herself with gold or the stone of India or of any other place, nor will she braid her hair with artful device; nor will she anoint herself with Arabian perfume; nor will she put white makeup on her face or rouge her cheeks or darken her brows and lashes or artfully dye her graying hair; nor will she bathe a lot. For by pursuing these things a woman seeks to make a spectacle of female incontinence. The beauty that comes from wisdom and not from these things brings pleasure to women who are well born. Let a woman not think that noble birth and wealth and coming from a great city and having the esteem and love of illustrious and royal men are necessities. For if a woman is well off, she has nothing to complain about; if not, it doesn't do to yearn. A clever woman is not prevented from living without these benefits. Even if allotments be great and marvelous, let not the soul strive for them, but let it walk far away from them. For they do more harm than good when someone drags a woman into trouble. Treachery, malice, and spite are associated with them, so that a woman so endowed could never be serene. A woman must reverence the gods if she hopes for happiness, obeying the ancestral laws and institutions. And I name after these [the gods], her parents, whom she must honor and reverence. For parents are in all respects equivalent to gods and they act in the interest of their grandchildren. A woman must live for her husband according to law and in actuality, thinking no private thoughts of her own, but taking care of her marriage and guarding it. For everything depends on this. A woman must bear all that her husband bears, whether he be unlucky or sin out of ignorance, whether he be sick or drunk or sleep with other women. For this latter sin is peculiar to men, but never to women. Rather it brings vengeance upon her. Therefore, a woman must preserve the law and not emulate men. And she must endure her husband's temper, stinginess, complaining, jealousy, abuse, and anything else peculiar to his nature. And she will deal with all of his characteristics in such a way as is congenial to him by being discreet. For a woman who is affectionate to her husband and treats him in an agreeable way is a harmonious woman and one who loves her whole household and makes everyone in it well disposed. But when a woman has no love in her, she has no desire to look upon her home or children or slaves or their security whatsoever, but yearns for them to go to perdition just as an enemy would; and she prays for her husband to die as she would a foe, hating everybody who pleases him, just so she can sleep with other men. Thus, I think a woman is harmonious if she is full of sagacity and temperance. For she will not only help her husband but also her children, relatives, slaves, and her whole household, in which reside all her possessions and her dear kin and friends. She will conduct their home with simplicity, speaking and hearing fair words and holding views on their common mode of living that are compatible, while acting in concert with those relatives and friends whom her husband extols. And if her husband thinks something is sweet, she will think so too; or if he thinks something bitter, she will agree with him. Otherwise she will be out of tune with her whole universe.[33]

In contrast to Neopythagoreanism and Stoicism—especially as exploited by the Romans—Epicureanism and Cynicism were oriented toward the happiness of the individual rather than the well-being of the family and the state. Neither Epicurus nor Diogenes, one of the earliest Cynics, favored conventional marriage, although Epicurus admitted that marriage could occur in special circumstances.[34] Diogenes advocated a community of wives, but unlike earlier utopian theorists he also considered the will of the woman essential, "recognizing no other marriage than that of the man who persuades with the woman who is persuaded." [35]

## Expanding Opportunities for Education

Epicurus admitted women to the school in his garden on the same terms as men. The Cynics were never organized in a conventional school, but we know of one female philosopher who lived according to Cynic principles. She was Hipparchia, wife of Crates, who went about with her husband, appeared with him in public, went to dinner parties, and was proud to have spent her time in education rather than in working at the loom.[36]

Hipparchia, the philosopher, was an aristocrat from Maroneia in northeastern Greece, and there is evidence that in other parts of the Greek world some women were given at least a rudimentary education in athletics, music, and reading, in imitation of the time-honored curriculum for boys.

Physical education was now available to women. Athletics were an essential part of the male curriculum that was opened to women in the Hellenistic period precisely because the Classical ideal no longer prevailed. Classical athletics had provided an opportunity for the assertion of individual prowess by amateurs, while the Hellenistic and Roman periods saw professionals supplant amateurs and athletics become a spectator sport. [Plate 13]

Apart from some races at Olympia segregated from the men's events, and footraces in honor of Hera at Elis for maidens classified by age, women in Greece did not personally participate in athletic competitions until the first century A.D., when their names begin to appear in inscriptions. An inscription erected at Delphi honoring three female athletes from Tralles proclaims that one of them, Hedea, won prizes for singing and accompanying herself on the cithara at Athens, for footracing at Nemea, and for driving a war chariot at Isthmia.[37]

More important than the possibility of participating in professional athletics was the acquisition of the ability to read and write. During the Hellenistic and Roman periods, we find from Egyptian papyri that some women are able to sign their names to contracts, although the number of illiterate women who have to resort to another person to sign on their behalf is proportionately higher than for men.[38]

Not surprising against the background of increased literacy and education for women is the reemergence of poetesses. One poetess of the period won high praise. Erinna, of the Dorian island of Telos, can be compared to Sappho.[39] Both speak of private worlds, and both are masterful artists. Erinna showed her originality in using the dactylic hexameter for a poem of lamentation, when tradition dictated the elegiac couplet or a choral meter. By the age of nineteen, Erinna had written her famous pom "The Distaff":

> You leaped from the white horses
> And raced madly into the deep wave—
> But "I've got you, dear!" I shouted loudly,
> And when you were the Tortoise
> You ran skipping through the yard of the great court.
> These are the things that I lament and

Sorrow over, my sad Baucis—these are
Little trails through my heart that are
Still warm—my remembrances of you.
For our former delights are ashes now.
When we were young girls we sat in our rooms
Without a care, holding our dolls and pretending
We were young brides. Remember—at dawn
The "mother," who distributed the wool
To the attendant servants, came and called
You to help with the salting of the meat.
And how afraid we were, when we were small,
Of Mormo—she had huge ears on her head,
Walked about on four feet,
And was always changing faces.
But when you mounted your husband's bed
You forgot all about those things,
All you heard from your mother
When you were still a little child.
Dear Baucis, Aphrodite set forgetfulness
In your heart.
And so I lament you and neglect my duties.
For I am not so irreverent as to set foot out-of-doors
Or to look upon a corpse with my eyes
Or let my hair loose in lamentation—
But a blush of grief tears my [cheeks].[40]

This fragment of a longer poem is sufficient to show why Erinna
was acclaimed in antiquity. The poem is a lament for her lifelong
friend Baucis. The title "Distaff" refers to the theme of wool-work-
ing, which is mentioned only once in the extant fragment but
probably occurred more frequently in the full poem. Recurring
expressions of grief punctuate the reminiscences about the childhood they enjoyed together: the game of Tortoise, playing with
dolls, and being frightened by the bogey Mormo. (In the fantasies of
Greek children bogies were mature females, who, having lost their
own children, desired to devour others. They were sexually insatia-
ble as well.[41] Thus, the mention of Mormo provides a transition from
girlhood to married life.) Erinna could not pay a last visit to her
friend's corpse either because of some religious taboo or, more
likely, because it was not seemly for a young unmarried woman to
enter the house of Baucis' husband, who was not her relative.
Baucis died shortly after marriage. Erinna elaborates on the

traditional theme of the bride of Hades, god of death, in an inscription she wrote for Baucis' tomb:

> I am the tomb of Baucis, the bride. When you pass by the tombstone which causes much lament, say this to Hades in the underworld: "Hades, you are jealous." And you see the fine inscription announcing the savage fate of Baucis, how her bridegroom's father lighted her pyre with the same torches that had burned while the bridal hymn was sung. And you, Hymenaeus, changed the harmonious wedding song to the gloomy sounds of lamentation.[42]

Erinna, like her friend Baucis, died young, shortly after writing the few poems that give evidence of her talent. She died unwed, for a later poet described her as "the maiden bride of Hades." [43]

Who was Erinna? Was she an ordinary woman endowed with the gift of the Muse? Was she an eccentric aristocrat like Hipparchia who chose to live as she pleased, not to marry but to write poetry? Was Erinna, like Sappho, the outstanding member of a group of cultivated women?

## Courtesans, Concubines, and Prostitutes

The special status accorded upper-class women continued with little relation to the attitudes toward women in less respectable areas of Hellenistic society. These women were the courtesans, who, with the exception of the royal and aristocratic women, were the most sophisticated females of their time—and the most notorious. To a large degree, however, the picture we have of the lives of prostitutes in the Hellenistic Age has been unduly embellished and enhanced by their presentation as characters in New Comedy.

New Comedy, which succeeded tragedy and Old Comedy as the national drama of Athens, and purported to hold up a mirror to life, is peopled with prostitutes. Since the scenes, by convention, are set out-of-doors, and respectable city women, especially unmarried girls, were required to stay inside, courtesans and slaves were the only females available to participate in the intrigue of this drama. In the romantic atmosphere of New Comedy one plot is repeated *ad nauseam:* a free young man is smitten with passion for a young slave woman. He intrigues to buy or steal her from the pimp who owns her and keep her as a concubine. Her father appears and identifies her as his long-lost daughter by means of trinkets she was wearing when found in infancy. When her parentage is known, she is thereby rendered freeborn, with no taint attaching from her former employment. The father explains the hardships that forced him to expose his daughter in infancy, and furnishes a dowry so that the couple can marry.

Thus the comedy has a happy ending, and the bride, now a "good" woman, can no longer figure in the adventures typical of this sort of drama. If she were a mythical heroine of tragedy, doubtless her marriage would have been of interest. But ordinary respectable women were not intended for representation; stage settings therefore were not designed for interior scenes, and the New Comedy —in true Cinderella fashion—usually closes with marriage.

Needless to say, in reality the careers of few prostitutes ended in such bliss, and the question of their parentage was, for most prostitutes, a sore point indeed. The prostitute's choice of career was often not her own: exposure of unwanted infants was widely practiced, probably more so than in the Classical period. J. Lawrence Angel has estimated the number of births per female in the Hellenistic period as 3.6, with 1.6 survivors (as compared with 4.6 and 3.0 for the Classical period).[44] According to Tarn, inscriptional evidence from the third and second centuries B.C. also shows that the one-child family was commonest, that sons were preferred, and that seldom more than one daughter was reared.[45] No doubt the necessity for providing a dowry for the daughter when she was of age contributed to a family's decision to expose a daughter. Some of the exposed infants were collected by others, and given to a wetnurse to tend. An abandoned infant automatically had slave status, unless proven freeborn. Despite the arguments of modern scholars that rearing an infant was more expensive than buying a full-grown slave, the evidence shows that some slave dealers made this investment.[46] The fate of many of these infants, if they were female, was to work as prostitutes, thus alleviating the disparity in numbers between free males and females which exposure of females had created. These women could not, however, become legitimate wives, and many freeborn men were doomed to a life of celibacy, owing to the lack of marriageable women.

The happiest ending a slave prostitute could hope for was manumission, but even so, like any freedwoman, she would continue to owe service to her former mistress or master.[47] Her children could be claimed as her master's property, perhaps to be sold to a brothel. Neaira, however, who had been a notorious courtesan in Corinth, got to keep her children and owed only one obligation to the ex-lovers who contributed money to her freedom: to stay out of Corinth.[48] Whether a prostitute was a slave or freedwoman, clients were more likely to be slaves, freedmen, or obscure freeborn men than wealthy, dashing young swains.

Prostitution was potentially lucrative for the prostitute herself, or for her owner if she was a slave. The tariff inscription of A.D. 90 from Coptos in Roman Egypt states that the passport fee for prostitutes was 108 drachmas, while for other women it was only 20 drachmas.[49] This differential is not likely to be indicative of social policy or a fine for immorality; rather, it should be attributed to the prostitute's ability to pay.

A few prostitutes, euphemistically referred to as companions (*hetairai*), led a more glamorous life. The stories told about them are reminiscent of the legends about Aspasia, the courtesan of Pericles, probably due to the unimaginativeness of some of the ancient gossip-mongers.[50] Like Aspasia, Hellenistic courtesans mingled with many of the leading men in the state; these were primarily members of the Macedonian courts. The famous courtesan Thaïs was rumored to have captivated Alexander, and then Ptolemy I, to whom she bore three children. Some courtesans were as learned as Aspasia. Leontion, the companion of the philosopher Epicurus, rivaled Theophrastus in writing philosophy.

Naturally, courtesans had to be beautiful. Phryne was the model for Apelles' painting of Aphrodite rising from the sea and for Praxiteles' famous nude, the Cnidian Aphrodite. Like Aspasia, Phryne was prosecuted in Athens. She was charged with organizing an immoral club devoted to the worship of the Thracian god Isodaetes and thereby corrupting young women. The orator Hyperides, who happened to be one of her lovers, successfully defended her.

The Ptolemies, at least according to the gossip, were particularly susceptible to the attractions of courtesans, whether or not they had married their own sisters. Resembling the charge that Aspasia caused the Peloponnesian War is the report that Agathoclia not only ruled Egypt through her influence on Ptolemy IV but also was partially responsible for the mob uprising in Alexandria early in the minority of his heir, Ptolemy V.[51]

## Sexuality: Its Representation in Art, Pornography, and Literature

The literature and visual art of the Hellenistic period, when compared with either the restrained or lewd depictions of women in the preceding ages, reveal a new interest in the eroticism of women. It is difficult from this vantage point to determine the extent to which these changed sexual mores touched the lives of respectable women, but it may be assumed by analogy with Roman women that, to a degree, some Greek women implemented the advice in the manuals for courtesans—such as Ovid's *Art of Love*—for their personal gratification.

The various portrayals of the female figure—draped, naked, or nude—in the visual arts of the Archaic, Classical, and Hellenistic periods are good indicators of changing social attitudes. While art historians have carefully catalogued the stylistic changes (which were not always simultaneous in sculpture and vase painting), only a few have ventured an interpretation of their psychological or social significance.[52] For our purposes, the most striking feature of Hellenistic art was the development of the nude female figure in sculpture. To examine this phenomenon it is necessary at this point to review briefly the earlier depictions of women in Archaic and Classical art.

The draped female figure appears in Greek art in both sculpture and vase painting. The unclothed female is found in the vase painting of all periods, but begins to be shown with some frequency in sculpture only in the fourth century B.C. These images will be discussed chronologically according to the date of their Greek originals, although some of the sculptures are known to us only through Roman copies.

As we have seen in the discussion of the *kouros* and *korē* (p. 47), in Archaic Greek sculpture the male figure was regularly nude and the female heavily draped. The Athenians gloried in male nudity, for it symbolized a distinction between Greek and barbarian, implying the superiority of the former. In earlier times, Greek and barbarian athletes exercised with loincloths, but the Greeks first stripped for their calisthenics around 720 B.C.[53] This "heroic" nudity, as it is commonly labeled, was confined to men at Athens, and is understandable in the context of male homosexuality or bisexuality. Respectable Greek women, except Spartan, did not participate in athletic activities, and there was no occasion for them to strip. One of Plato's more outlandish proposals was that women exercise in the nude.[54] Probably this attitude was of Eastern or Ionian origin. Herodotus, in the first story of his *History*, tells of the change in regal succession at Sardis because of the wrath of a queen who, with her husband's connivance, was viewed unclothed.[55] Similarly, death was the penalty meted out to Actaion, who happened to see Artemis nude, while Tiresias, according to some authors, was struck blind because he caught sight of Athena bathing. Accordingly, the female figure—both mortal and goddess—in Archaic and Classical Athenian sculpture is draped, with very few exceptions. The best-known totally nude female figures in fifth-century sculpture are the Esquiline Venus and the Flute Player of the Ludovisi Throne. Slightly more numerous are the females depicted in partial nudity to indicate pathos, among them the Barberini Suppliant, the Dying Niobid, and the Lapith women being raped.

However, sculpture is a public art. In the more intimate representations of vase painting, many naked women are represented. These figures occur most frequently on wine cups which began to be produced in the late Archaic period, around 530 B.C. Because wine was the province of Dionysus, scenes depicting the intercourse of Satyrs and Maenads—who formed part of the god's train—are popular. [Plate 14] There are also many representations of group sex which took place at the symposia. Wine drinking was an activity ideally reserved for men, as the male burials associated with drinking cups and kraters for mixing wine demonstrated (Chapter III above). The cups with erotic painting were designed for the symposia of upper-class men, parties to which respectable women were never invited. A wide variety of men's sexual activity is recorded on these cups, some homosexual, but more heterosexual.

There can be little doubt that the women depicted in erotic vase paintings were prostitutes. Aside from scenes of conventional intercourse, they are shown more frequently giving pleasure to men than receiving it. Cunnilingus is depicted more rarely than fellatio, and I have yet to see any portrayal of these activities occurring simultaneously. The vase paintings show that the Greeks practiced intercourse in many positions. In literature, especially comedy, the positions are named, many names deriving from traditional wrestling postures; other names are incomprehensible to the modern scholar.[56]

Noticeable in the portrayal of the female figures on the drinking cups are very prominent buttocks. There are also numerous occurrences of heterosexual anal penetration, probably in some cases a transference from the males' homosexual activities.

In addition to the pornography of the drinking cups, pictures of women bathing provided an opportunity to show the naked female. These depictions can in no sense be compared to the heroic nudity of the idealized male figure appearing in the sculpture of the same period. The vase paintings do indicate that models were available, if sculptor and patron had wished to portray the nude female in their medium.

T. B. L. Webster has traced a startling increase in the number of depictions of women in the second quarter of the fifth century B.C.[57] Before this time, vase paintings of athletes and horsemen were three times as common as portrayals of women and men or of women alone. After the Persian Wars, paintings of women and men or of women alone are at least twice as numerous as those of athletes and horsemen. Many of these vases were intended for use by women, and thus depicted their activities. But since they were manufactured and purchased by men for women, they reveal men's notions of women's tastes. Men may also have been increasingly interested in women's daily private lives. The segregation between the sexes may have fostered a sort of "voyeurism" in men. If Webster is correct, this focus on women appears in vase painting earlier than in the literature of the fifth century B.C.

The hypothesis about the voyeurism of Greek males may be borne out by the emergence, in the second quarter of the fifth century B.C., of large-scale paintings intended for public viewing that depicted women in transparent or wet, clinging drapery.[58] The actual paintings have not survived, but some vase paintings—which probably follow the style of the larger works—show women dressed in clothing of gauzelike transparency. Some of the scantily attired women are spinning, weaving, and visiting tombs. It is difficult to decide whether these were portrayals of respectable women or of prostitutes. On their tombstones, citizen wives are shown modestly garbed, but in their homes they often wore light garments.[59] On the other hand, prostitutes, especially those living as concubines, had to perform domestic chores such as spinning and weaving.

Another possible interpretation is that the artist was not drawing actual transparent garments, but rather adopted this convention as a means of revealing the shape of the body beneath clothing that was actually opaque. The transparent drapery was also employed in sculpture; the best-known representations of the female figure in wet drapery at this period are the Aphrodite of the Ludovisi Throne [Plate 15], the Nike of Paionius, and the Venus Genetrix.

The female nude appeared in large-scale painting in the early fourth century B.C. When Zeuxis wished to paint a nude Helen, he found five models in the city of Croton and assembled his figure from the best features of each of them.[60] Sculpture soon followed suit in the depiction of the totally nude female. In the mid-fourth century Praxiteles sculpted a nude Aphrodite, using his mistress Phryne as the model.[61] [Plate 16] The statue was placed in a shrine at Cnidus, where it could be admired from every side. She was totally nude, in preparation for a bath, but held one hand in front of her pelvis as a gesture of modesty (which also drew attention to the concealed area). The canonical proportions for the female nude established by Praxiteles were that the same distance should exist between the breasts, from the lower breast to the navel, and from the navel to the crotch. Pliny relates that one man became so enamored that he embraced the statue during the night and left a stain on it. Yet no one denied that the statue was that of a goddess, deserving of respect.

Other female nudes were sculpted thereafter. Most of these statues are called "Aphrodites," and portray the goddess partially or totally unclothed in preparation for a bath. [Plate 17] With these statues the female nude finally took its place beside the male nude in Greek sculpture, although the male was more commonly portrayed throughout classical antiquity. These nude images operate on two levels: as the nude male embraced a medley of elements, both homosexual and heroic, so the Aphrodite figure was sexually attractive while she simultaneously embodied religious ideals.

Erotic vase paintings of the Hellenistic Age also proclaim changes in sexual relationships. Earlier vases had depicted group sex scenes in stark physical surroundings. Hellenistic art shows fewer representations of male homosexual activity, and focuses instead on tender heterosexual scenes of couples in bed in a private and comfortably furnished setting. The furnishings are essential prerequisites, for a sophisticated etiquette of romance was developing which was to culminate in handbooks on the art of love.[62]

Nudity may be interpreted as a more open acknowledgment of women's erotic impulses and their gratification. The sculptured female nudes are in far more erotic and suggestive poses than males: crouching, stretching—desirable and desiring.

The eternal question of which sex enjoys intercourse more was as much a concern of the Greeks as it is of people today. According to a myth related by Hellenistic and Roman authors, Zeus and Hera asked the prophet Tiresias to settle this dispute: Zeus asserted that the female experiences more delight, Hera insisted that the male does. Tiresias, who was considered an expert since he had experienced part of his life as a male and part as a female, answered: "Women enjoy intercourse nine times more than men." According to ancient authors, Tiresias had been successively male, then female, then male again, but he combines both sexes simultaneously in T. S. Eliot's "The Waste Land," where he is described as an "old man with wrinkled female breasts." Eliot's description suggests another creature of both sexes, the Hermaphrodite, a bisexual deity whose figure appears with relative frequency in the Hellenistic Age and was especially appealing to the literate and wealthy classes. [Plates 18 and 19] The sculpture of the Hermaphrodite evolved from two sources. Either breasts were added to the figure of the ephebe, a youthful male with a feminine body, or male genitals were added to a nude female sculpture of the Aphrodite type. The Hermaphrodite embodied wholeness, transcending the imperfection of belonging to one sex or the other. This marks a new variation in Greek thought: in the Classical period the male was clearly the superior being, and to taint him with the characteristics of "the inferior" would have been a lessening of perfection. The Hermaphrodite's sensual depictions in sculpture remind us that the Greeks considered the young, both male and female, sexually desirable. Although in the Classical period the emphasis had been on males, Hellenistic art depicts the female as well as an object of sexual desire.

Women's sexual capacities were obviously noted in the verdict of Tiresias, and there are indications in literature that the satisfaction of women's desires was also considered in the Hellenistic period. Aristotle had described women's pleasure in intercourse, distinguishing between the place from which discharges are emitted (presumably the vagina) and the place where pleasure is produced (presumably the clitoris).[63] Ovid (43 B.C.-A.D. 17), a Roman influenced by Hellenistic poets, thus instructed lovers:

> Believe me, the pleasure of love is not to be rushed, but gradually elicited by well-tempered delay. When you have found the place where a woman loves to be fondled, don't you be ashamed to touch it any more than she is. You will see her eyes gleaming with a tremulous brightness like the glitter of the sun reflected in clear water. Then she will moan and murmur lovingly, sigh sweetly, and find words that suit her pleasure. But be sure that you don't sail too fast and leave your mistress behind, nor let her complete her course before you. Race to the goal together. Then pleasure is complete, when man and woman lie vanquished side by side. This tempo you must keep when you dally freely, and fear does not rush a secret affair. When delay is dangerous, then it is useful to speed ahead with full power, spurring your horse as she comes.[64]

Some literature of the Hellenistic period, notably the mime, depicted women's sexuality in a manner more vulgar than Aristophanic comedy, but other literature investigated the psychology of passionate women with a sympathy reminiscent of Euripides. The masterpiece in the second category is the *Argonautica* of Apollonius of Rhodes. The description of Medea's desire for Jason, which led her to deceive her father and murder her brother, became a model for later authors, including the Roman Virgil, who adapted it for his description of Dido's ruinous passion for Aeneas.

The turning inward toward a private sexual relationship, which we today take for granted, was of little interest to Greeks of the Classical period, but was fully explored in Hellenistic literature and art. This change in the relationship between the sexes can be attributed, with varying degrees of speculativeness, to a number of factors examined in this chapter: the influence of philosophers, the actions of royal women, and women's increasing economic power. The *polis* system of such a city as Athens—requiring a marital arrangement protective of women—had changed, allowing to men a familiarity with respectable women, especially in the areas recently settled by Greeks. At the same time, a new permissiveness was granted to respectable women. In his second *Idyll,* the poet Theocritus (300-260 B.C.) describes the activities of Simaetha, a virgin, perhaps an orphan, who went to a festival chaperoned by another woman. On the road she caught sight of and fell in love with a young man. He made love to her and later jilted her. In his fifteenth *Idyll*, Theocritus shows two respectable Greek housewives in Alexandria going to see "The Loves of Venus and Adonis," where they are jostled and addressed by men in the throng. Here, it is necessary to raise the question whether nudity in the visual arts connoted not only greater freedom for but also less respect toward women.

# ILLUSTRATIONS

1. Wounded Amazon. Roman copy of a Greek work of 440–430 B.C. (New York, Metropolitan Museum of Art [gift of John D. Rockefeller, Jr., 1932])

2. Belly-handled Geometric amphora with *prothesis*, ca. eighth century B.C. Female mourners raising arms in a formal gesture of mourning. (Athens, National Museum)

3. Shoulder-handled Geometric amphora with *prothesis*, ca. eighth century B.C. Female mourners are distinguished by their nudity; the corpse may be female. (Athens, National Museum)

4. *Kouros* from Anavysus, ca. 540–515 B.C. Sculpture of a male nude typical of the late Archaic period. (Athens, National Museum)

5. "Peplos *Korē*," ca. 540–530 B.C. Statue of a girl wearing a *peplos* over an Ionic *chiton*. (Athens, Acropolis Museum)

6. *Korē*, ca. 510 B.C. Elegantly adorned statue of a girl, found on the Acropolis. (Athens, Acropolis Museum)

7. Caryatid from the Erechtheum in Athens, 420–413 B.C. (London, British Museum)

8. Demeter, Triptolemus, and Korē. Votive relief from Eleusis showing Demeter with hair loosened in mourning, and Korē teaching the cultivation of grain to Triptolemus and crowning him. Roman copy of Greek sculpture of 450–440 B.C. now in Athens, National Museum. (New York, Metropolitan Museum of Art [Rogers Fund, 1914])

9. Woman suckling child. Red-figure hydria, ca. 440–430 B.C. A rare scene of a mother nursing a child in the courtyard of her house as her husband looks on. She is the legitimate wife, as indicated by her high-backed chair. Her

bracelet and embroidered cloak reveal that the household is fairly well off. A woman slave or relative stands by, holding a spindle in her right hand. Her left hand is reaching back to pull unspun wool from the wool basket behind her. The names of mythical personages are added: the man is Amphiareus, the seated woman his wife Eriphyle, and the baby Alcmeon; over the woman who is spinning is the inscription "Demo." (Berlin, Staatliche Museum) I am grateful to Elfriede Knauer for drawing my attention to this vase, and to Claireve Grandjouan for interpreting the scene. The vase is published in Ulrich Gehrig, *Führer durch die Antikenabteilung* (Berlin: Staatliche Museen Preussicher Kulturbesitz, 1968), F2395.

10. Grave stele of a woman, ca. 400 B.C. An intimate scene of a slave girl holding a casket of jewels for her mistress. The woman is wearing a *chiton* with sleeves, a *peplos,* and a *himation,* but her clothing is transparent and revealing. (New York, Metropolitan Museum of Art [Fletcher Fund, 1936])

11. Grave stele of Hegeso, ca. 400 B.C. Comfortably seated on a *klismos*, with her feet resting on a stool, Hegeso selects a necklace from her jewelry box, held by a slave (Athens, National Museum).

12. Woman using two artificial phalli. Red-figure drinking cup of the late Archaic period, by the Nicosthenes painter, showing a nude woman with African features. (London, British Museum)

13. Women athletes, second quarter of the fourth century A.D. Detail from a mosaic of Villa Romana del Casale, near Piazza Armerina, Sicily. (Photograph by Scala, Florence)

14. Satyr and Maenad. Red-figure drinking cup of the late Archaic period (ca. 490–480 B.C.), attributed to the painter Macron. (New York, Metropolitan Museum of Art [Rogers Fund, 1906])

15. Birth of Aphrodite. Front panel of the Ludovisi Throne, ca. 460 B.C., showing Aphrodite rising from the sea, aided by two Graces. (Rome, National Museum)

16. Aphrodite of Cnidus. Roman copy of the Greek original (ca. 350 B.C.) by Praxiteles. (Rome, Vatican Museum)

17. Aphrodite of Melos, ca. second quarter of the second century B.C. (Paris, Louvre)

18. and 19. Sleeping Hermaphrodite. Roman copies of Greek originals of the second century B.C. (Rome, Terme Museum)

1

2

3

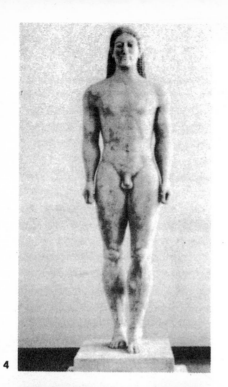

4

5

6

7

**11**

**12**

**13**

14

15

16

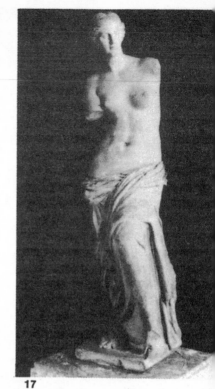

17

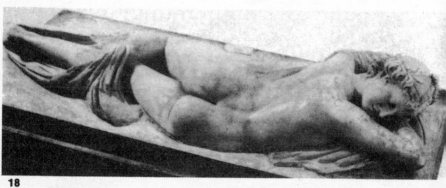

18

19

# VIII

## THE ROMAN MATRON
## OF THE LATE REPUBLIC
## AND EARLY EMPIRE

THE MOMENTUM of social change in the Hellenistic world combined with Roman elements to produce the emancipated, but respected, upper-class woman.[1] The Roman matron of the late Republic must be viewed against the background of shrewd and politically powerful Hellenistic princesses, expanding cultural opportunities for women, the search for sexual fulfillment in the context of a declining birthrate, and the individual assertiveness characteristic of the Hellenistic period. The rest of the picture is Roman: enormous wealth, aristocratic indulgence and display, pragmatism permitting women to exercise leadership during the absence of men on military and governmental missions of long duration; and, as a final element, a past preceding the influence of the Greeks—a heritage so idealized by the Romans that historical events were scarcely distinguishable from legends, and the legends of the founding of Rome and the early Republic were employed in the late Republic and early Empire for moral instruction and propaganda. The result was that wealthy aristocratic women who played high politics and presided over literary salons were nevertheless expected to be able to spin and weave as though they were living in the days when Rome was young. These social myths set up a tension between the ideal and the real Roman matron, and were responsible for the praise awarded a woman like Cornelia, who lived in the second century B.C.

Among Roman matrons, Cornelia was a paragon. We are told that she turned down an offer of marriage from a Ptolemy. A widow, she remained faithful to the memory of her husband, Tiberius Sempronius Gracchus, to whom she had borne twelve children. She continued to manage her household and was praised for her devotion to her children's education. Only three of her children survived to adulthood, but through her two sons, Tiberius and Gaius Gracchus, Cornelia exercised a profound influence on Roman politics. Some say that she goaded her sons to excessive political zeal by insisting that she was famous as the daughter of Scipio Africanus—conqueror of Hannibal—rather than as the mother of the Gracchi. It was even rumored, though much after the fact, that, with the aid of her daughter Sempronia, Cornelia suffocated Scipio Aemilianus, Sempronia's husband, because he opposed the legislation of Tiberius Gracchus. This allegation did not tarnish Cornelia's reputation. She endured the assassination of both her adult sons with fortitude, and continued to entertain foreign and learned guests at her home in Misenum. She was herself educated, and her letters were published. A bronze portrait statue inscribed "Cornelia, daughter of Africanus, mother of the Gracchi," was erected in her honor by the Romans and restored by the Emperor Augustus.[2]

## The Letter of the Law . . . and the Reality

Looking beyond the picture of Cornelia—independent, cultured, self-assured even in her widowhood—we find a long history of Roman legislation affecting women, especially in the areas of guardianship, marriage, and inheritance.

The weakness and light-mindedness of the female sex (*infirmitas sexus* and *levitas animi*) were the underlying principles of Roman legal theory that mandated all women to be under the custody of males. In childhood, a daughter fell under the sway of the eldest male ascendant in her family, the *pater familias*. The power of the *pater familias* was without parallel in Greek law; it extended to the determination of life or death for all members of the household. Male offspring of any age were also subject to the authority of the *pater familias*, but as adults they were automatically emancipated upon his death, and the earliest Roman law code, the XII Tables (traditionally 451–450 B.C.), stated that a son who had been sold into slavery three times by his father thereby gained his freedom. Among females, however, the only automatic legal exemption from the power of the *pater familias* was accorded those who became Vestal Virgins, a cultic role reserved for a very few.

Upon the death of the *pater familias,* the custody over daughters (and prepubertal sons) passed to the nearest male relative (agnate), unless the father had designated another guardian in his will. Guardianship over females was theoretically in force until the time of Diocletian (reigned A.D. 285–305), but this power was gradually diminished by legal devices and ruses and by the assertiveness of some women interested in managing their own concerns. A guardian was required when a woman performed important transactions, such as accepting an inheritance, making a testament, or assuming a contractual obligation, and all transactions requiring *mancipatio* (a ritual form of sale), including selling land and manumitting a slave. But if the guardian withheld approval, a woman could apply to the magistrate to have his assent forced, or to have a different guardian appointed.

By the late Republic, tutelage over women was a burden to the men acting as guardians, but only a slight disability to women. The virtuous Cornelia managed a large household and is not reported to have consulted any male guardian even in her decision to turn down Ptolemy Physcon's proposal of marriage. Similarly, a century later, much is said about the financial transactions of Terentia, Cicero's wife, but nothing about her guardian.

The legislation of Augustus provided a way for women to free themselves of the formal supervision by male guardians. According to the "right of three or four children" *(jus liberorum)*, a freeborn woman who bore three children and a freedwoman who bore four children were exempt from guardianship. This provision incidentally impaired the juridical doctrine of the weakness of the female sex, by expressing the notion that at least those women who had demonstrated responsible behavior by bearing the children Rome needed could be deemed capable of acting without a male guardian.

The right of three children was not a response to demands from liberated women yearning to free themselves from male domination, nor did it act as much of an incentive. As we have seen, the famous women of Roman society who had wanted to be free of the influence of guardians had managed to do so before the reign of Augustus, and without the tedious preliminary of bearing three children. Moreover, papyri from Roman Egypt, where women were less sophisticated, show a large number of women proudly announcing that they have gained the *jus liberorum,* but nevertheless availing them-selves of male assistance when they transact legal business.[3] Even after a law of Claudius in the first century A.D. abolished automatic guardianship of agnates over women, the majority of guardians or men who were present at transactions of women possessing the *jus liberorum* and who signed documents in behalf of illiterate women continued to be male relatives.[4]

The laws of guardianship indicate that the powers of the *pater familias* surpassed those of the husband. The *pater familias* decided whether his daughter would remain in his power, or would be emancipated from his power to that of another man, and if so, who would be her guardian. The guardian was not necessarily a relative, nor was the married daughter inevitably in the power of her hus-band. The *pater familias* decided whether or not she would be mar-ried according to a legal form that would release her from the authority of her father and transfer her to the power (*manus*) of her husband. If the marriage was contracted with *manus,* the bride became part of her husband's family, as though she were his daughter, as far as property rights were concerned.

A wife could become subject to a husband's *manus* in three ways: either by the two formal marriage ceremonies known as *confarreatio* (sharing of spelt—a coarse grain), and *coemptio* (pretended sale), or by *usus* (continuous cohabitation for a year). In ancient times, a vital feature of *manus* marriage for the bride was the change in domestic religions.[5] A family's religion was transmitted through males, and the *pater familias* was the chief priest. Upon marriage, a girl re-nounced her father's religion and worshiped instead at her hus-band's hearth. His ancestors became hers. The guardian spirit of the *pater familias* (known as the *genius*) and that of the *mater familias* (the *juno*) were worshiped by the household. Conversely, the woman married without *manus* was not a member of the husband's agnatic family, and hence theoretically excluded from the rites celebrated by her husband and children. In that case, she would continue to par-ticipate in her father's cult.

The *pater familias,* as we have noted, held the power of life and death over his daughters. Two stories from the history of early Rome related by Livy—who lived during the time of the Emperor Augus-tus—give a glimpse of the stern judgments inflicted upon daughters because of their fathers' expectations of moral behavior. One tale concerns Horatia, who was engaged to one of the Curiatii. When her three brothers fought the Curiatii, killing all three of them at the expense of two of their own number, Horatia grieved at the death of her fiancé. Hearing this, her surviving brother stabbed her, declaring, "Thus perish every Roman woman who mourns an enemy [of Rome.]" [6] Though the brother was forced to do penance for his impulsive act, his father affirmed that if his son had not slain Horatia, he would have killed her himself by the authority allowed fathers. In another story, from 449 B.C., Appius Claudius—one of the decemvirs who had published the XII Tables—was seized with desire for a young woman named Verginia. After exhausting his efforts to keep Verginia from falling into the hands of Appius Claudius, her father slew her—announcing later that because she could not have lived chastely, his act provided her with an honorable, though pitiful, death.[7]

It is fairly certain that the guardian did not have such authority over the person of his ward.[8] Whether the husband in a *manus* marriage held absolute power over the wife is unclear. In early Rome, we are told, all wives were subject to their husbands' authority, and marriages were stable and women virtuous. Cato the Censor claimed that husbands did have an unlimited right to judge their wives and could inflict the death penalty for drinking or adultery. One such incident took place in the days of Romulus himself. A husband cudgeled his wife to death because she drank wine. He was not censured because people believed that she had set a bad example.[9]

Our source for the statement on the powers of the husband is the report by Aulus Gellius of one of Cato's orations.[10] This passage is preceded by a paragraph where Gellius mentions that women were customarily kissed on the mouth by their male blood relations in order to determine if they had alcohol on their breath.[11] There is a slight inconsistency in this report of the blood relatives' remaining involved when a woman was supposedly under her husband's authority.

The testimony on the issue of the husband's powers in comparison with those of the blood relatives varies. Dionysius of Halicarnassus—who, like Livy, wrote during the reign of the Emperor Augustus—states that, according to the laws of Romulus, married women were obliged to conform themselves to their husbands, since they had no other refuge, while husbands ruled over their wives as possessions.[12] Plutarch gives the additional information that, according to the regulations of Romulus, only the husband could initiate a divorce, and then only on the grounds that his wife had committed adultery, poisoned his children, or counterfeited his keys. If he divorced his wife for another reason, she took half his property; the other half was consecrated to the goddess Ceres.[13]

Dionysius of Halicarnassus further confuses the question by stating that her husband, after taking counsel with a woman's relations, could inflict capital punishment on a wife guilty of adultery, or of drinking, since drinking inspired adultery.[14] The elder Pliny relates that a married woman was forced by her family to starve herself to death because she had stolen the keys to the wine cellar, but it is not clear whether "family" refers to the husband or blood relatives.[15]

So it is uncertain whether the husband had the right to kill the wife, or merely to divorce her, or to kill her only with the agreement of her male relatives. In 186 B.C., when thousands of men and women were sentenced to death for participating in Bacchic rites, the women were handed over to their blood relatives or to those who had authority (*manus*) over them to be executed in private. But here, each husband merely carried out the execution ordered by the state. He did not himself condemn her.[16]

What does emerge from this investigation is the concept that when "wives had no other refuge," as Dionysius puts it, or when they were totally under the authority of their husbands, as envisioned by Cato, marriages were more enduring. This power of husbands over wives—if, in fact, it had ever been prevalent in early Rome—was idealized and became an element in the marriage propaganda of Stoics and Augustan authors, both concerned with promoting marriage among their contemporaries.

What is also striking to anyone who lives in a society where a father's control over a daughter terminates when she reaches the age of majority, but where certain other laws make the wife subordinate to the husband, is that the situation may have been reversed at Rome, and the husband's authority more ephemeral than that of the father and blood kin. Thus, even in *manus* marriage, the bride's blood relatives continued to be involved in her guidance and welfare. The surveillance over her drinking is only one aspect of this. Some legends point to continued involvement by fathers of married women: among them are the raped Lucretia's appeal to both her father and husband and their joint vengeance in her behalf, and the story of the Sabine fathers who, when coming to reclaim their pregnant married daughters, were told by them that they did not want to be forced to choose between their fathers and husbands.

The marriage without *manus* has a long history. The XII Tables already provide for marriage without *manus,* and by the late Republic it was the common form, although marriage with *manus* was still occasionally found. It has been thought that because marriage with *manus* gave the wife some rights to her husband's property, the groom's family would stipulate a marriage arrangement without *manus.* Similarly, when the wife was wealthy, her family was likely to prefer a marriage arrangement without *manus* so that her property remained in her family of birth. Thus there may be a connection between the increase in wealth among the Romans in the second century B.C. and the decrease in *manus* marriage in the same period. The marriage without *manus* was a tentative arrangement, and was largely responsible for the instability of marriage evident in the late Republic. The concept ascribed to Romulus that wives were more obliging when they had "no other refuge" had a true converse. A wife who could readily return to her father for refuge was less amenable to the control of her husband.

The marriage without *manus* gave a woman more freedom. She was under the authority of a father or guardian who lived in a different household, while her husband, whose daily surveillance was available, had no formal authority over her. Moreover, even if she were married with *manus*, the abiding involvement of the father and other blood relatives can be viewed positively as a means of protecting the wife and her dowry against the abuses of a husband. Plutarch, pondering why Roman—unlike Greek—women did not marry close relatives, suggested that women needed protectors; if their husbands wronged them, then their kinsmen could aid them.[17] Aside from considerations of affection and protection, men could continue to reap profit from their female blood relatives, since their ties were not irrevocably severed by marriage.

As was true at the Hellenistic courts, betrothals, marriages, and divorces among the upper class were usually arranged between men for the political and financial profit of the families involved, rather than for sentimental reasons. The more children a man had, the greater the number of potential connections with other families. No doubt Ptolemy's proposal to Cornelia was motivated by a desire to form an alliance with some influential Roman families. Betrothals were broken or divorces were dictated when alliances between men became animosities. Pompey divorced his first wife to marry Sulla's stepdaughter Aemilia.[18] She was at that time pregnant and living with a husband. She died in childbirth soon after her marriage to Pompey.

Large numbers of connubial alliances in the late Republic are reported. When Caesar tried to gain the favor of Pompey, he betrothed his daughter Julia to him. Julia had been previously betrothed to a Servilius Caepio. In compensation, Pompey offered his daughter to Servilius Caepio, although she too was not free but was engaged to Faustus, the son of Sulla. (In the end, Pompeia did marry Faustus.) Caesar himself married Calpurnia and arranged for her father, L. Piso, to be made consul.[19] Cato, although he had used his wife to further his friendship with Hortensius, protested against using women to cement political alliances.[20] Nevertheless, the practice continued after the assassination of Caesar with the formation of the triumvirate of Antony, Lepidus, and Octavian.

Octavian broke his engagement to Servilia when he became engaged to Marc Antony's stepdaughter Clodia. But he broke this engagement as well in order to marry Scribonia, who was related to his onetime opponent Sextus Pompey, although it is not clear that this was part of the peace arrangements between them. Octavian, in turn, had arranged a marriage between his sister Octavia and Marc Antony. When Antony became his adversary, Octavian urged his sister to divorce her husband. She disobeyed him, and after Antony's death even took care of his children by his first wife and by Cleopatra. If the situation was not entirely a political game, then Octavia's show of disobedience to Octavian may indicate that she no longer wanted to be used as a tool in her brother's diplomacy, or that she felt some affection for Antony. Plutarch faithfully reports dynastic marriages, and sometimes describes a great affection developing between wife and husband, possibly because he can scarcely resist the temptation to praise marriage. It is likely that Virgil in the *Aeneid* comes closer to the truth when he shows Aeneas losing his first wife, Creusa, at Troy, and abandoning Dido (whom, it is true, he did not formally wed) to suicide, in order to find a dynastic marriage with Lavinia—the daughter of a king in Italy—who cares nothing for him.

Men's use of their female relatives to procure political allies was nothing new in the ancient world. Homeric kings, Greek tyrants of the Archaic period, and Hellenistic monarchs did the same. But among the Romans there is a new phenomenon: women in the late Republic at times initiated marriage alliances and chose lovers carefully, with a view to benefiting their own families. One of these ambitious women was the aristocrat Valeria, who captivated the dictator Sulla when they were both attending a gladiatorial spectacle.

As she passed behind Sulla she leaned on him with her hand and picked off a bit of lint from his cloak. Then she went to her own seat. Sulla looked at her in surprise. "It is nothing, Dictator," she said, "but I merely wish to share a little in your good fortune." Sulla was not displeased when he heard this, for he was clearly aroused. He sent to find out her name, her family, and her background. After that, they exchanged gazes, kept on turning their heads to look at each other, interchanged smiles, and finally there was a formal proposal of marriage.[21]

This marriage brought about a dramatic improvement in the fortunes of Valeria's family.[22]

When political situations were more stable, and, we presume, among people whose ambitions were not served by marriage alliances, there seem to have been fewer divorces. However, marital arrangements continued to be an acute problem where imperial succession was involved. Octavia, the daughter of Claudius, was betrothed when she was one year old to Lucius Silanus, a desirable partner since he was the great-great-grandson of Augustus. The turbulent events of the early Empire resulted in the suicide of Silanus and Octavia's marriage at the age of thirteen to Nero, who was then sixteen.

The consent of both partners was necessary for the betrothal and marriage, but the bride was allowed to refuse only if she could prove that the proposed husband was morally unfit.[23] It is unlikely that girls of twelve (the minimum age for marriage determined by Augustus) were in fact able to resist a proposed marriage. Some women, as they grew older, and their fathers were distant or dead, actually chose their own husbands. Cicero arranged two marriages for his daughter Tullia; but the third husband, the charming, degenerate Dolabella, was selected by Tullia and her mother in Cicero's absence. The marriage was legal, but a disgruntled Cicero contemplated dissolving it by not paying the installments on his daughter's dowry.

Divorce was easily accomplished, theoretically at the initiation of either or both parties to the marriage. Beginning in the late Republic, a few women are notorious for independently divorcing their husbands, but, for the most part, these arrangement were in the hands of men. As we have seen, divorce could be initiated by fathers whose married children were not emancipated from their authority. We may note a parallel to Classical Athenian law, where the father retained the right to dissolve his daughter's marriage (see p. 62). Not until the reign of Antoninus Pius was it made illegal for fathers to break up harmonious marriages.[24] If the marriage had involved *manus,* then the *manus* had to be dissolved, but this situation was infrequent. The major concern was the return of the dowry, as it had been in Classical Athens and Hellenistic Egypt. If the husband were divorcing the wife for immoral conduct, he had the right to retain a portion of her dowry; the fraction varied according to the gravity of her offense. A few husbands did attempt to profit by this procedure.[25]

In divorce, children remained with their fathers, since they were agnatically related to him, but, as we have seen in our discussion of *manus,* blood relationship was an important bond. Thirty-seven years after her divorce from Augustus, Scribonia voluntarily accompanied her daughter Julia into exile.[26] After his parents had been divorced, and he himself adopted into another family, Scipio Aemilianus shared his wealth with his mother.[27] Marcia had been divorced by the younger Cato because he wanted to let his friend Hortensius breed children with her. Nevertheless, after the death of Hortensius she remarried Cato, probably motivated by a wish to look after her daughters by him while Cato went off to join Pompey.[28] After her divorce from Claudius Nero to marry Augustus, Livia's children by her first marriage lived with their father, but following his death they joined their mother.

Most of the divorces we read about were prompted by political or personal considerations. No reason was legally required, but sterility of the marriage was often a cause, and a barren marriage was considered to be due to the wife. Sulla divorced Cloelia for alleged infertility.[29] However, a woman who died at the end of the first century B.C. won extravagant praise from her husband for offering him a divorce after a barren marriage that had lasted forty-three years. She is called "Turia." though her name is not definitely known.[30] Her funerary encomium describes her heroism in her husband's behalf during the civil wars, and then praises her self-effacing offer to divorce her husband on the condition that she—with her fortune—would continue to stay with him and be as a sister, and treat his future children as though they were her own. Her husband indignantly turned her down, preferring to remain married although his family line would thereby become extinct. This is one of the many interesting aspects of the document. The husband regards his preference for his wife and married life over his duties to perpetuate his family line as untraditional, yet by this period morally acceptable, indeed commendable.

Some men divorced their wives for flagrant adultery. Thus, Pompey divorced Mucia, and Lucullus divorced Claudia; Caesar divorced Pompeia because her notorious involvement with Publius Clodius at the rites of the Bona Dea, which were supposed to be confined to women, created a scandal. Caesar was High Priest at the time, and proclaimed that "the High Priest's wife must be above suspicion." We have little information on wives' divorcing husbands for adultery. This may have been due to a double standard, or to the discretion of some adulterous husbands, or to the upper-class men's opportunities for involvement with women of lower social classes —liaisons that were accepted as not threatening to legitimate marriages.

Augustus declared adultery a public offense only in women. Consistent with the powers of the *pater familias,* the father of the adulteress was permitted to kill her if she had not been emancipated from his power.[31] The husband's role, as we have seen in other areas of Roman law, was more limited than the father's. The husband was obliged to divorce his wife, and he or someone else was to bring her to trial.[32] If convicted, she lost half her dowry, the adulterer was fined a portion of his property, and both were separately exiled. According to the Augustan legislation, a wife could divorce her husband for adultery, but she was not obliged to, and he was not liable for criminal prosecution. The law may have been more stringent than the real situation, for the jurist Ulpian later commented: "It is very unjust for a husband to require from a wife a level of morality that he does not himself achieve." [33] Stoic theory as well condemned adultery in either man or wife.[34] The younger Cato, a man of Stoic and Roman principles, carried the doctrine still further:

he believed that sexual intercourse was only for the purpose of begetting children. Since he had a sufficient number of children and Marcia was worn out by childbearing, his second marriage to her was chaste.[35] No doubt the long absences from home imposed by the civil wars facilitated Cato's continence in his relations with his wife during the five-year duration of the remarriage.

Like the Augustan rule on adultery, the regulation on criminal fornication (*stuprum*) perpetuated a double standard. No man was allowed to have sexual relations with an unmarried or widowed upper-class woman, but he could have relations with prostitutes, whereas upper-class women were not allowed to have any relations outside of marriage.[36] Under some emperors, the penalties for breaking these laws were very severe. Augustus himself exiled both his daughter and granddaughter for illicit intercourse and forbade their burial in his tomb.[37] Some upper-class women protested against the curtailment of their freedom by registering with the aediles (magistrates whose duties included supervision of the markets and trade) as prostitutes. Then the laws of *stuprum* would not apply to them, but such women were excluded from legacies and inheritance. In any case, this legal dodge was eliminated when Augustus' successor, Tiberius, forbade women whose fathers, grandfathers, or husbands were Roman knights or senators to register as prostitutes.[38]

Rape could be prosecuted—under the legal headings of criminal wrong (*iniuria*) or violence (*vis*)—by the man under whose authority the wronged woman fell. Constantine was explicit about the guilt of the victim. In his decision on raped virgins, he distinguished between girls who were willing and those who were forced against their will. If the girl had been willing, her penalty was to be burned to death. If she had been unwilling, she was still punished, although her penalty was lighter, for she should have screamed and brought neighbors to her assistance.[39] Constantine also specified capital punishment for a free woman who had intercourse with a slave, and burning for the slave himself. This penalty was the outcome of a perpetual concern that free women would take the same liberties with slaves as men did. These liaisons were a real possibility, since unlike Athens, where women lived in separate quarters, in Rome wealthy women were attended by numerous male slaves, often chosen for their attractive appearance. The legendary virtuous Lucretia, according to the Augustan historian Livy, was so intimidated by Tarquin's threat that he would kill her and a naked slave side by side in bed that she submitted to Tarquin's lust. Though raped, she was technically an adulteress; therefore she made the honorable decision to commit suicide.[40]

Augustan legislation encouraged widows, like divorcées, to remarry. There was some tension between the emperor's concern that women bear as many children as possible and the traditional Roman idealization of the woman like Cornelia who remained faithful to her dead husband. The epitaphs continue to praise the women who died having known only one husband (*univira*), some of whom easily earned this recognition by dying young. The ideal of the *univira* and the eternal marriage was strictly Roman, and without counterpart in Greece. Two lengthy encomia of upper-class women of the Augustan period—one of "Turia," the other of Cornelia, wife of Lucius Aemilius Paullus—stress this ideal. In both cases, the women predeceased their husbands, who composed or commissioned the encomia.[41] Even Livia, the widow of Augustus, although she had had a previous husband, was praised for not remarrying. Virgil, writing the national Roman epic, depicts a disastrous climax to Dido's decision not to remain faithful to her dead husband. In Rome, unlike Athens, a woman could lead an interesting life without a husband, as Cornelia, mother of the Gracchi, did in entertaining guests and pursuing her intellectual interests. But Cornelia earned praise because she bore twelve children first, and then chose not to remarry.

A further refinement of the ideal-wife motif stresses that not only should a woman have only one husband, but she ought not to survive him—especially if he has been the victim of political persecution. Thus Arria, the wife of A. Caecina Paetus, upbraided the wife of another member of her husband's political faction for daring to continue to live after seeing her own husband murdered in her arms. She also advised her own daughter to commit suicide if her husband predeceased her. When Arria's own husband was invited to commit suicide during the reign of Claudius, she plunged the dagger into her own breast to set an example, and spoke her celebrated last words, "It does not hurt, Paetus." [42]

Roman law regulated the succession to property in great detail. Often the same regulation was passed again and again, with little change in the wording, because people either ignored the law or had found a loophole through which to evade it. Despite the continuous redefinition of the laws, room remained for interpretation, resulting in voluminous commentary on the legislation from antiquity to the present. During the Republic, when jurisdiction over women was mainly in the hands of their male relatives, their succession to property was the only major area in which they were subject to public law. The Roman woman's rights to inherit and bequeath property are not excluded from debate, but the following information seems plausible. According to the XII Tables, daughters and sons shared equally in the estate of a father who died intestate. A daughter married without *manus* would likewise share in her father's estate, but if married with *manus* she would share in her husband's estate as though she were his daughter. Until the legislation of Hadrian, Roman women could make wills only by a very complicated procedure, and they were not permitted to make legacies to female infants. Only in A.D. 178, according to the law entitled Senatusconsultum Orfitianum, could mothers inherit from children and children from mothers in intestacy. Thus preference concerning her inheritance was given to a woman's children over her sisters, brothers, and other agnates. Taken together with the legislation forbidding the father of the bride from dissolving her marriage against her will, it is evident that the second century A.D. was a period of change from the identification of a woman as a member of her father's family to the recognition of her as belonging to the same family as her husband and children.

The Voconian Law of 169 B.C. had restricted the wealth that could be inherited by upper-class women. In cases of intestacy, the only female agnates allowed to succeed were sisters of the deceased, and a woman could not be designated as heir to a large patrimony. She could receive property as a legacy, but in an amount not to exceed what was left to the heir or joint heirs. The previously existing provisions for equal inheritance by daughters in the XII Tables and the freedom to write wills favoring women, combined with a growing trend toward small families, had allowed a great deal of wealth to fall into the hands of women. Moreover, the second century B.C. was a period of increased luxury and wealth for the upper class, among women as well as men. Polybius relates that Aemilia, Cornelia's mother, became rich by sharing the prosperity of her husband Scipio

Africanus, and describes her ostentation when she went out to participate in ceremonies that women attend:

> Apart from the adornments she wore, and the decoration of her chariot, all the baskets, cups, and other implements for the sacrifice were either silver or gold, and were carried in her train on solemn occasions. The crowd of female and male slaves in attendance was suitably large.[43]

Aemilia would not have been embarrassed to have her assets compared not only with those of her husband but with those of her brother. When her brother died in 160 B.C., he left 60 talents, and when his two sons wished to return their mother's dowry of 25 talents—since they rightly regarded her dowry as her property—they were hard pressed to find the money immediately.[44] On the other hand, when Aemilia herself died in 162 B.C., she left so much wealth, probably including liquid assets, that her heir, Publius Scipio Aemilianus, was able within ten months to pay out the 25 talents each outstanding on the dowries of his two adoptive aunts. The dowry of each aunt was 50 talents, and they probably owned additional property on a par with the luxurious villa at Misenum on the bay of Naples where Cornelia, mother of the Gracci, lived.[45]

Despite restrictive legislation, the female members of wealthy families continued to possess large amounts of property and to display it. Cornelia's lack of pretension was unusual enough for people to ask her why she did not wear jewels, to which she gave the now proverbial response that her children were her jewels.[46] The Romans found a number of legal loopholes by which wealth could be transmitted to women, and by which women could in turn bequeath their wealth. By the late Republic and thereafter, some women were in actual fact independently controlling large amounts of property, although the laws formally in force said that this was not permissible. For instance, the fortune of a woman like Lollia Paulina in the first century A.D. was so immense that her banishment at the instigation of Agrippina, mother of Nero, may have been prompted by the desire to confiscate her property.[47] Under the Augustan marriage legislation, childlessness reduced the amount that could be inherited, while motherhood increased it.

## *Facts of Birth, Life, and Death*

Marriage and motherhood were the traditional expectation of well-to-do women in Rome, as they had been in Greece. The rarity of spinsters indicates that most women married at least once, although afterward a number chose to remain divorcées or widows.

Augustus established the minimum age for marriage at twelve for girls and fourteen for boys. The first marriage of most girls took place between the ages of twelve and fifteen. Since menarche typically occurred at thirteen or fourteen, prepubescent marriages took place.[48] Moreover, sometimes the future bride lived with the groom before she had reached the legal minimum for marriage, and it was not unusual for these unions to be consummated. Marriages of young girls took place because of the desire of the families involved not to delay the profit from a political or financial alliance and, beginning with the reign of Augustus, so that the bride and groom could reap the rewards of the marital legislation, although some of the benefits could be anticipated during the engagement. Sometimes one motive outweighed another. Thus there are cases of dowerless daughters of the upper class who nevertheless found social-climbing men so eager to marry them that the husbands surreptitiously provided the dowry, to save the pride of the girl's family.[49] Another factor which we have traced back to Hesiod was the desire to find a bride who was still virginal.

Most upper-class Roman women were able to find husbands, not only for first marriages but for successive remarriages. One reason for this, apparently, was that there were fewer females than males among their social peers.[50] As in Greece, this disproportion was the result of the shorter lifespan of females, whose numbers fell off sharply once the childbearing years were reached. There were the additional factors of the selective infanticide and exposure of female infants and, probably more important, a subtle but pervasive attitude that gave preferential treatment to boys (see p. 202). This can be surmised from a law attributed to Romulus that required a father to raise all male children but only the first-born female. This so-called law of Romulus—while not to be accepted at face value as evidence that every father regularly raised only one daughter—is nevertheless indicative of official policy and foreshadows later legislation favoring the rearing of boys over girls. The attitude may be criticized as short-sighted in face of the manpower shortage continually threatening Rome; the policy of Sparta, where potential childbearers were considered as valuable as warriors, should be compared.

The law of Romulus incidentally shows that it was not inconvenient for a daughter to be automatically called by the feminine form of her father's name (*nomen*). But it was awkward when the father decided to raise two daughters, who thus had the same name, like Cornelia and her sister Cornelia. The Romans solved the problem with the addition of "the elder" (*maior*) or "the younger" (*minor*). In families where several daughters were raised, numerals, which in earlier times may have been indicative of order of birth, were added (e.g., Claudia *Tertia* and Claudia *Quinta*).[51] A wealthy father might decide to dispose of an infant because of the desire not to divide the family property among too many offspring and thereby reduce the individual wealth of the members of the next generation. Christian authors such as Justin Martyr doubtless exaggerate the extent to which contemporary pagans engaged in infanticide,[52] but, on the other hand, it is clear that this method of family planning was practiced without much fanfare in antiquity. An infant of either sex who appeared weak might be exposed; in his *Gynecology* Soranus, a physician of the second century A.D., gives a list of criteria by which midwives were to recognize which newborns should be discarded and which were worth rearing. In deciding to expose a daughter, the provision of a dowry was an additional consideration. However, there was enough of a demand for brides, as we have mentioned, to make even the occasional dowerless bride acceptable.

Additional evidence for a dearth of females in the upper classes is that in the late Republic some men were marrying women of the lower classes. We know of no spinsters, yet upper-class women are not known to have taken husbands from the lower classes. Studies of tombstones generally show far more males than females.[53] This disproportion is usually explained away by the comment that males were deemed more deserving of commemoration.[54] Such a factor might discourage the erection of tombstones for those low on the social scale, but at least among the wealthier classes—the very group where small families were the trend—we could expect that, once having decided to raise a daughter, her parents would commemorate her death. In our present state of knowledge we cannot finally say that women were actually present in Rome in the numbers one expects in an average pre-industrial society, and that their lack of adequate representation in the sepulchral inscriptions is totally ascribable to their social invisibility; but it should be noted that the existence of masses of women who are not recorded by the inscriptions is, at most, hypothetical.

The traditional doctrine, enforced by Roman censors, was that men should marry, and that the purpose of marriage was the rearing of children.[55] The example of Hellenistic Greece, where men were refusing to marry and consequently children were not being raised (see p. 132), had a subversive influence on the ideal, although Stoicism affirmed it. A decrease in fecundity is discernible as early as the second century B.C., a time when the production of twelve children by Cornelia became a prodigy—probably because her son Gaius harped on it—although only three lived to adulthood Metellus Macedonicus, censor in 131 B.C., made a speech urging men to marry and procreate, although he recognized that wives were troublesome creatures. The speech was read out to the Senate by Augustus as evidence that he was merely reviving Roman traditions with his legislation.[56]

Augustus' legislation was designed to keep as many women as possible in the married state and bearing children. The penalties for nonmarriage and childlessness began for women at age twenty, for men at twenty-five. Divorce was not explicitly frowned upon, provided that each successive husband was recruited from the approved social class. Failure to remarry was penalized, all with a view to not wasting the childbearing years. Women were not able to escape the penalties of the Augustan legislation as easily as men. A man who was betrothed to a girl of ten could enjoy the political and economic privileges accorded to married men, but a woman was not permitted to betroth herself to a prepubescent male.[57]

But the low birth rate continued, and the Augustan legislation on marriage was reinforced by Domitian and reenacted in the second and third centuries A.D. It appears that women as well as men were rebelling against biologically determined roles. One reason for the low birth rate was the practice of contraception.

Not only infanticide and neglect of infants, but contraception and abortion were used by the married Romans to limit their families, and by unmarried and adulterous women to prevent or terminate illegitimate pregnancies.[58] Among the upper classes, the essential element in contraception—the wish not to have children—was present. Contraception was obviously preferable to abortion and infanticide, since the mother did not endure the burden and dangers of pregnancy and childbirth. There was a long tradition of medical and scientific writing on contraception and abortion, but most of our evidence comes from authors of the early Empire, who collected earlier knowledge and added their own recommendations.

Techniques for contraception were numerous; some were effective, more not. Among the ineffective were potions drunk for temporary or permanent sterility, which could, of course, be administered to unsuspecting parties to render them infertile. Amulets and magic were recommended. Pliny gives a recipe for fabricating an amulet by cutting open the head of a hairy spider, removing the two little worms which were believed to be inside and tying them in deerskin. Aëtius recommends wearing the liver of a cat in a tube on the left foot, or part of a lioness' womb in an ivory tube.[59] It was also thought possible to transfer the qualities of the sterile willow or of sterile iron for contraception.

The rhythm method was also practiced, but this was ineffective since the medical writers believed that the most fertile time was just when menstruation was ending, as that is when the appetite was said to be strongest. Conversely, it was thought that conception was not likely to occur when the woman did not have a desire for intercourse. Among other contraceptive techniques mentioned are for the woman to hold her breath at ejaculation, and post-coitally to squat, sneeze, and drink something cold.[60] Lucretius recommends that whores, but not wives, should wriggle their hips and so divert the plow and the seed.[61]

Mixed with ineffective techniques were effective methods, including the use of occlusive agents which blocked the os of the uterus. Oils, ointments, honey, and soft wool were employed.

Contraception was overwhelmingly left to women, but a few male techniques were recommended. Certain ointments smeared on the male genitals were thought to be effective as spermicides or as astringents to close the os of the uterus upon penetration. The bladder of a goat may have been used as an early version of a condom, although this item would have been costly.[62] Whether men practiced coitus interruptus is debatable. The sources do not mention this technique. Two explanations for this omission are equally plausible, but mutually inconsistent: coitus interruptus is not mentioned either because it was not used, or, more likely, because it was so much used and so obvious that it needed no description.

Abortion is closely associated with contraception in the ancient sources, and sometimes confused with it.[63] Keith Hopkins suggests that the reason for the blurring of abortion and contraception was the lack of precise knowledge of the period of gestation. Some Romans believed that children could be born seven to ten months after conception, but that eight-month babies were not possible. A contributing factor in the failure to distinguish between contraception and abortion was that some of the same drugs were recommended for both. Abortion was also accomplished by professional surgical instruments or by amateur methods. Ovid upbraids Corinna: "Why do you dig out your child with sharp instruments, and give harsh poisons to your unborn children." [64]

The musings of philosophers on when the foetus felt life and whether abortion was sanctionable will not be reviewed. In a society where newborns were exposed, the foetus cannot have had much right to life, although it is true that in the early Empire the execution of a pregnant woman was delayed until after the birth of her child. Literary testimony, including Seneca, Juvenal, and Ovid, shows both that some men were dismayed about abortions and that some upper-class women and courtesans had them.[65] Not until the reign of Septimius Severus was any legislation enacted curtailing abortion, and this was merely to decree the punishment of exile for a divorced woman who has an abortion without her recent husband's consent, since she has cheated him of his child.[66] In the reign of Caracalla, the penalty of exile (and death if the patient died) was established for administering abortifacients, but this law was directed against those who traded in drugs and magic rather than against abortion itself.[67]

Medical writers were concerned as well with methods of promoting fertility in sterile women and with childbirth. The writings of Soranus, a physician of the second century A.D., cover a sophisticated range of gynecological and obstetrical topics. He did not adhere to the Hippocratic Oath which forbade administering abortifacients, but stated his preference for contraception. At a time when wealthy women usually employed wetnurses, Soranus declared that if the mother was in good health, it was better that she nurse the child, since it would foster the bonds of affection. Of interest are his recommendations for the alleviation of labor pains, his concern for the comfort of the mother, and his unequivocal decision that the welfare of the mother take precedence over that of the infant.[68] In childbirth, most women who could afford professional assistance would summon a midwife, although if the procedure was beyond the midwife's ability, and funds were available, a male physician would be employed. In Rome the skilled midwives, like the physicians, were likely to be Greek. Midwives not only delivered babies, but were involved in abortions and other gynecological procedures, and as we have mentioned, they were supposed to be able to recognize which infants were healthy enough to be worth rearing.

Women—even wealthy women with access to physicians—continued to die in childbirth. Early marriage, and the resultant bearing of children by immature females, was a contributing factor. Tombstones show a marked increase in female mortality in the fifteen-to-twenty-nine-year-old group. In a study of the sepulchral inscriptions, Keith Hopkins claims that death in childbirth is to some extent exaggerated by the reliance upon evidence from tombstones.[69] He suggests that women dying between fifteen and twenty-nine were more likely to be commemorated, because their husbands were still alive to erect tombstones. In his sample he found that the median age for the death of wives was 34; of husbands, 46.5. J. Lawrence Angel's study of skeletal remains in Greece under Roman domination shows an adult longevity of 34.3 years for women and 40.2 for men.[70] Stepmothers are mentioned more than stepfathers, though this may reflect not only early death of mothers but the fact that children stayed with their father after divorce.

The wealthy Roman woman played a different role as wife and mother than her counterpart in Classical Athens. The fortunes of Romans were far greater, and they had not only more but more competent slaves. The tasks enumerated by Xenophon for the well-to-do Athenian wife were, even among the traditional-minded Romans, relegated to a slave, the chief steward's wife (*vilica*).[71] Nevertheless, the Roman matron bore sole responsibility for the management of her town house, and although her work was mainly the supervision of slaves, she was expected to be able to perform such chores as spinning and weaving (see p. 199). Household duties did not hold a prominent place in a woman's public image: the Roman matron could never be considered a housewife as could the Athenian. In fact, the writer Cornelius Nepos, who lived in the first century B.C., states in his "Preface" that the principal contrast between Greek and Roman women is that the former sit secluded in the interior parts of the house, while the latter accompany their husbands to dinner parties.

Freed from household routines, virtuous women could visit, go shopping, attend festivals and recitals, and supervise their children's education. There was a tendency among authors of the early Empire to castigate the mothers of men whom they wished to present to posterity as thoroughly evil. Outstanding examples are the portraits in Tacitus of Livia, mother of Tiberius, and the younger Agrippina, mother of Nero. In contrast and (like Cornelia) an exemplar to all mothers was Julia Procilla, the mother of the venerable Agricola. She was credited by Tacitus with supervising his education so closely that she checked his enthusiasm when he became more interested in studying philosophy than was suitable for a Roman senator.[72]

## Education and Accomplishments

Upper-class women were sufficiently cultivated to be able to participate in the intellectual life of their male associates. A little is known about how girls received their education. The story of Verginia (see p. 153) indicates that it was not unusual for the daughter of a lowly plebeian centurion to attend elementary school in the Forum. Both daughters and sons of well-to-do families had private tutors. Pliny the Younger, a senator and author active in government at the end of the first and the beginning of the second centuries A.D., included in his portrait of a girl who died at thirteen, just before she was to be married:

> How she loved her nurses, her preceptors, and her teachers, each for the service given her. She studied her books with diligence and understanding.[73]

Unlike boys, girls did not study with philosophers or rhetoricians outside the home, for they were married at the age when boys were still involved in their pursuit of higher education. Some women were influenced by an intellectual atmosphere at home. Ancient authors give the credit to fathers of girls, as they had to mothers of talented boys. Cornelia, we are told, acquired her taste for literature from her father, Scipio Africanus, noted for his philhellenism. (Cornelia's mother, as we have observed, was famous for her displays of wealth.) The eloquence of Laelia and Hortensia was a tribute to their fathers, who were leading orators.[74]

Intellectual and artistic achievements did not endanger a woman's reputation; instead, education and accomplishments were thought to enhance her. Plutarch, in a lost work, discussed the education of women. He wrote in complimentary terms of many women: for example, of Cornelia, the last wife of Pompey, who was particularly charming because she was well read, could play the lyre, and was adept at geometry and philosophy.[75] Pliny the Younger was pleased that his unsophisticated young wife was memorizing his writings, and was setting his verses to music and singing them to the accompaniment of the lyre.[76] Quintilian recommended that for the good of the child both parents be as highly educated as possible.[77] The Stoic Musonius Rufus asserted that women should be given the same education as men, for the attributes of a good wife will appear in one who studies philosophy.[78]

Epictetus, a pupil of Musonius Rufus, reported that at Rome women were carrying around copies of Plato's *Republic* because they supposed he prescribed communities of wives. Women, he noted, were quoting Plato to justify their own licentiousness, but they misinterpreted the philosopher in supposing that he bid people have monogamous marriages first and then practice promiscuous intercourse.[79] Although the Romans saw no essential connection between freedom and education, it was obvious that many cultivated women were also enjoying sexual liberty. Sallust gives a detailed description of the aristocrat Sempronia, who is probably faulted as much for her connection with the conspirator Catiline as for her lack of inhibitions:

Now among these women was Sempronia, who had often committed many crimes of masculine daring. This woman was quite fortunate in her family and looks, and especially in her husband and children; she was well read in Greek and Latin literature, able to play the lyre and dance more adeptly than any respectable woman would have needed to, and talented in many other activities which are part and parcel of overindulgent living. But she cherished everything else more than she did propriety and morality; you would have a hard time time determining which she squandered more of, her money or her reputation; her sexual desires were so ardent that she took the initiative with men far more frequently than they did with her. Prior to the conspiracy she had often broken her word, disavowed her debts, been involved in murder, and sunk to the depths of depravity as a result of high living and low funds. Yet she possessed intellectual strengths which are by no means laughable: the skill of writing verses, cracking jokes, speaking either modestly or tenderly or saucily—in a word, she had much wit and charm.[80]

The women addressed by the elegiac poets not only possessed the usual attractions of mistresses, but were learned as well. They could be of any class: courtesans or freedwomen or upper-class wives, widows, or divorcées. In any case, they were free to make liaisons with whomever they chose. The poets were drawn to women who would appreciate their work, which was crammed with erudite literary allusions. Catullus called his mistress by the pseudonym Lesbia, while Ovid's poems are addressed to Corinna, both poets alluding to venerated Greek poetesses. Delia and Cynthia, the names given to their mistresses by Tibullus and Propertius, are suggestive of Apollonian inspiration and the Greek poetic tradition.

On the other hand, Juvenal's criticisms make it clear that the bluestocking was not rare:

> Still more exasperating is the woman who begs as soon as she sits down to dinner, to discourse on poets and poetry, comparing Virgil with Homer: professors, critics, lawyers, auctioneers—even another woman—can't get a word in. She rattles on at such a rate that you'd think all the pots and pans in the kitchen were crashing to the floor or that every bell in town was clanging. All by herself she makes as much noise as some primitive tribe chasing away an eclipse. She should learn the philosophers' lesson: "moderation is necessary even for intellectuals." And, if she still wants to appear educated and eloquent, let her dress as a man, sacrifice to men's gods, and bathe in the men's baths. Wives shouldn't try to be public speakers; they shouldn't use rhetorical devices; they shouldn't read all the classics—there ought to be some things women don't understand. I myself can't understand a woman who can quote the rules of grammar and never make a mistake and cites obscure, long-forgotten poets—as if men cared about such things. If she has to correct somebody, let her correct her girl friends and leave her husband alone.[81]

Some women were authors themselves. Among prose writers were Cornelia, whose letters were published (although the extant fragments are probably not genuine), and the younger Agrippina, who wrote her memoirs. Propertius reports that his beloved Cynthia was a poet comparable to Corinna. A certain Sulpicia, who was a contemporary of Martial, also wrote poetry, although the attribution to her of a satire on the expulsion of the philosophers from Rome under Domitian is questionable.[82] Six love elegies totaling forty lines of another Sulpicia are preserved along with the works of Tibullus.

The latter Sulpicia was the daughter of Cicero's friend Servius Sulpicius Rufus and the niece and ward of Messalla Corvinus, whose literary circle included Ovid and Tibullus. She composed her poetry in 15 or 14 B.C., when she was probably at most twenty years old. She was not a brilliant artist; her work is of interest only because the author is female.

Sulpicia combines the deliberate simplicity of Greek lyric poetesses with some conventions of the elegiac genre. It is not clear whether she was married when she wrote her elegies, but she scarcely hesitates to publicize her love.

> Love has come to me, the kind I am far more ashamed
> To conceal than to reveal to anyone.
> Cytherea, won over by my Muses' prayers,
> Has brought him to me and placed him in my arms.
> Venus has fulfilled her promises. Let my joys
> Be told by those said to lack joys of their own.
> I won't entrust my thoughts to tablets under seal
> For fear that someone may read them before he does.
> But I'm glad I've erred; falsely posing disgusts me:
> Let me be called worthy, him worthy as well.[83]

Like the mistresses of the male elegists, the beloved of Sulpicia has a Greek pseudonym, Cerinthus. His true identity has not been discovered, and he may be a literary fiction. Sulpicia's poems do not describe him at all, but rather she reports her feelings about him in a straightforward style. Her only mythical allusions are obvious— Camenae (Muses) and Cytherea (Venus)—compared to the abstruse references of the male elegists. In the elegiac tradition, she speaks of the triumph of love, twice of her own birthday, and of illness, the sadness of separation, and love as slavery:

> The day which gave you to me, Cerinthus, to me
> Will be sacred, a holiday forever.
> At your birth the Fates sang of new slavery for girls

And bestowed exalted kingdoms upon you.
More than others I burn. That I burn, Cerinthus,
Brings joy, if you too blaze with flame caught from me.
May you too feel love, by our sweet stolen moments,
By your eyes, by your Birth-spirit, I ask you.
Great Birth-spirit, take incense, heed my vows kindly—
If only he glows when thinking about me.
But if perchance he's panting for other lovers,
Then, holy one, leave faithless altars, I pray.
And you, Venus, don't be unfair: let both of us
Serve you in bondage, or lift off my shackles;
But rather let us both be bound by a strong chain
Which no day to come will be able to loose.
The boy wishes for what I do, though he wishes
In secret—it shames him to utter such words.
But you, Birth-spirit, since as a god you know all,
Grant this: what difference if he prays silently?[84]

Like all the elegists, she berates her beloved for infidelity and
insists upon her own superiority, especially her noble lineage: "For
you prefer the prostitute's toga and a whore loaded with woolbaskets
to Sulpicia, Servius' daughter. My friends are greatly concerned lest
I surrender my place to a baseborn mistress." [85]

Sulpicia and Cerinthus are also known through five elegies
written by an anonymous poet who belonged to Messalla's coterie.
He does not mention Sulpicia's poetry, but celebrates her beauty and
claims that she is an inspiration for poets. Sometimes he writes as
though he were Sulpicia, and he manages to express her sentiments
at least as vividly as she did.

Lesbia, both Sulpicias, and the Empress Julia Domna (died A.D.
217) are known to have organized or been members of literary
salons.[86] This is one of the most important developments in women's
intellectual history: from Lesbia's coterie of amateurish bohemian
aristocrats of the late Republic, to the splendor and elegance characteristic of the court of the Flavian empresses, to the settled respectability, if not distinction, of the circle of Julia Domna. Though a
continuous history for these literary salons cannot be documented,
the few that are known were not considered eccentric, and we may
therefore suppose that others existed.

Greek antiquity supplied precedents for female poets, but female orators were singularly Roman.[87] Valerius Maximus gives three examples from the first century B.C. The first is Maesia Sentia, who, surrounded by a crowd, successfully defended herself against some unknown charge. Valerius labels her an "androgyne." Afrania, wife of a senator, became infamous for her lack of modesty in pleading cases before the praetor. But Hortensia, the daughter of the famous orator, was praised for the speech she delivered in 42 B.C. She was one of the 1400 wealthy women whose male relatives had been proscribed and who were themselves being taxed to pay the expenses of the triumvirs. The women beseeched Octavian's sister and mother and won them over, but failed to persuade Marc Antony's wife Fulvia. Rudely repulsed by her, the women forced their way into the Forum and Hortensia spoke in their behalf. The speech she delivered was preserved, and earned the approbation of Quintilian, a literary critic of the first century.[88] Appian, a second-century historian, purports to give her speech in a Greek translation. Though the speech as reported is most likely a rhetorical exercise of the second century, possibly incorporating some of the more memorable statements of Hortensia, it is of interest in that some of the themes reappear in the political speeches of modern women:

You have already deprived us of our fathers, our sons, our husbands, and our brothers on the pretext that they wronged you, but if, in addition, you take away our property, you will reduce us to a condition unsuitable to our birth, our way of life, and our female nature.

If we have done you any wrong, as you claimed our husbands have, proscribe us as you do them. But if we women have not voted any of you public enemies, nor torn down your house, nor destroyed your army, nor led another against you, nor prevented you from obtaining offices and honors, why do we share in the punishments when we did not participate in the crimes?

Why should we pay taxes when we do not share in the offices, honors, military commands, nor, in short, the government, for which you fight between yourselves with such harmful results? You say "because it is wartime." When have there not been wars? When have taxes been imposed on women, whom nature sets apart from all men? Our mothers once went beyond what is natural and made a contribution during the war against the Carthaginians, when danger threatened your entire empire and Rome itself. But then they contributed willingly, not from their landed property, their fields, their dowries, or their houses, without which it is impossible for free women to live, but only from their jewelry. . . .

Let war with the Celts or Parthians come, we will not be inferior to our mothers when it is a question of common safety. But for civil wars, may we never contribute nor aid you against each other.[89]

Appian explains that the triumvirs were angry that women should dare hold a public meeting when men were silent, and that they should object to contributing money when men had to serve in the army. Nevertheless, the crowd seemed to support the women, and the following day the triumvirs reduced the number of women subject to taxation to 400, and imposed a tax on all men who possessed more than 100,000 drachmas.

## Political Roles: Public Life and Status-Seeking

Public gatherings of women like the one at which Hortensia supposedly spoke were not without precedent, in both fact and fiction. Groups of matrons were involved in political and religious action in the earliest events of Roman history, related principally by Livy. Roman women, in contrast to Athenian, were not sequestered, and it is not difficult to believe that the affairs of state were of interest to them. Moreover, they were accustomed to all-female gatherings for religious purposes. Whether all the events actually took place, or if they occurred as Livy relates, does not concern us here; even as social myth they are of value in considering the political influence of Roman women. Livy tells a number of stories about honorable women congregating at critical points in Roman history, and performing acts that were crucial to the safety of the state. The first group was the Sabine wives of the early Romans, whose intercession not only prevented war between their husbands and fathers but brought about a profitable alliance between the two. Then there are the stories about the deputation of women who persuaded the traitor Coriolanus not to make war on Rome, and the matrons in the Forum who supported Verginius in his fight against the tyrannical Appius Claudius. Often the women ask for and win the favor of the gods for the state's benefit. Rarely, groups of women are shown to gather for malevolent purposes. However, in 331 B.C., 116 women were condemned for gathering to concoct charms or poisons.[90] Women's collective lamentations were disruptive in time of war, but that was forgivable, and Livy uses the women's mourning to underline particular disasters. The women who gathered in 195 B.C. to demand the abrogation of the Oppian Law which had been in force for twenty years staged the first women's demonstration.

At Trasimene and Cannae, in the two years preceding the passage of the Oppian Law, the Roman army had suffered the most debilitating defeats in its history. At the battle of Cannae alone, Hannibal destroyed so many men that, as Livy puts it, "There was not one matron who was not bereaved." In 216 B.C. the annual rite of Ceres, which could be celebrated only by women, had to be cancelled, since mourners were not allowed to participate. Owing to the dearth of freeborn men, an emergency military levy was made of adolescents and 8000 slaves.[91]

Hannibal offered another 8000 Roman prisoners for ransom. Women entreated the Senate to ransom their sons, brothers, and kinsmen. Many upper-class men were among those lost, either through battle or through the Senate's decision not to pay ransom. Many of the prisoners were related to the senators, and the next year the number of people eligible to pay the property tax was so diminished by the losses at Trasimene and Cannae that the tax was insufficient to meet the needs of the state.[92]

As the men died, we assume, their property was apportioned among the surviving members of the family. Women and children will have been numerous among the beneficiaries. Some Romans died intestate, and according to the laws of intestate succession sons and daughters shared equally.[93] To put it crudely, when their fathers and brothers were eliminated by Hannibal, women's portions of wealth increased.

One may consider whether the women availed themselves of the opportunity to flaunt any new-found wealth in the vulgar manner characteristic of Romans. As Plutarch remarks, "Most people think themselves deprived of wealth if they are prevented from showing off; the display is made in the superfluities, not the essentials of life." [94] Women were certainly prone to this vice. As one example, we may consider that Papiria, the mother of Publius Scipio Aemilianus, did not hesitate long after Aemilia's funeral to drive out in the dead woman's carriage which her natural son, Aemilia's heir, had given her.[95]

It could be argued that the specter of Hannibal and the

general misery contributed to inhibit boisterous displays. On the other hand, this period is replete with queer portents and indications of hysteria. But in 215 B.C., the year following the battle of Cannae, the state not only took most of the women's gold but deprived them of the opportunity to indulge in other displays of wealth. The Oppian Law was passed, limiting the amount of gold that each woman could possess to half an ounce, and forbidding women to wear dresses with purple trim or ride in carriages within a mile of Rome or in Roman country towns except on the occasions of religious festivals.[96]

Thus, although the state had curtailed the period of mourning and women were not to wear the sordid dress of the bereaved, they were to display the behavior and costume more appropriate to a dismal military situation. By this compromise, the requirements of religion and decorum could be met.

The next year all the funds of wards, single women, and widows were deposited with the state.[97] And that was the end of the windfall of any woman or minor who had become rich up to that time through the intervention of Hannibal. We also note, in passing, that the state readily commandeered the wealth of all those without close male relatives to defend them. The war continued for thirteen years, and we assume that after the passage of the Oppian Law some women continued to be fortuitously and disproportionately enriched by the deaths of male members of the family.

Appian's report of women's patriotism during the Second Punic War is slightly inconsistent with Livy's version. Hortensia states that women gave freely, but then only from their jewelry and not from their dowries and other possessions. One could suppose that, threatened by Hannibal, women would voluntarily make donations even from their dowries. Livy indicates that the women's wealth was taken through taxes, and that in 207 B.C. they were forced to invade their dowries and make an offering to Juno Regina to elicit her aid. He also highlights the generous patriotism shown by men in 210 when the senators, followed spontaneously by the knights and the plebs, contributed almost all their gold, silver, and coined bronze; Each reserved only rings for himself and his wife, a bulla (a gold locket) for each son, and an ounce of gold each for his wife and daughters. These reports of competitive patriotic zeal are suspect, and almost certainly mask official confiscations, including women's dowries and other possessions. Livy's report brings to mind the anger of the triumvirs after Hortensia's oration, when they thought that women were concerned about hoarding their money while men were actually serving in the army.[98]

One may wonder who exercised authority over the women when their male kin were deceased. Guardians were probably appointed, but, as we have noted, a guardian's concern with a woman's virtue is less than the concern of male relatives who regard female members of the family as extensions of themselves. Livy notes that "women's servitude is never terminated while their males survive."[99] Conversely, are there indications that their servitude was abated when their males were deceased? We remarked, in our discussion of the last phase of the Peloponnesian War, that women were less constrained in the absence of men. At Rome, too, they dared to mingle in the Forum with crowds of men, and even to make entreaties of the Senate.[100]

The loss of male relatives was conducive to the formation of irregular liaisons which the state attempted to punish or discourage. In 215 B.C. the cult of Venus Verticordia (Changer of Hearts [toward virtue]) was founded (see pp. 208–209). In 213 B.C. a number of matrons who were charged by the tribunes with immoral conduct were driven to exile.[101] These women should have been dealt with in domestic tribunals by their husbands and male relatives. Probably they had none left, and the tribunes did the job instead, hoping that the publicity would discourage future derelictions.

An incident toward the end of the war underlines the aspersions cast upon the moral character of even the highest born of Roman women. When the stone representing the Magna Mater, an Oriental mother goddess, was brought to Rome from Asia, its transfer was assigned to the noble matrons. The patrician Claudia Quinta used the opportunity of moving the stone as an ordeal to prove her chastity, for she had been popularly charged with promiscuity though she had not been—and could not be—prosecuted. Her success in moving the stone was considered the testimony of the goddess to Claudia's chastity.[102] It was the turmoil of the war that led to suspicion of Claudia and that then provided her with an opportunity to make a public demonstration of her chastity.

After the defeat of Hannibal in 201 B.C., Rome swiftly recovered. Men were allowed to display their prosperity. They wore purple, and their horses could be magnificently equipped. But the Oppian Law

remained in effect, curtailing displays by women. The law was an
irritant, despite some hints that it was not strictly enforced at all
times.[103] In 195 B.C. the repeal of this law was proposed, and women
demonstrated in the streets.[104] The issue, obviously, was of concern
only to the wealthy, and presumably they alone were the demon-
strators. This demonstration may have been orchestrated by men
and have resulted from factional disputes among them. Men may
have also wished to avail themselves once more of the opportunity of
displaying wealth through the adornments of the female members of
their families. But we cannot discount the idea that women were
demonstrating in their own behalf. The Second Punic War had given
them an opportunity to develop independence. Their pleas before
the Senate more than twenty years earlier had been a rehearsal in
political activism. At the time when they demonstrated for the repeal
of the Oppian Law, some of them, having lost their fathers and
husbands, may have been under the authority of a relatively unin-
terested guardian. These women will have been freer to mill around
in the streets and make demands of the government.

We may speculate whether it was likely that all the women
bereaved by the war found new husbands. The speech of Cato
arguing against repeal of the Oppian Law cannot be taken as
evidence for the actual situation in 195 B.C., for the words are Livy's
own, and there is no proof that Cato even spoke on the occasion. It is
in this speech that Cato declares that the women's husbands should
have kept them in the house. After the loss in Roman manpower
resulting from the Second Punic War, it does not seem likely that all
women would have had husbands in 195 B.C. Two thousand
Romans, whom Hannibal had sold into slavery in Greece, returned
in 194 B.C.[105] Did they find their wives remarried? To compare the
situation at Rome with that of Russia after World War II, when
virtually a generation of women could not find husbands, would be
extreme, but we cannot assume that all the women had husbands.

The condition of women without husbands and fathers is considered in the speech that Livy represents as winning the repeal of
the law. The Aristotelian view of the unequal relationship between
women and men is recognizable. The argument is that women, even
without the control of the Oppian Law, would not take advantage of
the freedom they could enjoy, "for they abhor the freedom that loss
of husbands and fathers provides." The speaker also points out that
even Roman men would be dismayed if they were not permitted to

flaunt their wealth in the face of their Latin neighbors. Naturally, weak women, who become disturbed over the merest trifles, would be all the more upset over their lost opportunities.

The twenty-year period when the Oppian Law was in force offers an opportunity to consider the effects of prolonged war on women. The Second Punic War did not resemble the Trojan War. The city of Rome was never captured and Roman women were not sold into slavery, although deprivation, famine, and disease were suffered by army and civilians alike.[106] The absence of men, which was an abiding feature of history as Rome conquered and governed distant territories, encouraged independence among women and unstable marriages.[107] The parallel with Sparta, where men were constantly engaged in warfare, is pertinent here (see p. 39). At Sparta (as in Rome), women were left to manage domestic matters; by the Hellenistic period they were very wealthy and influenced affairs of state, although they could not hold office. Spartan women exhibited their wealth in frivolities such as race horses.[108] Roman women sought status by dress and ownership of valuable slaves and costly vehicles. Roman men, of course, were no more restrained, but their lavish dinners and entertainments ultimately had the socially approved goal of furthering their political careers.

To the extent that a Roman woman was emancipated from the male members of her family, her display of wealth redounded to her own reputation among other women as well as men. Polybius' report of Aemilia's ostentation reflects that she grew wealthy as her husband became prosperous, and there is a hint that Aemilia's own pride is at issue when she shows off. A little later it appears that Papiria wins compliments among women for her new-found magnificence, although they end by praising her son's generosity. Livy also reports that there is a contest between women in displaying their finery, because they have no political offices, no priesthoods, no triumphs, no gifts, no spoils of war to give them prestige.[109] Sumptuary legislation at Rome, then, unlike Athens, is to a small extent directed against independent wealthy women as well as against men. In 184 B.C. Cato, as Censor, imposed an assessment on obvious displays of luxury, including certain carriages, women's adornments, costly slaves, and dinner plate.[110] Later Cato supported the Lex Voconia, curtailing women's inheritances, but, as we have noted, women continued to acquire wealth. The second century B.C. saw additional sumptuary legislation aimed primarily at curbing men's lavishness in dining, but no further attempt was made to limit women's ostentation.

The explanation for the lack of further sumptuary legislation against women may be found in women's increasing independence from male relatives. Wealthy upper-class women were considered less as appendages of men, and their displays of wealth brought them status in the eyes of women. But whatever women did independent of men was futile and, though potentially irritating to men, ultimately of minor importance to the state.

When men participated in status-seeking by means of the clothing of their women, then regulation was required. Wealthy women continued to parade their own wealth or that of their fathers or husbands until the eccentric Emperor Elagabalus, in the first quarter of the third century A.D., regulated the dress and etiquette appropriate to women belonging to various ranks. Daughters of senators or knights were classified according to their father's rank and maintained their status even after marriage. A woman usually married a man of the same rank; but even if she married a man of lower status, the evidence, though inconclusive, shows that she tended to keep her father's rank.[111]

According to an immensely amusing story—not to be accepted as factual—Elagabalus, prompted by his mother, Julia Soaemias, constituted a senate of women to decide what kind of clothing women of a particular rank could wear in public; who could ride in a chariot, on a horse, a pack animal, or an ass; who could be carried in a litter; who could use a litter made of leather or of bone; and other details. This senate was dissolved at the death of Elagabalus, though briefly revived by the Emperor Aurelian.[112]

Praising the female members of their family was another way that men used to gain status through women. Gaius Gracchus was criticized for using the name of his mother Cornelia with too much rhetoric, but he profited politically by it.[113] Ever since the *laudatio* pronounced in 102 B.C. by Q. Lutatius Catulus (consul 78 B.C.) over his mother, it had become acceptable to pronounce funeral orations over elderly women,[114] but the encomium delivered by Julius Caesar in 69 B.C. on the death of his aunt, the wife of Marius, marked a turning point in his political career. In the next year, Caesar's wife died, and he became the first man to deliver a eulogy over a young woman, winning great favor with the multitudes by this action.[115] At the precocious age of twelve, the boy who was destined to become the Emperor Augustus followed in the footsteps of his uncle Julius Caesar by delivering an oration in honor of his grandmother Julia. When Octavia, the sister of Augustus, died, she was honored by two orations, one delivered by Augustus himself and one by Nero Claudius Drusus, and public mourning was declared.[116] This practice of honoring women of distinguished families after death was common, and some of the themes of such eulogies have been pointed out in our discussion of the eulogies of "Turia" and Cornelia, wife of Lucius Aemilius Paullus (p. 161).

In the Empire, women, both living and after death, were decreed magnificent honors. Those honored while alive enjoyed their privileges, to be sure. But, living or dead, the usual purpose of honoring women was to exalt the men to whom they were mothers, wives, or sisters. Imperial coinage clearly demonstrates that the women of the emperor's family are viewed as his appendages, and their qualities are his. On the verso of an emperor's coin, the portrait or figure of an imperial woman is often depicted as a personification of an attribute of the emperor or an aspect of his reign. Thus some women are shown as Concordia, Justitia, Pax, Securitas, or Fortuna, these qualities actually accruing to the emperor to whom she is related. Because these abstract qualities are denoted in Latin by nouns of the feminine gender, and were honored as female divinities, imperial women could impersonate them.

Imperial women were also flattered by honorific titles. After the death of Augustus, his widow Livia was termed Augusta ("venerable"), because by testamentary adoption Augustus had acknowledged the old custom that at times considered a wife an integral member of her husband's family. Agrippina the Younger—wife of the Emperor Claudius—became the first to be so distinguished during her husband's lifetime. Some of the titles were *pro forma* honors, but in the early third century A.D. "Mother of Augustus," "Mother of the Army," and "Mother of the Army and the Senate" referred to the real political power of two unusual women, Julia Soaemias and Julia Maesa.

The most extraordinary honors bestowed on the women of the imperial court were those implying that they were goddesses. In their lifetime both Livia and Julia, the wife and daughter of the first emperor, were termed divine in the provinces, and a temple was erected in honor of Livia and her son Tiberius by the cities of

Asia.[117] A number of empresses were deified after death in order to strengthen the belief that their descendants, the reigning emperors, were divine, and the consecration was commonly announced on coins. The assimilation of imperial women to goddesses was also publicized on coins. Thus women served to promote the revival of the traditional Roman religion, which was supported by the emperors in the face of the popularity of foreign cults. Ceres, goddess of marriage, is the divinity to whom imperial women are most frequently assimilated. The characteristics of fertility and nurture associated with Ceres were those which the emperors wanted to instill in women in accordance with the official policy of improving the birthrate. (Ears of grain surrounding the portrait of Ceres also refer to the grain dole, an imperial gift to the male members of the urban population of Rome.) After Ceres, Vesta is the goddess to whom imperial women were most commonly assimilated on coins. These coins commemorate the grants of privileges of Vestals to nonvirginal women of the royal family. Occasionally women are shown as Juno or Venus, even more rarely as Diana.

The female members of influential families were also honored by the erection of statues and buildings. Statues of many women were erected in the late Republic and Empire, although Cato had inveighed against the practice,[118] and the Emperor Tiberius ordered that official compliments paid to women be kept within limits.[119] The women most represented are the members of the imperial court and Vestal Virgins. In the provinces, this practice was imitated by the erection of statues of wives of provincial governors and a proliferation of decrees in honor of various women, including athletes, musicians, and physicians (see pp. 125, 137).[120] Augustus named the Porticus Liviae and the Macellum Liviae in honor of his wife. He also dedicated the Porticus Octaviae to his sister, and placed there the statue of Cornelia mentioned at the beginning of this chapter.

The ideal of fecundity represented by Cornelia was perpetuated during the Empire. Aside from coins announcing their deaths and consecrations, the coinage of imperial women most frequently commemorated their fecundity. Of course, their children were potential successors to the throne, and thus childbirth had political implications, but the implicit lesson was that all women should bear children. The inscriptions on other coins of the imperial women also refer to the traditional virtues Romans sought in women: Pietas, indicating their loyalty to the traditional religion; Fides, denoting their faithfulness to one man, continuing after his death; and Pudicitia, asserting that their sexual conduct was beyond reproach.

## Women in Politics

Obviously, if women were actually conducting themselves in accordance with the ideal, there would have been no need to urge them continually by such means as the Augustan marriage legislation and the reminders on imperial coinage. We cannot review here the fortunes and failings of famous Roman women individually, but they can be analyzed in a general way, since the historical accounts of women show certain patterns of moral polarity. Interestingly enough, the wives of Marc Antony provide the paradigms: Fulvia, the evil wife; Octavia, the virtuous wife. Cleopatra, who was Antony's last wife, was, however, unique. The stories of all three women were distorted by political propaganda emanating from Octavian, or from historians hostile to Antony, who was Octavian's rival.

Fulvia was Antony's first wife, but she had been married twice before to husbands of distinguished backgrounds and brilliant political careers. She was the daughter of Sempronia (see p. 171). Fulvia did not inherit her mother's charm, but she attracted three husbands by her wealth. She bore children in each marriage, but, like her mother, Fulvia was described as female in body only. Fulvia's "masculinity" consisted in entering spheres reserved for men. Her political manipulations in behalf of her various husbands were of benefit to them, but Fulvia's ambitions provoked hatred of her. The antagonism she aroused is a measure of the real political power that women like her wielded, whether through wealth or influence. It also resulted from the hatred accruing to the men with whom they were connected; for example, Sempronia's aid to Catiline and Fulvia's to Antony implicated the women in the odium felt toward these men. Moreover, despite the long tradition of Roman women playing a role in politics, there remained a feeling traceable back to Homer that women and men should have distinct roles in society. But Fulvia did not care about spinning or housekeeping; rather, she preferred to accompany her husbands even in the army camps. Her cruelty during the proscriptions was equal to Antony's and her rudeness to the female relatives of the proscribed men has already been noted (see p. 175); but the stories about Fulvia are derived from biased testimony. Plutarch charges Fulvia with initiating the deterioration of Marc Antony and preparing him to be dominated by Cleopatra, for Fulvia wished to rule a ruler and command a commander, and she schooled Antony to obey women. While Antony was campaigning in the East, with Antony's brother Fulvia maintained his interests in Italy against Octavian until the defeat at Perusia in 40 B.C. She was devoted to her husband's career although Cleopatra had begun her liaison with Antony. In 40 B.C., soon after the birth of Cleopatra's twins and after she herself had suffered many rebuffs from Antony, Fulvia died. Her death prepared the way for his second marriage.[121]

Octavia, the sister of Octavian, was newly widowed and hence available for a marriage alliance with Antony. Their marriage was the result of the agreement between Octavian and Antony in 40 B.C., known as the Treaty of Brundisium. While Fulvia's policy had been to steer Antony against Octavian, Octavia's was to mediate between the two men, and for her efforts she won the approbation of her brother and later historians. Her precedents for female intercession between factions of men were, of course, the legendary women of the early Republic, including the Sabine women and the delegation of women that dissuaded Coriolanus from attacking Rome. This was the only traditionally commendable, active political role for women in Rome. Octavia bore two children to Antony in the three years they lived together, but he grew bored with her sober intellectual character. In 37 B.C. Antony married Cleopatra, and in 36 B.C. their son Ptolemy was born. Since Cleopatra was not a Roman citizen, Octavia, like Fulvia before her, was able to view the marriage as not legitimate. She continued to aid Antony, it is claimed, despite her brother's wishes. In 32 B.C. Antony formally divorced Octavia, and this insult gave Octavian a reason to declare war. Octavia was ejected from Antony's house, weeping lest she be considered a cause of war. After Antony's death she raised her children by her two marriages and Antony's children by Fulvia and Cleopatra, with the exception of Antyllus, Fulvia's elder son by Antony, whom Octavian had had murdered. Cleopatra's two sons by Antony also were never heard of again. Octavia was not the ordinary hateful stepmother, and her reputation was unblemished. When Octavia died, as we have noted, two public eulogies were delivered and public mourning declared. In contrast, the suicide of Cleopatra was greeted by Octavian and Rome with jubilation. Some rejoiced that the prophecy that the Egyptian queen would conquer Rome, reconcile Asia and Europe, and reign in a golden age of peace, justice, and love had been thwarted by her death.[122] Many were jubilant and ready to accept the rule of Octavian, for his propaganda against Cleopatra—the *fatale monstrum*—made Octavian himself seem like a divine savior when he defeated her.

In 41 B.C. Antony summoned Cleopatra to meet him in Cilicia. Cleopatra had not been able to persuade Caesar to abandon his respectable Roman wife, but she lured Antony from both Fulvia and Octavia. When she first met Antony she sailed on a golden barge, dressed like Aphrodite. She was not so beautiful as some earlier Macedonian queens, but she possessed a magical charm and a beautiful voice. She was well educated and spoke many languages including Egyptian (unlike many male Ptolemies), despite the fact that she was Greek by culture as well as heredity. Since Antony did not have intellectual aspirations, Cleopatra entertained him as he desired. The two of them enjoyed Oriental luxury, Cleopatra playing the exotic companion to Antony's pleasure, though the debauchery and drunkenness ascribed to her are not in keeping with the traditions of Hellenistic queens and, as far as we know, she had sexual liaisons with only Caesar and Antony. Legends built up by her enemies are doubtless the source of unflattering accounts, since Cleopatra's competence as a ruler was never questioned, and Egypt remained loyal to her.

Cleopatra resembled Octavia in her devotion to her country, Fulvia in her ruthlessness and masculine daring, and earlier Hellenistic queens in her unbridled ambition. She also resembled Alexander the Great in her ability and quest for world empire. She posed a major threat to Octavian and Rome, for she had the only living son of Caesar—Caesarion, Marc Antony—a triumvir and famous general who was widely popular among troops and aristocracy alike, and the riches and resources of Egypt at her command. When Octavian finally declared war after Antony had formally divorced Octavia, he declared war on Cleopatra alone. Antony was attracted to her personally, but politically he also hoped to profit by her support. Cleopatra aided Antony with her troops and supplies, but she never put her resources completely at his disposal. Rather, she participated in his campaigns and was present at the scene of battles, as were earlier Hellenistic queens. Her presence among the Roman troops was disturbing to them, since, as we have noted in our discussion of Fulvia, Romans, unlike the Macedonians, believed that the battlefield was no place for a woman. The Romans were also disturbed at Antony's transformation from a Roman soldier into a self-styled Hellenistic king, and believed that if he were triumphant the capital of the world would shift from Rome to Alexandria. As everyone knows, in 30 B.C., after being defeated by Octavian, Antony committed suicide and died in Cleopatra's arms. Rather than grace Octavian's triumph, Cleopatra killed herself by allowing an asp to bite her breast.

The asp was sacred to the Egyptian sun god, from whom Cleopatra as Queen of Egypt considered herself descended—though she did not deny her Macedonian descent. The divinity of Hellenistic rulers in Egypt had a long history. Cleopatra and Antony were also viewed as incarnations of Aphrodite and Dionysus, and of Isis and Osiris. As Isis, who championed the equality of women—and doubtless motivated also by what she considered to be her own interest—Cleopatra is known to have supported women twice in minor political disputes.[123]

The story of Dido and Aeneas related by Virgil in the *Aeneid* bears some resemblance to that of Cleopatra and Antony. Both women, by means of Oriental luxury and feminine charm, diverted men from political purposes which were to benefit Rome. The motivations of Dido and Cleopatra were quite different. Dido loved Aeneas. Though as queen she had managed to found the city of Carthage, she let her government disintegrate while she carried on her affair with Aeneas, and even offered to share her realm with him. Aeneas eventually showed his worth by abandoning Dido and Oriental softness to continue with his mission, which led to the founding of Rome. In contrast to Aeneas, Antony was permanently seduced by Cleopatra and her Oriental ways. Cleopatra herself was more like Aeneas in her devotion to her country and her ambitions for herself and her children. She dominated Antony, and, if she loved him, she certainly never let emotion divert her from her schemes. The Romans feared her as they had feared only Hannibal, and they created a legend that survives to this day.

It is apparent that the upper-class Roman woman—at least from the time of the late Republic—had far more freedom than the woman of similar status in Classical Athens. The Roman woman had choices; the Athenian had none. As we have seen, life styles varied and more than one role was tolerated by the society. A Roman matron could be a virtuous Cornelia, Octavia, or "Turia," or she could be free beyond the point of indiscretion. Like Dido or the daughter or granddaughter of Augustus, she might be forced to pay a price for her abandonment of propriety, but the choice was hers.

Roman women were given no true political offices and were forced to exert their influence through their men. Unlike Cleopatra, they were the power behind the throne, but the throne could never be theirs, and their interference in politics aroused resentment. Compared to Athenian women, Roman women were liberated, but compared to Roman men they were not.

On the other hand, Roman women were involved with their culture and were able to influence their society, whereas the Athenian women were isolated and excluded from activities outside the home. Roman women dined with their husbands and attended respectable parties, games, shows, and even political gatherings. Thus I believe that the notorious part of their lives has been exaggerated by historians who write of the silent, seething, repressed women taking out their fury in antisocial desecrations of tradition, in debauchery, and in cruelty at the games.[124] Roman women had access to money and power, and their fortunes were linked to those of the state. As men prospered, so did women.

# IX

## WOMEN OF THE
## ROMAN LOWER CLASSES

ROMAN LITERATURE tells us about the ruling classes, and preponderantly about the men within them. The length of this chapter, in comparison with the preceding one, will give a rough indication of the amount of both ancient material and modern scholarship that deals with lower-class as opposed to upper-class women. It must be evident that lower-class women were always more numerous, but less notorious—the activities of celebrities tend to captivate the historical imagination. Nevertheless, it is essential to acknowledge a new trend in Roman historical studies that is directed at finding out about the lower classes and which integrates women in its purview.

How can we know about the lives of lower-class women—slaves, ex-slaves, working women, and the poor? The literature does tell us the ways in which the lower classes pleased or displeased their social superiors. The sepulchral inscriptions that owners of slaves or members of the lower classes had carved for their associates and themselves give the messages they wanted to announce to posterity. Thus an epitaph may include not merely the name of the deceased, but the name of her owner or former owner if she were a slave or freedwoman (especially if she had belonged to an important family), the name of her husband, the duration of her marriage and the number of children in the family, her age at death, and her métier.

For the present chapter I have drawn heavily on the recent study of P. R. C. Weaver of the slaves and freedmen of the imperial household, which includes statistics on a control group of nonimperial slaves. Also of immense value have been S. M. Treggiari's studies of slaves and freedmen of the late Republic and the early Empire.[1] But the essential questions of how it felt to be a female slave among the Romans, and whether—if one were an ordinary slave—it was worse to be male or female, cannot be answered.

## The Exploitation of Slaves

The Roman household *(familia)* included not only kinsmen legally dependent on the head of the family, but also slaves. The number of slaves of course varied according to the means of the family, but even humble families might own a few. There is more abundant documentation on the slaves of the wealthy, as is true of the wealthy themselves. Wealthy families owned thousands of slaves, living on their various holdings, and the household of the emperor *(familia Caesaris)* was probably the largest. Owners of slaves invested in human property with the expectation that certain services would be performed, and that their own wealth would thereby be increased and their personal comfort enhanced. The complexities of Roman slavery were such that a woman might gain more prestige by marrying a slave than a free person, and that slaves and ex-slaves might be more highly educated and enjoy greater economic security than the freeborn poor.

The variety of the jobs held by female slaves was more limited than those of the males. Some women were enslaved only in adulthood, either by kidnappers or pirates, or because they were camp followers or ordinary citizens where the Romans made a conquest. In a population of captive Greeks, the Romans would find male scholars, historians, poets, and men with valuable skills. Owing to the limitations of women's education, a freshly captured woman may have been at most a midwife, an actress, or a prostitute. Most women did not have any training beyond the traditional household skills. In slavery, as in freedom, they could work as spinners, weavers, clothesmakers, menders, wetnurses, child nurses, kitchen help, and general domestics. The household duties of female slaves in Rome differed somewhat from those we observed in Greece. Because Roman engineers devised mechanical methods for transporting large quantities of water, Roman slave women did not carry water to the same extent that Greeks had done. Moreover, in Rome, unlike Greece, all clothing was not made at home.[2] In addition, female slaves were given special training in the wealthy Roman home and worked as clerks, secretaries, ladies' maids, clothes folders, hairdressers, haircutters, mirror holders, masseuses, readers, entertainers, midwives, and infirmary attendants.[3] Children born into slavery in a wealthy Roman home thus stood a fair chance of receiving some education.

Some female slaves, like males, were employed as attendants to enhance the splendor of the mistress' entourage when she went out of her home. Such slaves would clear the way before their owner. If her mistress was traveling on a litter, a female slave would put her sandals on for her and place a footstool next to the litter before the mistress alighted. A slave might carry a parasol for a mistress who was taking a walk. Naturally, slaves' functions on a farm or country estate would have differed from those in the urban household, but less is known about rural slave women. However, Cato the Censor does list the duties of the *vilica*, the chief housekeeper, a slave woman who held a supervisory position of great responsibility, subordinate to a steward who was a male slave.[4]

Women were always employable for sexual purposes, either in addition to their other domestic responsibilities, or as a primary occupation. The master had access to all his slave women. Scipio Africanus favored a particular slave girl, and when he died, his wife Aemilia, far from being vindictive, gave the girl her freedom. Cato the Censor, who was an authority on Roman virtue, was visited nightly by a slave girl after his wife died, and the emperors Augustus and Claudius consorted with numerous slave girls with their wives' explicit approval. Slave women were also available for sexual relations with the male slaves in the house, with the master's permission. Cato, who was always interested in financial gain, charged his male slaves a fixed fee for intercourse with his female slaves.[5]

Employment in the sex trade brought great profit to the owners of female slaves. Women worked as prostitutes in brothels or in inns or baths open to the public. Exposed baby girls and daughters sold by their parents were raised for this trade. In this same category, but at a higher level, were the women trained to work as actresses and entertainers of all types. Actresses sometimes appeared nude and performed sexual acts on stage. However, actresses were not invariably employed sexually. Eucharis, a young performer who had been given her freedom sometime before her death at the age of fourteen, performed in the chorus at respectable public games given as "Greek theater," and is described as "learned" and "skilled" in her epitaph.[6]

## Marriage, Manumission, and the Law

The fact of slavery disqualified a person from entering into a formal Roman marriage, but two slaves might have an informal marital arrangement known as "cohabitation" *(contubernium)*. Although the usual incest regulations applied just as if it were legal marriage, this arrangement had no legal validity: the children of the union were considered illegitimate, and the woman could not be accused of adultery.[7] But to the slaves themselves the marriages were valid, and in the epitaphs the partners refer to each other as husband and wife. It was in the master's interest to promote family life among his slaves, for it improved morale and produced slave children who were the master's to keep in his household or to dispose of as he wished.[8] Slaves tended to marry other slaves, and were likely to marry within their master's *familia*. With permission, a slave might marry a slave from another *familia* or a free person. However, if a male slave married a female outside his master's *familia*, the master lost the profit that might be gained from the offspring, since the children belonged to the mother if she were free, or to her master if she were a slave. Hence such a marriage might not be permitted. There was no security in a slave marriage—either partner or the children might be sold to another owner or moved to a different property owned by the original master. Broken marriages left no record. But sepulchral inscriptions show that many slave marriages survived over long periods of time, regardless of changes in habitation or changes in status from slave to freed of one or both of the partners. In lives subject to the whims of others, the stability of the marriage bond was welcome.

The study of imperial slaves and freedmen shows that almost half the marriages of freedmen whose duration is mentioned lasted at least thirty years. Moreover, their wives had married young, like the aristocrats discussed in the previous chapter. In order that the statistics on the duration of marriage be consistent with those on the age of death of wives, it is necessary to remember Keith Hopkins' hypothesis that the age of death of wives who die young is more likely to be recorded on a tombstone (see p. 169). Over half the wives of imperial slaves and freedmen were dead before thirty, with the highest proportion dying between twenty and twenty-five. Of the nine married women buried in the tomb of a wealthy family, the Statilii, studied by Susan Treggiari, five had died at age twenty or younger.[9] The mortality was probably even higher among the slaves belonging to poorer families.

The Roman household employed a far larger number of male slaves than female. Among children of imperial slaves and freedmen, the proportion is sixty or more per cent male, and among the adults the proportion of males is far higher, owing to the nature of the work of this elite group of civil servants. Susan Treggiari's study of the slaves and freedmen of Livia and of the Volusii likewise shows a ratio of roughly three males per female, with a slightly larger proportion of female slaves in a household owned by a woman than in the slave household belonging to a male owner. On the estates of the fictional Trimalchio were born thirty boys and forty girls in a single day. These statistics, like much in the *Satiricon,* are intended to be ludicrous, but nevertheless it is interesting to observe that all the slaves at Trimalchio's dinner are male.[10] Boy babies were retained to fill posts as their fathers were manumitted or died, but excess female children were disposed of in various ways. Some were sold to work as domestics in small households, many probably to brothels; others were perhaps exposed to die or be picked up by a slave-trader. Still others were given by the master to male slaves as marriage partners, with the expectation that children would be produced who would be the master's property; some girls were purchased by male slaves from their own funds. Perhaps Aurelia Philematium, a freedwoman who died at forty, was one of these girls. Her epitaph states that her freedman husband took her "to his bosom" when she was seven, and was like a father to her.[11] Apparently he was kind to her when she joined the household, and then married her. That this marriage could have been consummated when the bride was only seven is not impossible.[12]

Slaves were allowed to amass their own personal savings *(peculium),* and could use this money to buy other slaves. When a male slave purchased his wife, she had the status of a personal slave *(vicaria)* to her husband-owner—although, strictly speaking, like all her husband's possessions she belonged to his master—and the disaster of being sold to separate households was less likely. This arrangement also offered a path of upward mobility for the slave husband, since his master might free the slave's wife sooner than a valuable and industrious male slave.

The minimum age for manumission was thirty, according to the Lex Aelia Sentia of A.D. 4, but many slaves attained manumission earlier. Females were likely to be manumitted earlier than males for a number of reasons: consistent with the state's policy of encouraging marriage, the law allowed a master to manumit a slave in order to marry her.[13] Some masters will have manumitted and then married a woman with whom they were cohabiting so that their children would be free and legitimate. Marriage to women of slave or freed status was perfectly acceptable among the lower classes.[14] But such alliances were a cause for censure among the wealthy, and according to Augustan legislation, men of senatorial rank were not permitted to marry freedwomen at all.[15] Similarly, women of senatorial rank were prohibited from marrying freedmen. However, this restriction was not strictly observed in the first century A.D. The father of Claudius Etruscus was an imperial freedman of senior administrative grade, and he was able to contract a legitimate marriage with Tettia Etrusca, who was probably of senatorial rank.[16] An owner who was himself a slave might arrange for his master to free his slave wife *(contubernalis vicaria)* so that their children would be freeborn, though of course still illegitimate since the father remained a slave. Since a manumitted slave continued to have obligations toward his or her ex-owner *(patrona* or *patronus)*, the freed wife remained bound to her husband or his master, and could not desert him or remarry without his permission.[17]

Females could win their freedom through routes other than marriage. As we have mentioned, slaves were allowed to amass their own personal savings with a view to repaying their purchase price. A woman employed in domestic work would have less opportunity to collect tips than a male slave in an influential post, and her savings would grow rather slowly, although the master's favorite bedmate might receive gifts, and a lady's maid would be given tips from her mistress' lovers.[18] On the other hand, as she grew older and less attractive her value decreased, whereas the value of a highly trained male slave increased with years. Thus a woman might eventually be able to purchase her own freedom. In addition, Columella, who in the first century A.D. wrote a treatise on farming, considered that a slave woman had repaid her purchase price by bearing four children to be her master's property.[19] Some urban slaves might get away with fewer than this number. Freedom was often granted to slaves voluntarily by owners, or by last testament. The manumission of the actress Eucharis may be attributable to the good will of her owner; for example, the slave girl may have been granted freedom as she lay ill. A married couple might be manumitted simultaneously, or the partner who was freed first could amass enough funds to buy the partner still in slavery and manumit him or her.

When both husband and wife had been slaves together, and the wife was a freedwoman, the husband could in turn be manumitted by marriage. However, a freeborn woman who freed a male slave and married him was disapproved of, and such marriages were outlawed by Septimius Severus (reigned A.D. 193–211).[20]

The motives leading a freeborn woman or freedwoman to marry a slave are an indication of the complexity of slave society. Male slaves of the emperor or of important Roman families in administrative posts held positions of prestige and economic security. The wife had a good chance of being buried in the tomb of her husband's *familia,* and a place of burial was a concern to all Romans. The free woman who married an imperial slave was, in a sense, improving her status, while her husband also improved his. To the owner of the male slave, however, such an arrangement was detrimental, since the children were the property of the mother. Moreover, the prejudice against a free woman cohabiting with a slave extended even to slaves of high position within the slave hierarchy. Therefore a decree of the Senate was passed in A.D. 52 that discouraged freeborn and freedwomen from marrying slaves by reducing such a wife to the status of slave or freedwoman of her husband's master. This regulation was aimed at slaves of the imperial household. The loss of status gave the husband's master—the emperor in particular—financial advantages in regard to the wives and children of his male slaves.[21]

In contrast to male slaves, female slaves in upper-class families were less likely to marry above their station. Females, even in important households, were used only for domestic service and did not hold positions of influence. There was therefore little incentive for freeborn men or freedmen outside their households to unite with them. In a lower-class family a female slave could be freed to marry her master, but in senatorial or imperial households this route of upward mobility was closed. Men of senatorial status could not marry freedwomen, although they could, of course, cohabit with them.

A few female members of the imperial household attained positions of influence as the freedwoman concubines of emperors. These relationships were known publicly, often of long duration, and not a cause for scandal except when the woman misbehaved.[22] Vespasian, Marcus Aurelius, and Antoninus Pius—all emperors of good reputation—lived with concubines after the death of their wives. They already had heirs to their throne, and, by choosing to live with women whom it was impossible for them to marry, they may have intended to avoid the squabbles between heirs descended from different wives which, as we have seen, characterized the Hellenistic monarchies.

## Daughters and Sons

A slave might have slave children, freeborn illegitimate children, and freeborn legitimate children. Children born in *contubernium* took the status of the mother. Thus, the children born while a mother was still a slave were slaves; those born after her manumission were freeborn, but not legitimate unless her husband was of freed or freeborn status. Freed parents might try to locate their children born into bondage, purchase them, and then manumit them.

A freedwoman's care for her illegitimate daughter can be seen in the case of Petronia Justa. The eruption of Vesuvius in A.D. 79 preserved tablets at Herculaneum that record a lawsuit concerning the claim of Petronia Justa to free birth. Her mother had been a slave, was manumitted, and left Justa in the home of her patron. Justa claimed that she had been born after her mother's manumission and was therefore freeborn, and that her mother had returned to reclaim her daughter from the patron and had reimbursed him for the expenses incurred in raising her. The expenses involved would not have been inconsiderable.[23]

The epitaphs of freedmen generally testify to small families of rarely more than two children, a tendency that we also observed among the upper class.[24] This statistic makes us wonder how many women could take advantage of the Augustan marital legislation which offered privileges including exemption from guardianship to the freedwoman who bore four children, as it had to the freeborn woman with three children. Freeborn men, on the other hand, needed three children; while two free children served to release freedmen from obligations to their former owner.[25] The stipulation requiring four children of freedwomen but only two of freedmen is probably a response to the fact that men could be manumitted fairly late in life, and might have the opportunity to produce only two additional children. But slave women as well were not manumitted until they were into their childbearing years, and they died at younger ages than men—conditions that made it rather unlikely that four additional children could be produced. However, as mentioned, it was theoretically possible for freedmen to find their own children born in slavery, buy them, adopt them, and have them count as legitimate children; the freedman would thereby be eligible for the privileges accruing to freedwomen with four children and freedmen with two children. The fact that the parents' epitaph mentions two children, then, may not reflect the actual number of children in the family; additional children may have grown up and married and been commemorated elsewhere by their spouses.

## Freedwomen and Working Women

Legislation concerning the right to bequeath property was applicable to freedwomen worth at least 100,000 sesterces, and the Emperor Claudius offered the privileges of women who had four children to freedwomen who invested in the grain market for the feeding of Rome.[26] Both of these provisions show that there were some wealthy freedwomen, and the resources of many freedwomen are obvious from the burial places they were able to construct for themselves and at times for their own slaves and freedmen. A few wealthy freedwomen are known by name. Lyde, freedwoman of the Empress Livia, owned at least four slaves,[27] and the fictitious Fortunata of the *Satiricon,* who wallows in riches, is probably a caricature of real freedwomen. Those freedwomen who were courtesans and consorted with wealthy men at bachelor parties and elsewhere were likely to have acquired some riches of their own. Volumnia Cytheris, a freedwoman who had been an actress in the mime, is one of the best known of the freedwoman courtesans. She was the mistress of Brutus the Tyrannicide, Marc Antony, the elegist Cornelius Gallus, and others. Cytheris was independent enough to be able to choose her lovers, and her desertion of Gallus provided the theme of Virgil's tenth *Eclogue*.[28]

Most freedwomen, however, were not spectacularly wealthy, but rather comprised a large part of the Roman working class, serving as shopkeepers or artisans or continuing in domestic service. The occupations pursued by freedwomen were commonly those for which they had been trained as slaves, and are not notably more varied than the occupations we have listed for working women in Classical Athens. Nevertheless, women were the tastemakers of textile manufacture throughout classical antiquity.

Working in wool was traditionally a woman's task, in Rome as well as in Greece. Spinning was so sex-stereotyped that, as we have observed, even in Dark Age burials spindle whorls served to identify corpses as female. The reader will be reminded of earlier references to woolworking by women: the tablets from Pylos, Homeric epic (Hector's admonition to Andromache to return to her loom), Xenophon's descriptions in the *Memorabilia* and *Oeconomicus,* the weaving of the *peplos* for Athena Polias, Erinna's titling her poem "The Distaff," and the predominance of woolworkers in a list of women manumitted in Athens between 349 and 320 B.C.[29] We also recall that the Greek Plutarch noted Fulvia's masculinity, pointing out that "she did not care for spinning." The Phoenician queen Dido, who in many ways is modeled on Homeric queens, has a subtle blemish: Virgil never shows her spinning or weaving.

So among the Romans spinning was always a woman's task. The sepulchral inscription of the archetypal Roman matron Claudia makes this association clear:

> Stranger, what I have to say is short. Stop and read it through. This is the unlovely tomb of a lovely woman. Her parents named her Claudia. She loved her husband with her whole heart. She bore two sons, one of whom she leaves on earth; the other she has placed beneath the earth. She was charming in conversation, yet her conduct was appropriate. She kept house, she made wool.[30]

The old-fashioned Roman bride wreathed the doorposts of her new home with wool. When Augustus wished to instill respect for old-fashioned virtues among the sophisticated women of his household, he set them to work in wool and wore their homespun results.[31] Many women of the lower classes, slave and freed, were also employed in working wool both at home and in small-scale industrial establishments where working-class men joined women as weavers and as weighers of balls of wool to be apportioned to weavers.[32] Spinning, however, continued to be solely women's work. But women were not restricted to spinning alone.

Laundry work was done by women and men, unlike the situation in Classical Athens, where this occupation was confined to women. That men worked as fullers and weavers is probably a result of the organization of this work into small-scale industries in the Roman period. At Pompeii, women worked at mills where grain was ground, and we find a landlady and a female moneylender.[33] Freedwomen, since they often came from the East, frequently sold luxury items or exotic merchandise, such as purple dye or perfumes. They also sold more mundane merchandise, such as clothing and food, and worked as butchers or even as fisherwomen—and afterward hawked their catch.

The occupations of women at Pompeii give a good sample of the types of economic activity open to women. Moreover, the sepulchral inscriptions of many women from the entire Roman world record how a woman had made her living. Métiers as lowly as "dealer in beans" or "seller of nails" and as lofty as "commercial entrepreneur" or "physician" are found. Women's names stamped on pipes and bricks also record their involvement with building activities—from the ownership of a brickmaking or stonecutting operation by an upper-class woman to actual participation in the making of building materials and construction work by working women of the lower classes.[34]

The best-known woman at Pompeii is Eumachia, a businesswoman whose family manufactured bricks. She was the patroness of the fullers, who set up her statue. She, in turn, donated to the town porticos, colonnades, and a crypt, and erected an imposing tomb for herself.

The selection of a woman as patroness *(patrona)* of a men's guild *(collegium)* was by no means unique. A few women are known to have served as patronesses of guilds, either by themselves or simultaneously with male patrons who frequently were their husbands; yet, women comprised less than five per cent of known patrons during the period of the Empire.[35] In return for the gratitude and praise awarded by the guild, the patrons and patronesses—who were wealthy and influential—were expected to bestow benefactions on their guilds. Women could belong to religious and burial guilds, and indeed a few held high office in them. At least two women were chosen as patronesses of synagogues. But there is no evidence that women were permitted to belong to the professional or craft guilds of men, even when they worked in the same occupation.

Many women worked as waitresses in taverns and at counters dispensing drinks and food. These women were selected, doubtless, for their ability to attract customers, and sometimes the taverns had rooms for prostitution upstairs. The names of waitresses and prosti- tutes are found scribbled on walls at Pompeii. The graffiti refer to the women's vices and attractions, and announce that some women can be had for two asses—the price of a loaf of bread. But these may be written as insults, rather than reflect a true price. The highest price of a woman is given as sixteen asses.[36]

Prostitutes came from a variety of ethnic origins. Foreign-born prostitutes would be attractive both to men of the native lands who happened to find themselves in Pompeii and to men who wanted to try out exotic women. It is impossible to determine the status of the women who worked in brothels from the information in graffiti, but it seems likely that they were slaves or freedwomen. Prostitution was recognized and taxed, and brothels were regarded by some as a respectable investment, but the Roman comedy shows that slave- dealers who traded in prostitutes were despised.[37] Relatively few respectable women wrote electoral graffiti, but women who mingled with the crowds—the waitresses and prostitutes—are responsible for numerous electoral endorsements (which incidentally indicate that they knew how to write): e.g., "Sucula [little sow] asks you to make Marcus Cerrinius aedile."

Many freedwomen continued working for their former owners after manumission. Within the household, there was a good chance that female slaves engaged in female-oriented activities—such as ladies' maids and midwives—would be freed by the mistress, and male slaves by the master. Freed slaves were legally obliged to provide service, so long as enough time remained to earn their own livelihood. Prostitutes were exempt from the obligation to continue service but often had no other way of making a living. Women of high status and those over the age of fifty were also exempt, and so, in practice, were women who had married with their master's consent.[38] Julia Phoebe, a freedwoman of Augustus' daughter Julia, remained close to her *patrona* and hanged herself when Julia was exiled.[39] Dorcas, the dresser *(ornatrix)* of Livia, was a freed-woman.[40] Freedwomen, particularly domestics or ladies' maids with no marketable skills, probably welcomed the opportunity to remain in the security of their patron's employ and to continue living in the house, for it was preferable to being released into the throngs of the poor.

The fate of very poor women can only be guessed at. They were probably worse off than slaves, for slaves at least were property, and were cared for in a manner commensurate with their value. Some freedwomen, as well, might have been able to count on the good will of their former owners. We assume that many unskilled poor women maintained themselves through prostitution. Some did not even have the security of a brothel but practiced their trade out-of-doors under archways.[41] Indeed, the word "fornicate" is derived from the Latin word for "arch."

## The Dole and Women's Worth

Beginning in the late Republic, a number of public-assistance programs were maintained by the Roman government, but most of them benefited free men and boys. The doles were motivated not so much by humanitarian reasons as by politicians' desires to keep men pacified and to curry favor with the crowds. Thus Publius Clodius proclaimed a free grain dole in order to win votes. Since women, though citizens, could not vote, and their hunger was not likely to drive them to revolution, there was little point in including them in the largesse. Moreover, including women would have meant reducing the portions of men, and the benefactor would not have won the good will of those he courted. As it was, the imperial grain dole could maintain only one man. For some men the dole supplemented other sources of income, and they could therefore support a family. But any man who was maintained totally by the dole at Rome could not have shared it with a wife and children.

Similar factors operated in the assistance programs, occasional distributions, and public feasts established by private benefactors in various towns in Italy. Women, if included at all, were usually given less; this discrimination existed even when the donor was female, for it was the gratitude of men that was desirable to wealthy women.[42] Only one public dinner for women to the exclusion of men is recorded. This was a dinner for the *curia mulierum* of Lanuvium in the late second or early third century, on an occasion when men were recipients of a cash distribution.[43]

Children were supported by special programs, in keeping with the state's policy of increasing the Italian birthrate. These programs, because they were aimed at the future recruitment of soldiers, also favored boys over girls. Augustus included boys under eleven among those eligible for the irregular distributions *(congiaria)* he made on special occasions, and Trajan added five thousand boys to the adults on the grain dole of the city of Rome.[44]

Regular alimentary distribution programs for the support of children in Italy were also established by Trajan. According to inscriptions of Veleia (Elea), a town in southern Italy, the monthly allowance was at the rate of sixteen sesterces for boys, twelve for girls, twelve for illegitimate boys, ten for illegitimate girls. Boys were probably supported until seventeen or eighteen, girls until fourteen, when they were expected to be married. Of the three hundred recipients, only thirty-six were girls. As Richard Duncan-Jones suggests, this ratio may not reflect the actual proportion of the two sexes in the population at Veleia.[45] The eligibility requirements for recipients of the *alimenta* are uncertain, but if each family was permitted to receive only one portion, it was likely that a boy rather than a girl would be enrolled, since the boy's allowance was larger and of longer duration.

Private alimentary schemes were initiated earlier than the state-supported ones. The first recorded alimentary foundation was established by T. Helvius Basila sometime in the third quarter of the first century A.D.[46] His gift was given to the children of Atina, in southern Italy, not distinguished by sex. At least a generation later, Pliny established a fund at Comum, in northern Italy, for the subsistence of freeborn boys and girls.[47] Perhaps seventy-five girls and one hundred boys were maintained by Pliny's foundation. The rates are known at a private foundation from the second century at Tarracina: following the government policy of giving more to boys than girls, this foundation, established by a woman, Caelia Macrina, provided monthly allotments to one hundred children at the rate of twenty sesterces for boys and sixteen for girls.[48]

The shortsightedness of the alimentary programs and doles which favored males would not have induced poor parents to raise the girls who might become the mothers of the next generation of soldiers. Therefore a few public and private funds were created solely for the benefit of girls. In memory of his wife, the elder Faustina, Antoninus Pius established the "puellae Faustinianae," and Marcus Aurelius endowed the "novae puellae Faustinianae" honoring the memory of his wife, the younger Faustina.[49] In the third quarter of the second century A.D., a daughter of C. Fabius Agrippinus established an alimentary fund at Ostia for girls in memory of her mother.[50] Fabia's grant probably supplemented a government-supported alimentary scheme at Ostia whose beneficiaries were principally boys. All the funds for girls were on a very small scale.

In the absence of information, the reader is free to imagine what it was like to spend most of one's life in slavery, with a few years as a freedwoman, or to be a poor woman in Rome. Marriage and friendships must have provided some satisfaction, particularly for slaves and ex-slaves who had lost track of their blood relatives. Marriage bonds among the lower classes were at least as stable as among the sophisticated Romans of the upper class, although owners did not always respect the connubial arrangements of slaves.

Despite the sexual availability which was a fact of slavery, there is no evidence that freedwomen were notably more promiscuous than women who had never experienced slavery.[51] A freedwoman remained under her patron's guardianship; her patron was sometimes her husband or her husband's master; and this surveillance, while keeping the woman in a subordinate position, was likely to have strengthened the marriage bond. The bonds of affection and obligation were so strong that they abided in some couples even after divorce, to the extent of seeing to it that a proper burial was awarded to an ex-spouse.[52]

A principal motive for marriage among the lower classes was likely to be affection. Thus the political alliances which encouraged successive marriages and divorces among the upper class would not be a significant factor, except for those who were social climbers. Whether divorce was frequent among the lower classes is difficult to ascertain, for divorces are not likely to be commemorated on tombstones. But some tombstones show that hoary Roman ideals could flourish among the very classes that were recruited from non-Roman or newly Romanized ethnic backgrounds: marriages were of long duration, and women were lauded for having been married only once.

# X

# THE ROLE OF WOMEN
# IN THE RELIGION
# OF THE ROMANS

My dear, I truly desire to see you as soon as possible, and to die in
your arms, since neither the gods whom you have piously worshiped
nor the men whom I have always served have shown us any thanks.
                                        —Cicero to his wife, Terentia,
                                        Brundisium, April 29, 58 B.C.[1]

THIS DIVISION of labor—the cultivation of the heavenly powers by
the woman and the care of the mundane by the man—would not
come as a surprise to anyone familiar with Italian customs even
today. But it is necessary to point out at once that Cicero has sim-
plified the facts for rhetorical effect, and that the dichotomy is more
ideal than real, for the life of a Roman man was also fraught with
religious duties, while a woman like Terentia was primarily concerned with the management of her family and finances. For Terentia, participation in religion could be both an obligation and a
pleasure.

Roman religion was basically of two kinds: there were the native
cults that supported and were supported by the state; and there were
the imported Oriental cults—including that of Isis, the most intriguing of all Roman deities. Religion afforded an outlet for those whose
lives were circumscribed in other ways: some cults—evidently the
more popular—offered opportunities for joy and release. The
Romans had festivals confined to women, analogous to the Thes-

mophoria of the Athenians, at which drunkenness, obscene jests, and lewd behavior were appropriate. They also had Mystery religions like those at Eleusis, which held out the comfort of a blessed resurrection. On the other hand, many cults that offered no particular pleasure to the worshiper had to be maintained in order to avert the wrath of a spurned deity. Often these cults had their own peculiar constellations of prescriptions for the devotee: abstinence from certain foods or from sex, and the punctilious performance of ritualized—but frequently inexplicable—ceremonies at designated times.

Among the numerous cults developed by the Romans to enlist divine aid for practical purposes were those designed to uphold ideals of female conduct. The Roman genius for organization is reflected in the categorizing of women and their desirable qualities, and in the creation of cults appropriate to the categories. Women were ranked according to the class distinction between plebeians and patricians, by a moral standard segregating respectable women from those who followed disreputable professions, by age, and by whether they were slave or free. Marital status was also a fundamental subdivision by which women were ranked, including the following distinctions: young virgin, celibate adult, wife, wife married only once *(univira)*, and widow.

## Protector of the Fortunes of Women

The several cults of Fortuna (Luck or Fortune) that emerged from that goddess' patronage of women's lives show the Romans' use of religious sanctions to promote socially desirable behavior.[2] Identifiable in the Roman pantheon by her rudder, globe, and cornucopia, Fortuna's significance for women centered on the last of her symbols, for she was the guarantor not only of the fruits of the earth but also of women's physical maturation and sexual fulfillment.

Fortuna Virginalis, or Virgo (Virgin), was the patroness of young girls as they came of age. Adolescent girls dedicated to this goddess the little togas they had worn in girlhood.[3] After the dedication, a girl donned the stola, the dress by which a respectable matron was distinguished from a toga-clad prostitute. Analogous ceremonies for boys, including the donning of the dress of men *(toga virilis)* and the dedication of the first beard, were clearly puberty rites and not concerned directly with marriage. But since puberty and marriage often came at about the same time in a girl's life, the dedication of her girlhood clothing may have marked both occasions.

Upon her marriage a bride passed to the protection of Fortuna Primigenia (firstborn, primordial, or first-to-sire) of Praeneste, who was a patroness of mothers and childbirth and an oracular deity as well. The cult of Fortuna of Praeneste, however, was not confined to women, for men were interested in her promise of virility, material success, and economic prosperity. She had several temples: her temple on the Quirinal, which was vowed in 204 B.C., before a battle against Hannibal, was actually dedicated in 194 B.C., along with a number of temples to various deities. This was the year following women's agitation for the repeal of the Oppian Law (see p. 180); the building of the temple served to confirm and advertise the traditional expectations the Romans continued to hold for their women, despite the repeal of the law.

Some Fortuna cults were linked to other exclusively female cults, and many of these were confined to *univirae*. A temple of Fortuna Virgo was built near a temple of the Good Mother (Mater Matuta) in the cattle market (Forum Boarium).[4] The foundation of both temples was considered to be in the hoary past, since it was ascribed by tradition to Servius Tullius, the sixth king of Rome; being closely located, both temples suffered the same history of burning and restorations. That the two cults were linked is shown by their location and by the facts that they shared the dedication day of June 11 and that *univirae* were concerned with both. The feast of the Mater Matuta—the Matralia—could be celebrated only by respectable matrons. In one rite they brought in a slave woman, whom they then expelled with physical abuse; a literal interpretation of this expulsion is that it was a demonstration that the worship of the Mater Matuta was confined to matrons. In another rite, the familial role of aunt was emphasized, for the women commended their brothers' and sisters' pubescent children to the care of the goddess. The temple of Fortuna in the cattle market was also confused or connected with a cult of Patrician Chastity (Pudicitia Patricia). The temple contained a veiled statue which could be touched only by *univirae*. There was some doubt about what the statue represented. Some believed that it was a figure of Servius Tullius, the founder of the cult; others supposed that it represented the goddess Fortuna; still others thought that the statue represented Chastity (Pudicitia). According to a story in Livy, Verginia, a patrician woman, was excluded from worshiping Pudicitia Patricia because other women considered that she had demeaned herself by marrying a plebeian.[5] In 296 B.C., in response to this insult, she dedicated a shrine and altar to Plebeian Chastity. This cult, confined to *univirae* of the plebeian class, asserted that plebeian matrons upheld the same conjugal ideals as patricians. But the next year, 295 B.C., was vexed with prodigies, including the discovery that a number of matrons were guilty of adultery. They were fined, and the money used to erect a temple of Venus the Compliant (Obsequens), which was to serve as a permanent admonition to women.[6]

The glorious deeds of the mother and wife of the infamous Coriolanus occasioned the founding of a cult of Womanly Fortune (Fortuna Muliebris). In 491 B.C. Coriolanus, a traitor, was threatening to lead the Volsci against Rome, when a deputation of women led by his mother and wife met him at his camp and dissuaded him.[7] The place where the meeting occurred, approximately four miles outside Rome, was the site of the founding of the cult; the cult of Fortuna Muliebris was also confined to *univirae*.

Virile Fortune (Fortuna Virilis) was a cult concerned with the sexual fortune of women. On April 1, crowds of women gathered in the public baths of men for ceremonies honoring Virile Fortune. Thus the goddess was probably identical with Fortune of the Baths (Balnearis). According to the traditional explanation, the baths were the appropriate location for a cult of sexual fortune, for there men exposed that part of the body with which the cult was concerned. It is not known whether men were banished from the baths during the ceremony, nor whether the worship of the goddess was always assigned to all "baseborn" (meaning plebeian) women or was confined to courtesans and prostitutes *(humiliores)*. But it seems likely that respectable women did not participate, at least after the cult of Venus, Changer of Hearts [toward virtue] (Verticordia), was instituted during the war against Hannibal, as a public admonition to adultresses.[8] Venus, Changer of Hearts, was honored for the sake of domestic harmony and a life of marital fidelity, and was worshiped by respectable women on April 1, the day sacred also to Virile Fortune. Thus the dichotomy between respectable women and whores was dramatized: the former worshiping an apotheosis of conjugal ideals, the latter worshiping sexual relationships having nothing to do with wedlock.

Even pagan sources for the history of the early cults are not objective. For example, Livy's report on religion, like his legends about the high-principled women of the early Republic, are colored by his view that Roman society had suffered moral degeneration. Livy noted, for example, that the altar of Plebeian Chastity was degraded by polluted women—not only matrons, but women of all classes—and thus at last fell into oblivion.[9] In the area of social history, Livy's purpose was not merely to record the events of the past, but to present them creatively as propaganda for the Augustan marital legislation. Augustus openly used religion to promote his social ideals. He restored many temples and, as far as women were concerned, he emphasized cults centered on childbearing, chastity, and familial bonds. Some women, especially members of the imperial household, went through the motions required by the religious ceremonies. But the religious restorations, like the marital legislation, do not appear to have had a discernible influence upon public morality. Augustus' lack of success in achieving any permanent change may be judged from the report of the satirist Juvenal at the end of the first century A.D. about the homoerotic relations of Tullia and Maura at the altar of Chastity itself, keeping in mind that Juvenal painted a distorted picture of the practices he wished to condemn:

Did you ever wonder why some women make crude remarks and lewd gestures as they pass the Temple of Chastity? That's where they stop every night to relieve themselves—and piss on the goddess. Then they strap a phallus on the statue and take turns riding it. Next morning, some husband on his way to work slips in the puddle.

My god! the sacred mysteries of the special Goddess of Women [Bona Dea] are no longer secret! Women get all stirred up with wine and wild music; they drive themselves crazy; they shriek and writhe —worshipers of Phallus. And sex. They moan, they quiver with lust; there's a steady stream running down their legs. The aristocratic matrons challenge the professional whores—and win. These aren't just games—it's a serious business. They could get a rise out of any old man, even Priam or Nestor. Now their lust can't wait; they drop their pretenses; the temple rings with the cry "Bring on the men." Soon they need replacements; when they run out, they jump the servants; if there aren't any servants, they'll drag in any old beggar. If they can't find any men, they raid the stables and rape the donkeys.

If only the ancient rituals of our public rites could be conducted free from such debaucheries; but the whole world knows how they were defiled when Clodius disguised himself as a woman and entered the sacred ceremony from which even male mice had fled, where even pictures of men used to be covered as part of the ritual. In the old days, who would dare defile sacred rites and ritual objects and scorn the gods? Now there's a Clodius for every temple. We can't even lock the women up to keep them in check. Who'd guard the guards? [10]

Juvenal points out that women had ceased paying honor to the old-fashioned cults designed for women as early as 63 B.C. by alluding to the time when a man, Publius Clodius, was present at the rites of the Bona Dea, a goddess whose worship was supposed to be celebrated exclusively by women. Caesar divorced his wife Pompeia after this scandal, for there were rumors that she had encouraged Clodius' profanation of the rites. Juvenal, in his encyclopaedic catalogue of vicious women, did not hesitate to include an empress, but he dared not criticize the Vestal Virgins. In their case, if the charge of unchastity were true, the consequences for the state would be profound.

## The Privileges of Virginity

Vesta (Greek Hestia) was the goddess of the hearth, both public and domestic. The hearth with its undying flame symbolized the continuity of both family and community, and extinction of the fire was a grave matter. Tending the family hearth was the responsibility of the daughter of the household. (Freud suggested that women guard the hearth because their anatomy, unlike that of males, removes the temptation to extinguish the fire by urinating on it.) [11]

Since a virgin belongs to no man, she can incarnate the collective, the city: she can belong to everyone. Thus the young daughters of kings of early Rome tended the royal hearth from which the state cult of Vesta probably evolved. At some point in the remote past, the service of the state cult of Vesta was assumed by virgin priestesses known as Vestals. Their principal duty was to tend the fire in the temple of Vesta, and any Vestal who let the fire go out incurred the penalty of scourging. In addition to the service of Vesta, the Vestals were active in other areas of Roman religion. Most paradoxical, perhaps, was their involvement in agricultural and fertility rites. It appears that virginity is not synonymous with sterility, and not incompatible with fertility. Purity and intactness can be viewed as stored-up fertility, although it cannot be assumed that the Romans had this idea clearly formulated when they assigned multifarious tasks to the Vestals.

In early Rome there probably had been only one Vestal serving at a time, for potential childbearers could not be reserved for the service of religion.[12] But in historical times there was a college of six Vestals who varied in age. All had been enrolled between the ages of six and ten, and were obliged to remain virgins throughout the thirty years of their service, after which they were given dowries and were free to marry, although most remained unwed.

The Romans were punctilious about religious matters; there was no latitude for mistakes. But chastity was difficult to maintain throughout the approximately one thousand years of the history of the Vestals until the order was dissolved in A.D. 394.[13] Even in the legends about early Rome, a Vestal became the mother of Romulus, the revered founder, and of his twin brother Remus.[14] Later, Vestals judged guilty of violating their chastity were condemned to be buried alive. The theory was that if the Vestal were innocent, Vesta herself would rescue her entombed priestess, but actually none was ever saved. Fewer than ten Vestals are known to have undergone this execution, both because the severity of the punishment was a deterrent and because during some periods of Roman history, when there was little enthusiasm for the archaic religion, the deportment of the Vestals was overlooked. However, attitudes fluctuated, and Vestals who entered the college in a period of laxity might find themselves, in the course of their service, confronted by a government interested in imposing moral restraints. At such times, the merit of the Vestals was imputed to the state whose hearth they tended. When calamities such as the Roman defeat at Cannae occurred (216 B.C.), Vestals came under suspicion, for it was conceivable that their misconduct had contributed to the disaster.[15]

The prosecution of the Vestals is a specific example of the firmly established principle of Greek and Roman thought connecting the virtue of women and the welfare of the state. Aristotle, we have noted, blamed Spartan women for the deterioration of Sparta;

Theopompus and Livy stressed the luxuriousness of Etruscan women as a factor aggravating the degeneracy of Etruria; Juvenal harped on the rottenness of Roman women as symptomatic of a sick society; and finally Tacitus, who is outspoken in his criticisms of the members of the Roman ruling class, also condemned them implicitly by praising the vigor of the Germans[16]:

> [The German women] live with their chastity protected, not corrupted in theaters with seductions, nor at dinner parties with enticements. Men and women both know nothing of secret letters.
>
> Adultery is very rare among this large population. Punishment is swift, and is the prerogative of the husband: in the presence of relatives, the husband expels the wife from the house nude, with her hair cut, and drives her through the whole village with a whip. There is no pardon for prostituted chastity; neither beauty nor youth nor wealth will find a husband for her. There, no one laughs at vice, nor calls seduction or being seduced the "trend of the times."
>
> Even better are those tribes where only virgins marry and make one lasting agreement, with the intentions and vows of a wife. Thus, they take only one husband, just as they have only one body and one life, so that there will be no further thought, no late-blooming desire; and so that they may love their husbands not so much as the condition of marriage itself.
>
> It is a disgrace to limit the number of children, or to kill any children born after the father has made his will. There, good habits prevail more than good laws elsewhere. . . . Children are nourished at their mother's breasts, and are not handed over to maids and wetnurses.

The Emperor Domitian (reigned A.D. 81-96), a contemporary of Tacitus and Juvenal, also perceived a connection between popular morality and female degeneracy. Domitian's campaign for virtue included the enforcement of the Augustan marriage legislation and the restoration of the shrine of Plebeian Chastity. He also made public examples of the Vestals by holding capital trials of Vestals and their lovers.[17]

The trials under Domitian give evidence of the role played by politics and the personal prejudices of judges in the prosecution of Vestals and their paramours. In the first trial, the Vestals were allowed to commit suicide, and their paramours to go into exile. The second trial shows increased severity on the part of the emperor, for the guilty Vestal was buried alive, and a lover of equestrian rank was scourged to death according to the ancient practice. On the other hand, one of her lovers who was a senator and had been a praetor was preferentially permitted to choose exile.[18] Political rivalry among men surely was responsible for many accusations against Vestals—for example, the prosecutions of 73 B.C. linking two Vestals to Catiline and Crassus.[19] In earlier periods as well, factional rivalry provoked attacks, and thus in 114 B.C. three Vestals were accused (but only one condemned) by the chief pontiff. A tribune—a plebeian magistrate—demanded a secular re-trial, and the next year the other two were condemned in turn.[20] The cult of Venus, Changer of Hearts, was reaffirmed at this time.

The lives of Vestals were severely regulated, but in some respects they were the most emancipated women in Rome. As noted in our discussions of unmarried goddesses, the most liberated females are those who are not bound to males in a permanent relationship. The emancipation of the Vestals was legal, rather than *de facto* like the emancipation of the upper-class women described in Chapter VIII. As early as the laws of the XII Tables (451–450 B.C.) it was stated that a Vestal was to be freed from the power of her *pater familias*.[21] Since a Vestal had no family for legal purposes, she could not inherit from an intestate kinsman, nor could anyone inherit from her if she died intestate. She did, on the other hand, have the right to make a will. The chief pontiff *(pontifex maximus)* chose, supervised, and some-times judged and scourged the Vestals, but he did not exercise legal guardianship *(tutela)* over them. Vestals could not be bound by oath, nor were they subject to the testamentary limitations of the Voconian Law of 169 B.C.[22] This emancipation probably evolved along principles analogous to those governing certain priests. The word *lex* ("law") is derived from *ligare* ("to bind"). Romans in the service of religion were subject to restrictions, but not the same ones that bound ordinary people.

Further evidence of the freedom from the restrictions of ordinary women is to be found in the privileges enjoyed by Vestals. They were the only women permitted to drive through the city of Rome in a *carpentum,* a two-wheeled wagon, which conferred high status on its occupant. Like magistrates, priests, and men of certain distinctions, they were preceded in the streets by a *lictor* (attendant) who cleared the way before them. When other women were relegated by Augustus to the top tiers of seats at theatrical performances and games, the Vestals retained places on the imperial podium.[23] These privileges had such implications of status that the "rights of Vestals" were often conferred upon female members of the imperial family, who were frequently portrayed as Vestals on coins.

Despite the privileges, candidates for the priestesshood became increasingly difficult to find. Vestals were traditionally recruited from the upper classes, though they were not necessarily patricians. Members of this group were relatively liberated, and probably did not wish to impose thirty years of chastity and monotonous tasks on their daughters. The penalties of scourging or death for the erring Vestal were also a deterrent. Moreover, upper-class families were small, and a daughter might make the difference between the survival or extinction of a family line. Fathers were so reluctant to offer their daughters that Augustus cleverly and paradoxically, as an incentive to increase the birthrate, exempted the father of three children from this obligation.[24] He also reduced the requirements for eligibility so that the daughters of freedmen could be enrolled,[25] although this was never necessary, for during the Empire the chief pontiff, who was in charge of enrolling Vestals, was usually the emperor himself, and few dared oppose him.

## A Goddess of Birth and Death

The priestesses of Ceres were the only women besides Vestals who had the prestigious duty of administering a state cult.

Ceres was an agricultural divinity whose name shows the same root as the Latin verbs *creare* and *cresco,* meaning "to produce" and "to grow." Thus Ceres was an important goddess in earliest Rome, when the principal occupation was farming and religion was devoted to agrarian prosperity. The goddess Tellus (Mother Earth) was closely associated with Ceres in the realm of agriculture, and both goddesses were especially concerned with the production of grain.

Ceres and Tellus were concerned with human fecundity as well as the productivity of the fields. Both were goddesses of marriage, for it is clear that the chief objective of marriage was procreation. Thus brides, who would be thought at fault if the marriage proved sterile, customarily honored Ceres and Tellus. There was also a tradition that Ceres protected wives, since the laws attributed to Romulus by Plutarch state that if a husband divorces his wife for any reason other than poisoning his children, counterfeiting his keys, or adultery, half his property will belong to his wife and the other half be consecrated to Ceres, and that whoever puts away his wife must make a sacrifice to the infernal deities.

The passage in Plutarch shows that Ceres was even more protective of wives than has been thought hitherto. The husband who "puts away his wife" is to be interpreted as one who not merely repudiates but actually sells her, and capital punishment was his penalty. The husband who sold his wife was himself consecrated to the infernal deities, and this consecration, it is to be understood, was normally followed by execution. That husbands might well have sold wives may only be inferred from the fact that they did sell their children into slavery in the days of the XII Tables.[26] A wife, of course, when she had entered into the kind of marriage that put her in the legal position of "daughter" to her husband, could theoretically be sold.

Ceres was associated with death as well as fertility, for the dead are returned to the earth. On the human level, as noted above in Chapters III and V, the female is particularly concerned with preparing and mourning the corpse; one is born of woman and on dying returns to woman. Following a death in a Roman family a sow was sacrificed to Ceres. Moreover, in public cult, Ceres was the guardian of the dead. Sacred to the goddess was the pit in the earth *(mundus Cereris)* considered to be the passageway to the underworld. This pit was uncovered three times annually to permit the spirits of the dead to visit the living. The pit was divided into two sections, and may have been used also for storing seed-grain.[27]

In 496 B.C. Rome had suffered a famine, and after consultation with prophecies collected in the Sibylline books, it was agreed to try to win the favor of the goddess of the growth of grain by building a temple for her. The temple was dedicated on the lower slopes of the Aventine in 493 B.C. In this temple, Ceres was associated with Liber and Libera, who were male and female spirits of fecundity, alluding to the sexual aspect of fertility. From earliest times the cult of Ceres had been administered by a priest *(flamen Cerialis)*, and owing to the conservatism of Roman religion, the *flamen*'s ministration continued. But with the founding of the temple on the Aventine, plebeian magistrates known as aediles also became important in supervising the cult. The temple proclaimed a victory of the plebeians, for the sphere of the aediles was political as well as religious, and the temple became a center of plebeian political activity. Ceres of the Aventine thus remained a goddess of grain, but her primary concern was with the seasonal yield of the earth *(annona)* for the feeding of all social classes in an urban population. The aediles supervised the provision and distribution of grain. Not only aediles but other politicians as well recognized that attention to the supply and free distributions of grain was a means of winning popular support, and the portrait of Ceres on their coins proclaimed their allegiance to the popular cause.

Rome's expansion brought her into contact with other religions, and in the case of Ceres, the Italian goddess was assimilated to the Greek Demeter. The old cult of Ceres was not eradicated; the *flamen* and aediles continued to function, and time-honored rituals such as tying lighted torches to the tails of foxes that were let loose in the Circus Maximus continued long after any observer understood their meaning. But in the second half of the third century B.C., Greek accretions were adopted with the endorsement of the state. The earliest mention of the enactment of these rites occurs in the description of events following the disastrous battle at Cannae, when it was questionable whether the annual rites of Ceres could be celebrated, for those polluted by death could not participate, and every Roman matron had been bereaved (see p. 177).

The cult of the Hellenized Ceres was exclusively in the hands of women. Greek priestesses were brought from Naples or Veleia (Elea) to supervise the new cult. These priestesses were granted Roman citizenship and held positions of prestige. Myths and rites surrounding Demeter were attributed to Ceres. Liber and Libera, who had been associated with Ceres in the earlier cult, were supplanted by Proserpina, the Romans' name for Persephone, daughter of Demeter. The central myth was the rape and marriage of Proserpina, the mourning of Ceres, and the joyous reunion of mother and daughter. The Roman rites, consisting of an annual celebration *(sacrum anniversarium Cereris)* and Mysteries *(initia Cereris)*, were reminiscent of the Thesmophoria and the Eleusinian Mysteries at Athens, discussed in Chapter IV. Like other all-female celebrations, they were not much described in literature, and in any case Mysteries were not to be divulged; therefore the details are far from clear. However, we do know that there were preliminary rites of purification and abstinence. Matrons and virgins participated in reenacting the myth; perhaps the matrons played the part of Ceres, and the virgins represented Proserpina. The sow, a prolific animal, was sacred to both Ceres and Demeter, and thus formed part of a ritual sacrifice. The ceremonies also included offering shoots of grain woven into wreaths and garlands.

Unlike the Eleusinian Mysteries, those of Ceres excluded men and people of low birth. The cult of the Greek god Bacchus at Rome had also once been exclusively female; when men were admitted, debauchery ensued. A national scandal had resulted, requiring the execution of thousands of participants, and a senatorial decree made it virtually impossible for men to attend Bacchanalia thereafter (186 B.C.). With this precedent, the Mysteries of Ceres at Rome remained confined to women, and for this reason they never attained the prominence of those at Eleusis. Moreover, as Cyril Bailey wrote, "[It was not] till the oriental cults came into prominence that the mystery-idea obtained any real hold on the Roman world. Possibly the vague hopes of immortality suggested in the Greek mysteries appealed less to the practical Roman than the surer promise of the oriental cults.[28]

## Sovereign Isis: The Loving Mother

The cult of Isis was one of the many Oriental mystery religions that stand in dramatic contrast to the traditional cults of Roman religion. The foreign cult of the Greek goddess Demeter had been easily accepted by the Romans, who assimilated her to their own goddess Ceres. The cult of Ceres and some Fortuna cults were controllable, for they were confined to female devotees. Likewise, the cults of Ceres, Fortuna, and the Vestals were entwined with the interests of the state, rather than directed toward the benefit of particular individuals. The cult of Isis is unlike the others we have discussed. Through it the religious and emotional needs of women and men of the Hellenistic and Roman worlds could be expressed and satisfied. Isis met with official resistance from the Romans, but ended by having a larger sphere of influence in religious ideas than any of the cults we have previously considered.[29]

Isis was a national divinity of ancient Egypt dating back at least to 2500 B.C., but she was a goddess with accretions of myths and rituals of many lands by the time she reached the shores of Italy at the end of the second century B.C. The cult of Isis had spread throughout the Mediterranean world, and easily adapted itself wherever it was carried. Unlike Roman cults, in which the details of worship and the categories of worshipers were rigidly prescribed, that of Isis was capable of unlimited flexibility. The goddess readily encompassed inconsistencies and mutually contradictory qualities. Thus she was identified with many other Mediterranean goddesses ranging from Astarte of Phoenicia, to Fortuna, Athena, Aphrodite, Hestia, Hera, Demeter, and Artemis. She was endowed with magical capabilities, could heal the sick, and promised blessed resurrection to her devotees after death.

Even more remarkable than her assimilation of the powers of female deities is Isis' acquisition of powers associated in the classical world with male divinities. She has the attributes traditionally assigned to the Indo-European sky god: dominion over lightning, thunder, and the winds. She is the creator, for she divided earth from heaven, assigned languages to nations, and invented alphabets and astronomy. Aretalogies surviving from antiquity give long lists of the attributes of the goddess; her epithets are innumerable, her powers limitless.

Owing to the influence of her worshipers in port cities such as Alexandria, Isis became a patroness of navigation and commerce. Her cult lent itself as well to philosophical interpretations. Plutarch explains the creativity of Isis with citations from Plato's *Timaeus,* and writes that the power of Isis "is concerned with matter which becomes and receives everything: light and dark, day and night, fire and water, life and death, beginning and end." [30] Thus Isis could be all things to all people, a quality that greatly enhanced her popularity. She was a single supreme goddess behind many manifestations; the prerogatives of other goddesses accrued to her, and she was worshiped in varying ways, but she remained Isis. In this sense her religion was henotheistic, but her worshipers were pagan and polytheistic, for they did not deny the existence of other divinities. An inscription found in Capua erected by a Roman senator described Isis succinctly as "you who are one and all" *("te tibi una quae es omnia dea Isis").*[31] But in her omnipotence she was not threatening, for she was loving and merciful.

The impressive history of the expansion of the cult both before and after it migrated to Italy has been traced in detail by the meticulous study of archaeological and inscriptional evidence. However, examining the cult from the viewpoint of women's history allows new questions to be posed relating to women's role in the religion, the emotional appeal of a supreme female divinity, and the ascendancy of a mother goddess at a particular point of Roman history.

The worshipers of Isis were everywhere, of all ages and both sexes. The only segment of society where Isis did not attract devotees was the Roman army, for whom the masculine god Mithras held more appeal. By contrast, the cult of Isis was especially attractive to women. Isis was a wife and mother, but she had also been a whore. Respectable women as well as prostitutes could identify with her. Isis also elevated the status of women. Male deities were sometimes worshiped in her temples, but in the Hellenistic and Roman worlds Isis was supreme among the Egyptian gods. Diodorus Siculus reported that because of the example of Isis, the Egyptian queens had more honor than the kings, and that among commoners the wives ruled the husbands.[32] No doubt the example of the domination of Cleopatra over Antony was fresh in the mind of Diodorus, who wrote in the time of Caesar and Augustus. Equality rather than domination is mentioned in a long hymn to Isis dating from the second century A.D. found in Oxyrhynchus, Egypt, which includes in its praises of the goddess that "she made the power of women equal to that of men." [33]

However, the worship of Isis was by no means confined to women. Like the Mysteries of Demeter and Persephone at Eleusis, those of Isis appealed to men as well. There were also Mysteries of male gods; in paganism it was possible to have one's choice. It may be suggested that one specific avenue of appeal that a loving maternal divinity held within a rigid patriarchal society was that she was accessible to entreaty—she could be yielding and merciful.

The intimate nature of the relationship between goddess and devotee is palpably expressed by Isidorus of the Fayum in one of his hymns written in the early first century B.C. He asks, "Share your gifts with me . . . your suppliant: fortune, and especially the blessing of children." Below his signature as author, Isidorus ingenuously adds a postscript: "The gods, hearing my prayers and hymns, have granted me the blessing of great happiness." Doubtless his prayer for a child had been answered. Like other aretalogies of Isis, the four hymns of Isidorus show the personal relationship of the poet to the goddess. Besides listing the repetitive motifs and conventionalized epithets of Greek hymns, the worshiper simply defines those qualities of the goddess that have special meaning to him.[34]

The story of the spiritual conversion of Lucius, told by Apuleius in the novel *The Golden Ass,* or *Metamorphoses,* in the second century A.D., illustrates on a larger scale the tenderness and closeness of Isis, and the love Lucius gave her in return. Lucius, a young man of a good family, meddled with the magic of Thessalian witches and was changed accidentally into an ass. He retained his human perceptions, and suffered vicissitudes, many of which included lewd and humiliating incidents, until, at last, by the agency of Isis, he was restored to human form. Isis visited him personally in dreams and invited him to be initiated into her Mysteries and to vow his life to her service. It is clear that the devotee had a private relationship with the goddess, and the worship of Isis suited the individualism of the Hellenistic and Roman worlds. Individuals were responsible for their own acts; they could be initiated, rewarded, forgiven, and granted eternal salvation. In contrast, traditional Roman religion was based on a communal responsibility, in which the unchastity of one Vestal jeopardized the entire population, while the expiation of her transgression would restore the favor of the gods to all.

The central myth of the Isis cult combines peculiarly Egyptian antecedents with Greco-Roman elements. According to one version, Isis and her brother Osiris had loved one another even within their mother's womb. Their marriage provided the paradigm for the brother–sister marriages common among Egyptian rulers. But Osiris, commonly identified with the sun, was killed and dismembered by his brother Set, god of darkness. Isis mourned and searched for the fragments of Osiris' body, and through her agency he was restored to life. But before his resuscitation Isis bore a child, and thus she is often depicted in visual representations nursing a baby. These portraits have led to comparisons between Isis with her infant Horus and the Virgin Mary with the baby Jesus. However, while Christian theologians held up Mary as a model of virginal maternity, the child Horus was clearly seen in the cult of Isis as being the offspring of his parents' union. The Isis myth also relates that when she searched for the pieces of Osiris' body, she failed to recover his phallus. Perhaps to compensate for that critical loss, Osiris is often represented as a phallus.

The emotional appeal of a divinity who has herself suffered such inestimable loss is undeniable. Worshipers could feel sympathy for and closeness to Isis, while they experienced only awe and fear in their distant relationships with most of the Olympian deities. Moreover, the worshiper could readily identify with Osiris—as Osiris suffered death and was born again, so the devotee of Isis could anticipate his own renewal after death. This appeal must have been especially potent among the most wretched members of society. Women were attracted, too, to the promises of exotic religions, as Juvenal disparagingly pointed out in his diatribe on women:

And watch out for a woman who's a religious fanatic: in the summer, she'll fill the house with a coven of worshipers of strange oriental deities. Their minister will be a weird apparition, an enormous obscene eunuch, revered because he castrated himself with a jagged hunk of glass. He'll use his prophetic powers and solemnly intone the usual warning:

> "Beware the Ides of September!
> Beware the arrival of December!
> Protect yourself! pledge me one
> hundred eggs and a warm woolen cloak."

He claims that whatever dangers threaten will be absorbed by the cloak and promises protection for the coming year.

In the middle of winter, at dawn, she'll go down to the Tiber, break through the ice, and piously immerse herself three times to purify her body, and then she'll crawl on her bleeding knees halfway across Rome—to atone for having slept with her husband the night before: this is the ritual prescribed by the deity in favor *this* month. If some Egyptian goddess instructs her to make a pilgrimage to the Nile, she'll leave at once, follow the river to its source, and return with a phial of sacred water to sprinkle on the temple (which, as you can see, desecrates one of our oldest historical landmarks). She actually believes that Isis speaks to her! As if any god would bother to talk with such a fool.

Women like this revere any Egyptian priest who cons his followers with elaborate rituals and meaningless taboos. He has them convinced that he has the power to obtain forgiveness for their sins. If they fail to abstain from marital relations on holy days, or if they owe a penance for violating the goddess' prohibitions, the goddess will reveal her displeasure by shaking her head; the priest, in tears, mumbling an empty litany, will intercede with the gods so that Osiris, bribed by a fat goose and a piece of cake, will forgive them.[35]

Eroticism and asceticism were mingled in the cult. Isis herself was said to have been a prostitute in Tyre for ten years, and the phallic representation of Osiris has already been noted. Her temples were located near brothels and marketplaces, and they had a reputation for being meeting places for prostitutes. There is a long history of official suspicion of sexual license in secret societies and mystery religions. Among the Romans, the scandals of the Bacchanalia provide the obvious example. Among the Greeks, the behavior of Pentheus, king of Thebes, at the coming of Dionysus can be cited. As Euripides dramatized the myth in the *Bacchae,* the women of Thebes followed Dionysus into the countryside, and Pentheus suspected that the new religion provided an excuse for sexual misconduct. The suspicion of the Romans was well founded; Pentheus' was not, at least in the Euripidean play. Nevertheless, the association of Dionysus with sexual license is clear from the vase paintings, from the god's entourage of satyrs and nymphs, and from the literary evidence of Euripides in the *Ion* and *Phoenician Women.* But the mystery cults also offered ample opportunity for abstinence, both from certain foods and from sexual intercourse, forever or for a limited period. A woman could devote herself to perpetual virginity in the service of Isis, and the elegiac poet Propertius complained of loneliness when his beloved Cynthia spent ten nights in the goddess' ceremonials.[36]

Social pleasure and sensual gratification were among the rewards of the devotees of Isis. Magnificent processions of worshipers and professional priests garbed in white linen proceeded to the edge of the sea to launch a sacred boat, accompanied by the rattle of the sistrum and the music of the flute. This ceremony was called the Navigium Isidis, and took place on March 5 to inaugurate the season of navigation. The rite was more purposeful to the businessman than the agrarian-based rituals of Roman religion, while to an urban population it assured the protection of ships laden with grain from the provinces of the Empire, in particular from Egypt. Also of major importance were the Mysteries at which the worshipers reenacted the lamentation of Isis and her subsequent joy when she found the body of Osiris. Here the rite of Isis is directly parallel to the Eleusinian Mysteries at Athens: empathy with the woman who lost what was dear to her and found it again. At this time the devotees of Isis exchanged embraces, danced in the streets, and invited strangers to dinner parties.[37]

For slaves and freedmen and anyone who lacked a family, the

conviviality of the cult was attractive. The social order was precious to Romans, but disregarded by Isis; her cult was open to all. There was a professional body of male priests, but others, both men and women, could hold high office within the cult. Of twenty-six functionaries termed minister *(sacerdos)* in extant inscriptions of Italy, six are women, including one woman of senatorial rank and one daughter of a freedman.[38] Frescoes of Herculaneum and Pompeii portray women participating fully in the ceremonies. In contrast, the state religion of Rome traditionally excluded slaves, freedmen, and of course women—with the exception of a few, including the six Vestals and two priestesses of Ceres—from its hierarchy, while those who did participate were carefully organized into separate categories.

Those Romans who idealized their traditional way of life nursed a hostility against foreigners and secret societies, fearing that their activities might erupt in antisocial behavior. No wonder that congregations such as those worshiping Isis could be considered potentially revolutionary, especially since so many votaries were those who had little stake in the perpetuation or revival of Roman traditions; worshipers were not viewed as part of a societal or governmental whole and, as we have noted, the cult was oriented to the well-being of the individual.

The worship of Isis can be traced in Italy during the late second and early first centuries B.C. in Pompeii, Herculaneum, and the Greek cities of Campania, and a college of the priests of Isis was founded at Rome in the time of Sulla.[39] Women as well were strong influences in the establishment of the cult. Nearly one-third of the devotees named in inscriptions in Italy are female.[40] It is likely that the establishment of the cult was promoted by the agency of Oriental slaves and freedmen, a number of whom were prosperous businessmen. Some slaves converted their owners, but even after it spread to the upper classes the Isis cult never abandoned its associations with the lowly members of society.

Egypt and her deities were anathema to Rome. Five times during the late Republic the shrines of Isis were ordered torn down. In 50 B.C., when no workmen could be found to carry out the order, the consul himself took an ax and began the destruction.[41] In 43 B.C. there was a temporary respite when the triumvirs, in a bid for popular support, ordered that a temple be built for Isis, but whether this temple was erected is not known.[42]

The hostility to Egypt was intensified by the confrontation

between Cleopatra and Antony on the one hand, and Octavian on the other. Cleopatra was Isis incarnate. Octavian had seen Cleopatra, and had viewed Egypt. He recognized the lure that had turned Antony into a "slave of withered eunuchs." [43] In 28 B.C. the triumphant Octavian, who became Augustus, forbade the building of temples to Isis within the boundaries of the city (the *pomerium*), and seven years later the prohibited territory was extended to the area close to the city of Rome. He intended thus to deprive the goddess of her worshipers, of whom the urban population constituted a large part. It is well known that in his settlement of Egypt, Augustus, for political and economic reasons, kept the country as a private possession, not to be administered like the other provinces of the Empire. There were moral reasons as well: Isis, like Cleopatra, was seductive. The gods of Egypt threatened to undermine the new moral foundations of society which Augustus hoped to establish by legislation. From this vantage point, it may be suggested that Augustus might have been more successful if instead of requesting sophisticated women to worship archaic abstractions of female virtues, he had co-opted the cult of Isis and exploited her as an example of a faithful wife and loving mother.

The antagonism of Augustus was continued by Tiberius, under whose reign the priests of Isis were persecuted. The ostensible cause was a scandal arising from an assignation between Paulina, an upper-class matron, and an equestrian, Decius Mundus. The priests of Isis arranged for the couple to meet in their temple, telling the woman that the Egyptian god Anubis wished to have intercourse with her. For this deceit they were paid handsomely by Decius Mundus, who impersonated the god. This incident suggests that the popularity of the goddess among the upper classes was increasing, since it was not unusual for a woman of high station to visit a temple of Isis. Mundus was exiled under the adultery laws, but the persecution of the cult of Isis was far out of proportion to the crime. The priests were crucified, the rites expelled, and thousands of worshipers deported from the city of Rome. There is little doubt that Tiberius intended to totally purge Rome of the foreign goddess.[44]

The cult of Isis, like other Oriental religions, competed too successfully with the imperial revival of traditional Roman religion. Isis was too popular to suppress. Instead, Romans and then Christians adopted elements of her cult, choosing to subordinate her power to the traditional abstract ideals of virginity, marriage, and motherhood. Perhaps it was Caligula who first decided to take advantage of the popularity that might accrue to an emperor who favored Isis. A temple was erected in the Campus Martius, and most of the successive Roman emperors continued to support the goddess.[45] By the second century A.D., magistrates and other functionaries of high status were establishing honorific monuments to Isis.[46]

The worship of Isis apparently developed among those who had little stake in the rewards of a religion based either on male dominance or on class stratification. Egypt, where the cult was born, was a land in which women are known to have enjoyed high status. The cult then migrated in the Hellenistic period through the Mediterranean world settled by the Greeks. There are strong indications that there were fewer restraints on Greek women in this Hellenistic world than there had been during the Classical period. The two most influential Greek women of the Hellenistic period—Arsinoë II and Cleopatra—interestingly enough considered themselves to be incarnations of the goddess. Further, some conclusion must be drawn from the fact that the establishment of the cult of Isis in Italy in the late Republic coincided with the growing emancipation of women. The cult continued to blossom among the Romans, especially those women and men who did as they pleased despite official prohibitions.

But Isis was not universally popular. One of her strongest rivals was Mithras, a male god whose worship was confined exclusively to men. The cult of Mithras stressed militant and masculine qualities and, as has been noted, became a favorite among the soldiers and officers of the Roman army. In some ways the existence of Mithras fostered the femaleness of the cult of Isis: those who might have diluted or changed the cult of Isis were actually siphoned off and diverted to their own god. Thus, in Isis-worship there remained latitude for uninhibited women, such as the mistresses of elegiac poets and others who are less well known now, to become both official magistrates and common devotees.

What can be said about a world in which two vastly different godheads—Mithras and Isis—were simultaneously popular, and in which the Mysteries of both this god and goddess and many competing cults, including Judaism and Christianity, could offer comparable promises of blessed immortality?

We must return to the speculations raised at the close of the first chapter of this book on the role of mother goddesses as a determinant of women's status in society. There is little information for prehistory—in fact, some deny that mother goddesses ever existed or were prevalent—but much more is known about the societies in which the historical Isis was worshiped. Certainly neither Greece nor Rome in historical times was a matriarchy; yet the growth of the cult was apparently greatest where some women, at least, attained a measure of emancipation. However, the strength of Isis in historical times could scarcely have any implications for prehistory, whether in support or denial of a theory of matriarchy. The external differences between the early culture and the sophisticated worlds of the Greeks and Romans were so vast as to militate against drawing parallels. That religious and social history repeated itself would be a remarkable coincidence, and it is not profitable to speculate on it. The most that can be proposed in this vein is that the human female has consistently evoked—at least among some elements of given societies—a psychological response with religious implications that transcend the varying statuses of mortal women at particular eras of history.

What is of more interest in a way is the adherence of men to the cult. The hymns of Isidorus and the conclusion of *The Golden Ass* show that the relationship of the male to the mother figure is very pronounced. In psychological terms, the appeal of Isis is comprehensible: in an age of unrest the yearning for total maternal protection is indeed a basic impulse. It is uncertain whether any true idea of equality for women would inevitably emerge in such circumstances, for the adoration of female divinities has not improved the circumstances of the women who worship them, nor has it raised mortal women in the eyes of the men who cultivate them.

In this respect Isis was different from other mother goddesses. She did stand for the equality of women, and one cannot help wondering about the nature of the subsequent history of Western women if the religion of Isis had been triumphant.

# EPILOGUE: THE ELUSIVE WOMEN
# OF CLASSICAL ANTIQUITY

In 18 B.C. according to the historian Cassius Dio there were more upper-class men than women.[1] Such is my perception of the ratio of males to females, not only in the Roman upper class in the days of Augustus, but, with few exceptions, in all social strata throughout classical antiquity.

A selection from the crude and haphazard data of various periods and places in antiquity shows that males outnumbered females by at least two to one. These are the sex ratios to be deduced from the funerary artifacts of the Dark Age and Archaic period, the prosopographical studies of propertied families in Classical Athens, sepulchral inscriptions of slaves and freedmen in the early Empire, and the list of children receiving the alimentary fund at Veleia.

Were there actually fewer females than males in antiquity, or is the apparent disproportion between the sexes illusory? Demographers point out that when a census is taken in an underdeveloped country, women are not adequately counted. Certainly statistics cannot be based on the sort of evidence cited here. Demography, in any case, is a dangerous field, and it would be incautious to argue that the disproportion between men and women was as vast as our evidence indicates. Either women were underenumerated when living and undercommemorated after death to an extent that can only be described as startling, or there actually were fewer women than men, or both of these factors operated simultaneously.

If, following years of civil war and proscriptions—when far more men than women were killed and, in the aftermath of war, huge contingents of veterans were exported as colonists—as Cassius Dio records, there were still more men than women at Rome, then it is likely that in periods of peace the disproportion between the sexes was even greater.

There can be little doubt that female infanticide was practiced, apparently more in Hellenistic than in Classical Greece; the parents' financial situation and the general political climate probably were the major determinants in deciding whether infant girls would be raised. Moreover, poor health resulting from a diet inferior to that accorded boys—as indicated by the writings of Xenophon, the Persepolis inscriptions, and the discriminatory alimentary allotments at Rome—followed by childbearing at an immature age, resulted in women's life expectancy being shorter than men's by five to ten years. If fewer female infants were raised, and if women's lives were shorter, the result would inevitably manifest itself in a disproportionate sex ratio.

Certainly the attitude of ancient society toward the relative importance of the activities of men and women was such that most women were less likely to be described by ancient historians or to be commemorated by enduring sepulchral monuments. The glaring exception to undercommemoration is noted by Keith Hopkins, who points out that, among women whose ages are recorded on their tombstones, wives who died in their childbearing years and predeceased their husbands are more likely than other women to be commemorated. We tend to forget that—despite a dazzling veneer of literary and artistic achievements—Greece and Rome were warrior societies. What really mattered, even to the Athenians, the most intellectual of all, was winning wars and maintaining an empire, along with the training that was an essential prerequisite for these goals. Except in their role as bearers of future soldiers, most women were peripheral to these concerns.

The women who are known to us are those who influenced matters of interest to men. Most is known—on the lowest level of society—about prostitutes, and—on the highest level—about women who played a role in politics: Hellenistic queens and those Roman women who asserted themselves in traditionally masculine spheres of activity. The names of a few poetesses have been immortalized but, for the majority of them, little remains beyond their names and the comments of later critics. It is no surprise that the only woman in antiquity who could be the subject of a full-length biography is Cleopatra. Yet, unlike Alexander, whom she rivals as the theme of romance and legend, Cleopatra is known to us through overwhelmingly hostile sources. The reward of the "good" woman in Rome was likely to be praise in stereotyped phrases; in Athens she won oblivion.

In contrast to the scarcity of reliable historical information about women are the abundant portrayals of women in art and literature, from the Neolithic figurines and nameless mourners and flute girls depicted on pottery to the well-known heroines of tragedy and the fictionalized mistresses of elegiac poets. It would appear that in Classical Athens, where respectable women were ideally in little evidence, artists were most prolific and inventive in creating them. Banished from participation in men's lives, women returned to haunt men's imaginations, dreams, and nightmares. Poets, Athenian and otherwise, were not uniformly misogynistic, and the literary portraits of women, even when monstrous, show self-assertion, self-esteem, dignity, and rage at injustice—and not all of them were monstrous. I can think of no other literature in which women are such compelling figures, beginning with Andromache and Penelope. These Galateas are so seductive that scholars have chosen to pursue them with greater zeal than they display in their attempts to study flesh-and-blood women: no one yet has adequately explained the relationship between, for example, the heroines of epic or Athenian drama and the women who were living contemporaries of the poets. It may be that the gulf between fact and fiction was so broad and the relationship so obscure that it is not to be perceived from this vantage point.

In this account I have attempted to find out about the realities of women's existence in the ancient world rather than concentrate on the images that men had of women. Yet to compose a polemic against the men of Greece and Rome and to write a brief in defense of their women are not the proper objectives of a historian. Nor would it be defensible to pronounce a verdict based on modern preferences, noting that although the basic patriarchal power structure was similar in Greece and Rome, Roman women appear to have led more satisfying lives as a result of the deepening of the marriage relationship and the transference of the possibilities of the finer kind of love from homosexual to heterosexual relationships. I hope I may be forgiven for suggesting that the modern woman would have felt more at home among the Romans, since despite the perspective of some 2,000 years the women of classical antiquity evoke an emotional response. For the ancient views of women, as well as what can be determined about their actual lives, remain valid paradigms for the modern world.

To redress the balance, something can be said in favor of the men of classical antiquity. The Greeks were the first we know of to consider and question women's role. This did not happen in other societies at the time or indeed much later. Whether they took actual notice of the women around them as they formulated their theories is debatable. The product is a variegated fabric so finely woven that we cannot tell how much to attribute to the living women of the period and how much is due to men's imagination.

A chasm gapes between the beastlike women in the verses of Semonides and the female watchdogs of Plato's *Republic;* yet, upon closer analysis, the attitudes of one of the most celebrated misogynists and one of the greatest philogynists of antiquity show more similarities than differences. Even Plato—of ancient authors one of the most sympathetic to women—found that the one sex was in general inferior to the other, although he allowed for exceptions. Plato had strayed far from the mainstream of Greek thought. The views of Aristotle were more representative: he elucidated in detail the range of woman's inferiority, from her passive role in procreativity to her limited capacity for mental activity. Serious intellectual thought about women continued: Stoicism, the most popular of the Hellenistic and Roman philosophies, directed women's energies to marriage and motherhood. The argumentation is brilliant and difficult to refute. And this rationalized confinement of women to the domestic sphere, as well as the systematization of anti-female thought by poets and philosophers, are two of the most devastating creations in the classical legacy.

# NOTES

For a bibliographical survey of modern scholarship on Greek and Roman women, see Sarah B. Pomeroy, "Selected Bibliography on Women in Antiquity."

## Introduction

1. M. I. Rostovtzeff, *Greece*, p. 176.

## Chapter I

1. The subject matter of mythology is vast and can be interpreted from numerous traditional and iconoclastic viewpoints. A valuable guide to literature on mythology is John Peradotto, *Classical Mythology*. For a possible psychoanalytic interpretation of some of the motifs, see Philip Slater, *The Glory of Hera*.

2. On Pandora, see D. and E. Panofsky, *Pandora's Box;* for an interpretation of Pandora differing from my own, see Frederick Brenk, "Hesiod: How Much a Male Chauvinist?"

3. Hes. *Theog.* 585–602; *Op.* 53–82. (Abbreviations follow the *Oxford Classical Dictionary*, 2d ed.) Translated by Judith Peller Hallett.

4. Hom. *Od.* 22. 205–10. Cf. 1. 105; 2. 401.

5. Helene Deutsch, *The Psychology of Women*, p. 292.

6. Hom. *Od.* 1. 275–78; 13. 379–82.

7. *Homeric Hymn* 5: "To Aphrodite." 24–32.

8. Hes. *Theog.* 188–92.

9. Pl. *Sym.* 180D–81.

10. Hes. *Theog.* 929–32; Hom. *Il.* 1. 590–94; 18. 394–99.

11. Dem. 59. 118–22.

12. Aesch. *PV* 901–6.

13. Eur. *Ion* 437–52. All citations from Euripides are according to the line numbers

in the Oxford Classical Texts, vols. 1–3, edited by Gilbert Murray (Oxford: Clarendon Press, 1902–13).

14. E.g., George Derwent Thomson, *The Prehistoric Aegean*.

15. Hom. *Il.* 6, 24; *Od.* 4, 6–8, 13.

16. Peter J. Ucko, *Anthropomorphic Figurines of Predynastic Egypt and Neolithic Crete*, p. 316.

17. M. I. Finley, "Archaeology and History."

18. E.g., Jacquetta Hawkes, *Dawn of the Gods*, p. 6.

19. Erich Neumann, *The Great Mother*. For a Freudian interpretation of the pathological relations between the Athenian mother and son, see Slater, *op. cit.*

20. See my article "A Classical Scholar's Perspective on Matriarchy."

## Chapter II

1. Hom. *Il.* 3. 156–60.

2. For an extensive bibliography on women in Homer, see Kaarle Hirvonen, *Matriarchal Survivals and Certain Trends in Homer's Female Characters*, pp. 198–209.

3. Hdt. 2. 112–20.

4. Thuc. 1. 9.

5. Hom. *Od.* 6. 180–85.

6. Hom. *Od.* 16. 77; 16. 391–92; 20. 335; 21. 161–62. Also, Finley, "Marriage, Sale and Gift in the Homeric World," and W. K. Lacey, "Homeric *Hedna* and Penelope's *Kurios.*"

7. Hom. *Il.* 9. 336; 9. 340–43; 9. 663–65; 19. 295–99.

8. Hom. *Il.* 9. 393–400.

9. Hom. *Od.* 8. 19; 15. 226–40.

10. Hom. *Od.* 6. 280–84.

11. Hom. *Il.* 22. 477–515.

12. Hom. *Od.* 11. 427–34. Cf. 3. 272.

13. Thuc. 1. 1–12.

14. Hom. *Od.* 6. 303–15.

15. Hom. *Od.* 7. 68.

16. Hom. *Il.* 6. 397; 6. 425; Pomeroy, "Andromache and the Question of Matriarchy."

17. Hom. *Il.* 3. 189; 6. 186.

18. Hdt. 4. 110–17.

19. Hom. *Il.* 1. 113–15.

20. Hom. *Il.* 2. 355–56.

21. Hom. *Il.* 1. 113–15; 23. 263; 23. 704–5; *Od.* 7. 8–11.

22. Hom. *Il.* 6. 425–28.

23. See Michael Ventris and John Chadwick, *Documents in Mycenaean Greek*, *passim.*

24. Laertes: Hom. *Od.* 1. 429–33; 19. 482–89. Megapenthes: *Od.* 4. 10–14. Eurycleia: *Od.* 4. 743–46; 19. 350–56; 19. 467–92.

25. Hom. *Od.* 6. 18–19; 6. 273–74; 19. 527.

26. Hom. *Il.* 16. 175–92.

27. Hom. *Il.* 9. 452–56.

28. Hom. *Od.* 14. 199–212.

29. Hom. *Od.* 1. 356.

30. Hom. *Od.* 11. 197–203.

31. Hom. *Il.* 22. 79–83; 24. 212–13.

32. Telemachus: Hom. *Od.* 16. Orestes: *Od.* 3. 306–12.

33. Hom. *Il.* 22. 105–10.

34. Hom. *Od.* 23. 232–40.

35. Hom. *Il.* 6. 410; 19. 287.

36. Hom. *Il.* 6. 490–93. Cf. *Od.* 1. 356–57.

37. Hom. *Od.* 7. 103; 22. 420–23.

38. Hom. *Od.* 7. 233–36.

39. Calypso: Hom. *Od.* 5. 265. Polycaste: *Od.* 3. 464–66. Helen: *Od.* 4. 252.

40. F. F. J. Tritsch, "The Women of Pylos"; Ventris and Chadwick, *op. cit., passim;* L. R. Palmer, *The Interpretation of Mycenaean Greek Texts*, pp. 96, 98.

41. Hom. *Il.* 18. 514–15.

42. Hom. *Il.* 22. 126–28.

## Chapter III

1. Libanius 12. 60. 387.

2. Jean Rougé, "La colonisation grecque et les femmes." Miletus: Hdt. 1. 146. Cyrene: Hdt. 4. 153; 4. 186. Cf. Hdt. 4. 108 for peaceful marriages.

3. On the marriage of tyrants, see Louis Gernet, *Anthropologie de la Grèce antique*, pp. 344–59.

4. Hdt. 6. 126–31.

5. Pisistratus: Plut. *Mor.* 189c, 457f; Val. Max. 5. 1. *ext.* 2. Periander: Ath. 13. 589f.; Hdt. 3. 50; 5. 92.

6. Theog. 185–91.

7. On Sparta, see H. Michell, *Sparta*, for the fullest documentation of ancient sources; also, Lacey, *The Family in Classical Greece*, pp. 194–208, and W. G. Forrest, *A History of Sparta*.

8. Plut. *Lycurgus* 27.

9. Xen. *Const. Lacedaemonians* 3.

10. Jean Charbonneaux, *Archaic Greek Art*, p. 145.

11. Hdt. 5. 88.

12. Plut. *Lycurgus* 3. 3.

13. Arist. *Pol.* 5. 6 (1306b). Cf. Strabo 6. 3. 2–3 and the intermarriage of the Scythian women with their slaves during their husbands' twenty-eight-year absence described in Hdt. 4. 1; also, the Argive women being taken over by inferiors after the disaster at Sepeia, Hdt. 6.83.

14. I owe this suggestion to W. K. Lacey, in a personal letter.

15. Ath. 13. 555c.

16. Arist. *Pol.* 2. 6. 8 (1270a).

17. Cic. *Tusculan Disputations* 2. 15. 36.

18. Forrest, *op. cit.*, pp. 134–37.

19. Plut. *Agis* 7.

20. Arist. *Pol.* 2. 6. 5–11 (1269b–1270a).

21. See R. F. Willetts, *The Law Code of Gortyn* (hereafter: *Code*), and Lacey, *Family*, pp. 208–16.

22. Arist. *Pol.* 2. 7. 5 (1272a).

23. Lacey, *Family*, p. 227 and note.

24. Strabo 10. 482.

25. *Code* 3. 40–44.

26. For an extensive survey, with bibliography, see Donna C. Kurtz and John Boardman, *Greek Burial Customs*.

27. See V. R. d'A. Desborough, *Protogeometric Pottery*, pp. 5–6; Evelyn Lord Smithson, "The Protogeometric Cemetery at Nea Ionia," p. 151. Professor Smithson, in a personal letter, disagrees with Desborough's suggestion that belly-handled amphoras were used to carry water.

28. For the Geometric period, see J. N. Coldstream, *Greek Geometric Pottery*, and Gudrun Ah!berg, *Prothesis and Ekphora in Greek Geometric Art*. Much of this data remains controversial.

29. Smithson, "The Tomb of a Rich Athenian Lady, ca. 850 B.C."

30. Hom. *Il.* 24. 720–26; *Od.* 24. 58–62. Cf. Margaret Alexiou, *The Ritual Lament in Greek Tradition*, pp. 10–14.

31. Hom. *Il.* 12. 433–35; Hes. *Op.* 602–3. Finley ("Was Greek Civilization Based on Slave Labour?" p. 53 note 4) believes that the woman referred to was a slave rather than a free laborer.

32. *Homeric Hymn* 2, 98–104.

33. J. Lawrence Angel, "Geometric Athenians," and personal letter.

34. Smithson, "Tomb."

35. Angel, "Ecology and Population in the Eastern Mediterranean," pp. 99–100.

36. K. Weiss, *Demographic Models for Anthropology*, p. 76.

37. Kurtz and Boardman, *op. cit.*, p. 222.

38. For this legislation, the date of which is disputed, see Cic. *Laws* 2. 26. 64 and G. M. A. Richter, *The Archaic Gravestones of Attica*, pp. 38–39.

39. Richter, *Korai*, p. 4.

40. Anthony E. Raubitschek, *Dedications from the Athenian Acropolis*, pp. 465–66.

41. Christine Havelock, "The Nude in Greek Art."

42. Archilochus: E. Diehl, *Anthologia Lyrica Graeca* (hereafter: Diehl), fragment 25; Semonides: Diehl, fragment 7, 65–66.

43. Hes. *Theog.* 603–12. Translated by Judith Peller Hallett.

44. Hes. *Op.* 373–75, 695–705.

45. Phocylides: Diehl, fragment 2. Bees: Arist. *Gen. An.* 10. 759–60; Virgil *Georgics* 4. 198–99.

46. Semonides: Diehl, fragment 7. Translated by Marylin Arthur.

47. Ael. *VH* 13. 25; Paus. 9. 22. 3. Corinna may have lived ca. 200 B.C.; see Denys L. Page, *Corinna*.

48. Denys L. Page, ed., *Poetae Melici Graeci*, fragment 664; *Suidas Lexicon, s.v.* "Corinna" and "Pindar."

49. Pindar *Pythian Odes* 9. 98–103.

50. See Page, *Sappho and Alcaeus*, and Mary Lefkowitz, "Critical Stereotypes and the Poetry of Sappho."

51. E. Lobel and Denys L. Page, eds., *Poetarum Lesborium Fragmenta*, fragment 31. Translated by Judith Peller Hallett..

52. Alcman, fragment 3. Translated by Judith Peller Hallett.

53. Page, *Sappho*, fragment 94 and pp. 79–80, 142–45; *olisb* in Lobel and Page, *op. cit.*, fragment 99, 5.

54. Quoted by Ath. 13. 599c = Anacreon: Diehl, fragment 5.

55. Ar. *Wasps* 1346, *Eccl.* 920, *Frogs* 1308; Pherecrates, fragment 149. However, in *Wasps*, where the context is heterosexual, *lesbizein* may make a particular reference to fellatio; these interpretations were suggested by Kenneth Dover in a personal letter.

56. Lobel and Page, *op. cit.*, fragment 132. Translated by Judith Peller Hallett.

57. Hdt. 2. 135.

58. Scholiast, on Lucian *Portraits* 18; Strabo 10. 2. 9.

59. *Palatine Anthology* 9. 506.

60. See Page, *Alcman: The Partheneion*, and C. M. Bowra, *Greek Lyric Poetry*, pp. 30–65.

61. Plut. *Lycurgus* 18.
62. Page, *Sappho*, p. 199, Cf. Ath. 13. 609e–f.
63. Diog. Laert. 1. 89. 91.

## Chapter IV

1. See the survey of discussions of status in Pomeroy, "Selected Bibliography on Women in Antiquity," pp. 140–43.
2. F. A. Wright, *Feminism in Greek Literature*, p. 1.
3. A. W. Gomme, "The Position of Women in Athens in the Fifth and Fourth Centuries B.C."
4. Moses Hadas, "Observations on Athenian Women"; H. D. F. Kitto, *The Greeks*, pp. 219–36. Cf. Charles Seltman, *Women in Antiquity*, pp. 110–11, and "The Status of Women in Athens"; and Donald C. Richter, "The Position of Women in Classical Athens," who gives a history of the controversy.
5. Lacey, *Family*, chap. 7, and Victor Ehrenberg, *The People of Aristophanes*, chap. 8.
6. Lacey, *Family*, p. 176.
7. This topic is competently surveyed by A. R. W. Harrison, *The Law of Athens*, pp. 132–38, 309–11, *et passim*, as well as by David Schaps, "Women and Property Control in Classical and Hellenistic Greece," pp. 49–83.
8. Dem. 30. 7; 57. 41.
9. Similarly, the lawgiver Charondas required that a dowry be provided for a poor *epiklēros* by her next-of-kin if he did not wish to marry her (Diod. 12. 18. 3–4).
10. Lacey, *Family*, pp. 202–3.
11. Arist. *Const. Athens* 58. 3. Cf. A. R. W. Harrison, *op. cit.*, pp. 195–96.
12. A. R. W. Harrison, *op. cit.*, pp. 30–32; Dem. 41. 4.
13. Evelyn B. Harrison, "Athena and Athens in the East Pediment of the Parthenon," p. 43 and note 134.
14. Dem. 59. 113; Men. *Dyscolus* 842–47; Ter. *Ad.* 729; Aeschines 3. 258; Plut. *Aristides* 27. 4. But cf. J. K. Davies, *Athenian Propertied Families 600–300 B.C.*, pp. 51–52, on the dowering of the daughters of Aristides. Davies, however, has a tendency to disbelieve stories about women, for example the story of the daughter of Pisistratus, who married the young man who kissed her on the street (Davies, p. 449) and the story of Socrates' marriage to Myrto (p. 52), while he finds credible the tale of the romantic connection between Solon and Pisistratus (p. 445).
15. Isae. 3. 8; 3. 36–38; 3. 78.
16. Ath. 13. 572a.
17. Plut. *Solon* 20. 4
18. Schaps, *op. cit.*, pp. 11–12, 148–49; Isae. 2. 9.
19. When the husband of Diogeiton's daughter died, he left her an inheritance which she brought to her father and he (presumably) handed over to her new husband (Lys. 32. 11–18). Likewise, the dowry of Demosthenes' widow, which was destined for Aphobus, was larger than her original one.
20. W. E. Thompson, "The Marriage of First Cousins in Athenian Society."
21. Plut. *Solon* 20. 3.
22. Lys. 1. 6.
23. Xen. *Oec.* 7. 5. Of course, these ages varied; Davies, *op. cit.*, pp. 336–37, draws attention to the short generations (ca. twenty-five years) and the long (ca. forty years) which existed simultaneously in Athens within the same social class.
24. Arist. *Hist. An.* 7. 1.(581b); *Pol.* 7. 14. 5 (1335a).
25. Dem. 30. 33; 27. 5; 30. 22; 36. 8; 57. 41. Plut. *Pericles* 34. 5–6.

26. Thompson, "Athenian Marriage Patterns: Remarriage."

27. Plut. *Alcibiades* 8. 5; Andoc. 4. 14. Cf. A. R. W. Harrison, *op. cit.*, pp. 39–44, and Eur. *Andr.* 984.

28. A. R. W. Harrison, *op. cit.*, pp. 39–44; Thompson, "Athenian Marriage Patterns," pp. 221–22.

29. Aesch. *Eum.* 658–66. Translated by Judith Peller Hallett. Cf. Arist. *Gen. An.* 1. 20 (729a).

30. Arist. *Const. Athens* 26. 4.

31. Thuc. 2. 44. 3–4.

32. Xen. *Hell.* 1. 6. 24.

33. Ar. *Lys.* 591–97.

34. Diog. Laert. 2. 26. Cf. Ath. 13. 555d–556; Aul. Gell. 15. 20. 6; A. R. W. Harrison, *op. cit.*, pp. 16–17; Contra C. Hignett, *A History of the Athenian Constitution to the End of the Fifth Century B.C.*, p. 345; H. J. Wolff, "Marriage Law in Ancient Athens," p. 85, n. 195; J. W. Fitton, "That Was No Lady, That Was..."

35. Bigamy and polygyny are often found in societies with an imbalanced sex ratio favoring women, as was likely to have been the case in wartime Athens. See M. Ember, "Warfare, Sex Ratio, and Polygyny."

36. Lys. 12–21. Cf. Dem. 59. 112–13; Hyperides 1. 13.

37. Eumelus, fragment 2, in F. Jacoby, ed., *Die Fragmente der griechischen Historiker* 2.2, p. 158 and Carystius, fragment 11, in C. Müller, ed., *Fragmenta Historicorum Graecorum* 4, p. 358. Cf. A. R. W. Harrison, *op. cit.*, p. 26.

38. D. W. Amundsen and C. J. Diers, "The Age of Menarche in Classical Greece and Rome." Presumably rags or wool were used to absorb menstrual blood. The female genitals were referred to by Aristophanes as *choiros* (pig), and he called a napkin for menstrual blood a *choirokomeion* (pigpen) (H. G. Liddell and R. Scott, eds., *A Greek-English Dictionary, s.v. choiros,* citing *Ach.* 773; *s.v.choirokomeion,* citing *Lys.* 1073). To my knowledge this is the earliest nonmedical reference to menstruation in classical literature.

39. Angel, "Paleoecology, Paleodemography, and Health," p. 29, and personal letter. A. E. Samuel, W. K. Hastings, A. K. Bowman, and R. S. Bagnall, *Death and Taxes,* pp. 11–12, have criticized Angel's work, giving, among other reasons, "that the data are few," but they do not seem to be aware of the major studies that Angel has conducted since his 1947 publication.

40. See, e.g., Thompson, "Athenian Marriage Patterns," p. 222.

41. See the survey in Norman E. Himes, *Medical History of Contraception,* Parts I and II.

42. Arist. *Pol.* 7. 14. 10 (1335b); E. Nardi, *Procurato aborto nel mondo greco romano;* W. A. Krenkel, "Erotica I: Der Abortus in der Antike."

43. On infanticide, see A. Cameron, "The Exposure of Children and Greek Ethics"; Lacey, *Family,* pp. 165–66; Ehrenberg, *op. cit.,* p. 199; A. R. W. Harrison, *op. cit.,* p. 71.

44. Isae. 11; Dem. 43. The dating of the adoption to 396 B.C. is argued by Davies, *op. cit.,* pp. 78, 82–83. Her inheritance should have facilitated finding a husband, but there is no proof that she married.

45. K. Weiss, *op. cit.,* makes it clear that this is a basic principle of population control.

46. Hignett, *op. cit.,* p. 346.

47. A. R. W. Harrison, *op. cit.,* pp. 16–17, gives the ancient evidence, but does not totally accept it.

48. J. J. B. Mulder, *Quaestiones Nonullae ad Atheniensium Matrimonium Vitamque*

*Coniugalem Pertinentes,* pp. 115–24. The families studied by Davies, *op. cit.,* likewise show a larger proportion of males than females.

49. Hdt. 5. Cf. Hes. *Op.* 519–21.
50. Hdt. 8. 40–41.
51. Thuc. 1. 10; 2. 52.
52. On women's work, see P. Herfst, *Le travail de la femme dans la Grèce ancienne.*
53. E.g., Eur. *Hel.* 329, 830; *Phoen.* 198.
54. Xen. *Mem.* 2. 7. 7–10; cf. *Oec.* 7–10.
55. Thuc. 2. 78. 3. Brides carried a pot for roasting barley, alluding to their kitchen duties (Pollux 1. 246).
56. Hdt. 6. 137.
57. Ernestine Friedl, "The Position of Women: Appearance and Reality," p. 98.
58. Xen. *Oec.* 9–10. 1.
59. J. D. Beazley, *Attic Red-figure Vase-painters,* p. 571, vase no. 73.
60. Helen McClees, *A Study of Women in Attic Inscriptions,* pp. 23, 31–32.
61. On women and property, see Schaps, *op. cit.;* A. R. W. Harrison, *op. cit.,* pp. 73 note 3, 108–9, 112–14, 141–47, 236; and the comments by G. E. M. de Ste. Croix, "Some Observations on the Property Rights of Athenian Women."
62. Lys. 13. 39–42; 32. 11–18. Dem. 36. 14; 47. 57.
63. Helen North, *Sophrosyne, passim;* Soph. *Ajax* 293; Arist. *Pol.* 1. 5. 8 (1260a); Eur. *Andr.* 364–65; *Hercules* 534–35; *Heracl.* 476–77; *Iph. Aul.* 830.
64. Thuc. 2. 45. 2.
65. Arist. *Pol.* 1. 2. 12 (1254b); 1.5 (1259–60). Arist. *Eudemian Ethics* 7. 10. 8–9 (1242a); 7. 3. 3 (1238b); 7. 5. 5 (1239b). In 1869 John Stuart Mill formulated a response to the sort of ideas about women expressed by Aristotle, in which Mill asserted that no one can know the real natures of the two sexes so long as they exist in their present relationship to each other (*On the Subjection of Women,* pp. 37–38).
66. For detailed discussions of Athenian cults, see *inter alios,* L. Farnell, *Cults of the Greek States;* L. Deubner, *Attische Feste;* M. P. Nilsson, *Geschichte der griechischen Religion.*
67. Hdt. 5. 72; 8. 41.
68. McClees, *op. cit.,* pp. 9, 36.
69. Thuc. 6. 56–58; Arist. *Const. Athens* 18.
70. C. J. Herington, *Athena Parthenos and Athena Polias,* pp. 32–33.
71. On Eleusis, see, in addition to the references cited in note 66 above, G. E. Mylonas, *Eleusis and the Eleusinian Mysteries.*
72. The priestesses of Hera at Argos were also eponymous.
73. Mylonas, *op. cit.,* p. 310.
74. In addition to the works cited in note 66 above, see Ar. *Thesm.* and Jane Harrison, *Prolegomena to the Study of Greek Religion,* pp. 120–62.
75. Isae. 6. 49–50.
76. Isae. 8. 19.
77. Isae. 3. 80.

## Chapter V

1. Pl. *Phd.* 3. 60A.
2. R. E. Wycherley, *How the Greeks Built Cities,* p. 187.
3. Dem. 24. 197.

4. Ar. *Lys.* 17–19, 880–81.

5. Arist. *Pol.* 4. 12. 9 (1300a); 6. 5. 13 (1323a); Xen. *Oec.* 7. 35–36.

6. Dem. 43. 62; Alexiou, *op. cit.,* pp. 15–22.

7. Lys. 13. 39.

8. E.g., Ehrenberg, *op. cit.,* pp. 27–28 note 2; 201. According to the *Life of Aeschylus,* probably written by Didymus in the first century B.C., women in the audience miscarried at a performance of the *Eumenides.*

9. This arrangement was peculiar to Athens, according to D. M. Robinson and J. Walter Graham, *Excavations at Olynthus 8: The Hellenic House,* pp. 167–68; but Hdt. 5. 20 describes women's quarters in the royal palace at Macedonia, and 3. 123 refers to men's quarters in the house of Polycrates. Plut. *Pelopidas* 9. 5 mentions women's quarters at Thebes.

10. Xen. *Oec.* 9. 4–5; in Dem. 47. 56, slave women live in a tower.

11. Andoc. 1. 124–27.

12. Andoc. 1. 16.

13. Lys. 3. 6–7; Dem. 47. 53.

14. Lys 1. 6–14.

15. On women's dress, see U. E. Paoli, *La donna greca nell'antichità,* pp. 13–35.

16. Xen. *Oec.* 10. 2; according to Angel, "Paleoecology," p. 29, the mean height of women was 61.5 inches and that of men 66.8 inches.

17. Ar. *Lys.* 88, 149; *Thesm.* 215–47, 538–40; Ehrenberg, *op. cit.,* pp. 34, 179. Some vase paintings show the hair.

18. Eur. *Med.* 250–51.

19. Eur. *Iph. Taur.* 1404–9.

20. Kurtz and Boardman, *op. cit.,* p. 139.

21. McClees, *op. cit.,* pp. 17–22.

22. Eur. *Alc.* 318.

23. Plut. *Lycurgus* 14; Xen. *Const. Lacedaemonians* 1. 3.

24. Richard T. Hallock, *Persepolis Fortification Tablets,* pp. 344–53, for mothers' rations (Ionian women in tablet no. 1224). I owe this reference to Ernst Badian.

25. Ar. *Lys.* 80–83.

26. Pl. *Republic* 5. 452; 5. 460E. Pl. *Laws* 6. 785; 8. 833D.

27. Arist. *Pol.* 7. 14. 4; 7. 14. 9 (1335a–b).

28. Amundsen and Diers, "The Age of Menopause in Classical Greece and Rome."

29. Dem. 43. 62. 4. A number of persons catalogued in Davies, *op. cit.,* reached advanced ages, but they were members of the propertied classes.

30. On these laws, see A. R. W. Harrison, *op. cit.,* pp. 32–38, and Lys. 1.

31. Plut. *Solon* 20. 3.

32. Ar. *Lys.* 26–28.

33. Pl. *Sym.* 190A–B.

34. Ath. 13. 569d–e.

35. Dem. 59. 30–32; Lacey, *Family,* p. 172 and notes.

36. Ar. *Ach.* 526–34.

37. Plut. *Pericles* 34. 3–6. Translated by Judith Peller Hallett.

38. Davies, *op. cit.,* pp. 458–59.

39. Pl. *Menex.* 4. 236B; 4. 237E–238B.

40. Xen. *Oec.* 10. 12.

41. Plut. *Alcibiades* 8. 3–6; Andoc. 4. 14.

42. Hdt. 2. 134–35.

43. Dem. 59. 18–20.

44. Aeschin. 1.28; Arist. *Const. Athens* 56.6.

45. Ps.-Dem. 59. 100. Cf. Lacey, *Family,* pp. 172–74.

46. Ar. *Lys.* 865–97; Ehrenberg, *op. cit.*, chap. 8; Eur. *Alc., passim.*

47. G. Kaibel, ed., *Epigrammata Graeca* 44. 2–3. Cf. R. Lattimore, *Themes in Greek and Latin Epitaphs*, p. 275.

48. E.g., Clive Bell, *Civilization*, pp. 238–45.

49. Xen. *Mem.* 3. 11. 1.

## Chapter VI

1. Gomme, *op. cit.;* Hadas, *op. cit.;* Kitto, *op. cit.*, pp. 219–36; Seltman, *Women in Antiquity*, pp. 110–11, and "Status of Women"; and Donald C. Richter, *op. cit.*

2. Soph. *Antigone* 61–62.

3. Candaules' wife: Hdt. 1. 10–13; Artemisia: 8. 87; Amestris: 9. 112. Cf. the vengeance of Tomyris on the corpse of Cyrus: 1. 214.

4. Slater, *op. cit.*

5. Ar. *Birds* 130–32 and *Clouds* 1382–90, 863–64. Ehrenberg, *op. cit.*, p. 197. Marie-Thérèse Charlier and Georges Raepset, "Etude d'un comportement social: Les relations entre parents et enfants dans la société athénienne à l'époque classique."

6. Arist. *Poetics* 15. 4.

7. A. Adler, *Understanding Human Nature*, pp. 124–25. For an analysis of Clytemnestra as a masculine personality whose motive for murder was jealousy of Agamemnon's power, see R. P. Winnington-Ingram, "Clytemnestra and the Vote of Athena."

8. Eur. *Or.* 553–57.

9. Simone de Beauvoir, *The Second Sex*, p. 73 note 8.

10. Hdt. 8. 88, 93.

11. R. Jebb, ed., *Sophocles: Antigone*, p. 91 note 464, p. 124 note 651. Cf. R. Kühner and B. Gerth, *Ausführliche Grammatik der Griechischen Sprache*, 2, part I, p. 83.

12. Hdt. 3. 119. Cf. Octavia's refusal to choose between brother and husband in Shakespeare, *Antony and Cleopatra*, III, vi, 15–20.

13. Jebb, *op. cit.*, p. 164. See C. M. Bowra, *Sophoclean Tragedy*, pp. 93–96; A. J. A. Waldock, *Sophocles the Dramatist*, pp. 133–42.

14. Deutsch, *op. cit.*, pp. 285–86, 289–92.

15. In the light of the heroine's cruel treatment of the female members of her family, it is surprising to read sentimental judgments of her "womanly nature, her absolute valuation of the bonds of blood and affection," and that she represents "the all-embracing motherly love" (C. Segal, "Sophocles' Praise of Man and the Conflicts of the *Antigone*," p. 70). Cf. E. Fromm, *The Forgotten Language*, p. 224.

16. Cf. Eur. *Hipp.* 525–63.

17. A. R. W. Harrison, *op. cit.*, p. 22; Soph. *Oed. Col.* 830–33.

18. Sigmund Freud, *Civilization and Its Discontents*, p. 73.

19. Aesch. *PV* 436–71, 476–506; but cf. Soph. *Oed. Col.* 668–719, where olive culture is included.

20. I owe these suggestions to Froma Zeitlin.

21. Eur. *Med.* 410–29.

22. Translated by Judith Peller Hallett.

23. Aul. Gell. 15. 20.

24. Ath. 13. 557e; cf. 13. 603e.

25. Eur. *Med.* 408–9.

26. Eur. *Or.* 605.

27. Eur. *Med.* 569–73.

28. Eur. *Med.* 285, 319–20.

29. Eur. *Ion* 1025, 1330; *Alc.* 304–19, 463–65.
30. Eur. *Hipp.* 409–10.
31. Eur. *Ion* 617, 844, 1003; *Andr.* 33, 157.
32. Eur. *Hipp.* 616–68. Translated by Judith Peller Hallett.
33. Hom. *Od.* 24. 196–202.
34. Eur. *El.* 1018–34. Translated by Judith Peller Hallett.
35. Eur. *Hipp.* 378–84.
36. E.g., Eur. *Hec.* 941 and *Tro.* 773; *Iph. Taur.* 326, 524; *Rhes.* 261.
37. Eur. *Heracl.* 979.
38. Eur. *Hec.* 237, 511, 1252–53.
39. Eur. *Iph. Aul.* 139.
40. Eur. *Hec.* 545–83.
41. Eur. *Supp.* 990–1071.
42. Eur. *Hel.* 352–56; *Tro.* 1012–14.
43. Eur. *Alc.* 623–24, 728.
44. Eur. *Andr.* 222–25; cf. 465–85, 911; *El.* 945–46, 1033; *Med.* 155–56. The wife of the elder Cato often suckled her slaves' children, so that, by being nursed together, they might feel affection for her own son (Plut. *Cato the Elder* 20. 3).
45. Eur. *Andr.* 1350.
46. Eur. *El.* 1039–40.
47. Eur. *Andr.; Tro.; Or.; Iph. Aul.,* 1148–56; *Hipp.; Alc.*
48. Eur. *Med.* 232–35; *Andr.* 675, 940.
49. The mother of Rhesus in Eur. *Rhes.;* Creusa in *Ion;* Melanippe in the lost *Melanippe the Wise.*
50. Hermione in Eur. *Andr.;* Creusa in *Ion.*
51. Eur. *Iph. Taur.* 219; *Supp.* 790–92; *Heracl.* 523, 579–80, 592–93; *Med.* 233–34.
52. Eur. *Phoen.* 355; *Iph. Aul.* 918; *Andr., passim; Hec., passim.*
53. Eur. *Tro.* 84, 792–85; *Med.* 1090–1115; *Andr.* 720–79; *Hec.* 650–56; *Hel.* 367.
54. Eur. *Supp.* 1132–35.
55. Eur. *Alc.* 303.
56. Eur. *Hec.* 924–26.
57. Eur. *Med.* 250–51; *Phoen.* 355; *Hipp.* 161–69; *Alc.* 315–19; *El.* 1107–8.
58. Eur. *Or.* 107; *Tro.* 646; *Heracl.* 476; *Iph. Aul.* 996.
59. Eur. *El.* 343–44, 1072–75; *Iph. Aul.* 830–34.
60. Eur. *Phoen.* 1485–86.
61. Eur. *Hec.* 975; *Tro.* 654.
62. An excellent sociological analysis of the women in Aristophanes is Ehrenberg, *op. cit.,* chap. 8.
63. Germaine Greer, in *The Female Eunuch,* p. 315, recommends the tactic of Lysistrata.
64. Ar. *Eccl.* 93, 156, 166, 243–44, *et passim.*
65. Ar. *Eccl.* 717–24, 1161.
66. Ar. *Clouds* 553–56; *Eccl., passim.*
67. E.g., Ar. *Thesm.,* 331–40, 395–423, 476–517; *Frogs* 1047–52.
68. Finley, "Utopianism Ancient and Modern"; Pierre Vidal-Naquet, "Esclavage et gynécocratie dans la tradition, le mythe, l'utopie."
69. Pomeroy, "Feminism in Book V of Plato's *Republic*"; Dorothea Wender, "Plato: Misogynist, Paedophile, and Feminist."
70. Arist. *Pol.* 2. 4. 2 (1266a–b).
71. Hdt. 4. 104. Cf. 1. 216 for a community of wives among the Massagetae; 4. 172 and 4. 180 for other groups practicing promiscuous intercourse.
72. Pl. *Republic* 5. 449C; 5. 457C–D.
73. Ar. *Eccl.* 468–70, 616–20.

74. Diog. Laert. 7. 131; Diod. 2. 58.

75. Ar. *Eccl.* 716–19.

76. Diod. 2. 55–60.

77. Frederick Engels, *The Origins of the Family, Private Property, and the State,* p. 120.

78. Pomeroy, "Feminism." Note that in his other works Plato does not see women as equal. For example, see *Timaeus* 90E–91A, where men who are cowardly and spend their lives in wrongdoing become women in their second incarnation.

79. P. Herfst, *op. cit.,* p. 99.

80. Joseph Vogt, *Von der Gleichwertigkeit der Geschlechter in der bürgerlichen Gesellschaft der Griechen,* pp. 211–55; R. Flacelière, "D'un certain féminisme grec"; Wender, *op. cit.,* pp. 84–85.

## Chapter VII

1. See Grace Macurdy, *Hellenistic Queens,* and W. W. Tarn and G. T. Griffith, *Hellenistic Civilization.*

2. Plut. *Alexander* 2. 4–5.

3. Some parallels from the Archaic period can be found in the marriage of Pisistratus and the daughter of Megacles. Pisistratus, who already had adult sons whose succession he did not wish to jeopardize by engendering new heirs, had agreed to a political marriage with the daughter of Megacles, but he had intercourse with her in an unnatural fashion. Megacles, insulted and enraged, was obviously deprived of the hope of having a grandson succeed to the tyranny and became the adversary of his son-in-law. Hdt. 1. 61.

4. App. *Syr.* 65; Pliny *HN* 7. 53; Macurdy, *op. cit.,* pp. 82–90.

5. Ptolemy II, IV, VI, VIII.

6. The marriage of Elpinice to her half-brother Cimon in Athens was irregular. See Davies, *op. cit.,* pp. 302–3.

7. Tarn and Griffith, *op. cit.,* p. 50.

8. Macurdy, *op. cit.,* p. 125.

9. See McClees, *op. cit.,* and the convenient collection of H. W. Pleket, ed., *Epigraphica II: Texts on the Social History of the Greek World* (hereafter: Pleket).

10. Pleket, no. 3; J. and L. Robert, "Bulletin épigraphique" 81, inscription nos. 444, 445.

11. E.g., *IG* 2. 5. 477d.

12. Tarn and Griffith, *op. cit.,* p. 99; *IG* 2. 1. 550.

13. *IG* 9. 2. 62.

14. Pleket, no. 2; J. and L. Robert, "Bulletin épigraphique" 76, inscription no. 170.

15. Pleket, no. 5; *I. Priene,* no. 208.

16. The legal position of women in the papyri has been reviewed by Claire Préaux, and some of her findings will be summarized here. Préaux, "Le status de la femme à l'époque hellénistique, principalement en Egypte." For an interpretation differing on some points, see Claude Vatin, *Recherches sur le mariage et la condition de la femme mariée à l'époque hellénistique,* pp. 241–54.

17. Citizen women of Alexandria, titled *astai,* were barred from making wills. See the *Gnomon of the Idios Logos,* line 15.

18. *P. Tebtunis* 776. 27–28; *P. Enteuxeis* 82. 7; *BGU* 648. 11–16.

19. *BGU* 1104.

20. *P. Elephantine* 1. The names of six witnesses are added at the bottom of the document.

21. *P. Giessen* 2; *BGU* 1052, acting with a guardian.

22. Athens: see p. 62 above. Rome: see p. 158 below. Roman Egypt: Naphtali Lewis, "On Paternal Authority in Roman Egypt."

23. *P. Tebtunis* 104.

24. For epigraphic documentation, see Schaps, *op. cit., passim*, and M. I. Finley, *Studies in Land and Credit in Ancient Athens, 500–200 B.C.*, pp. 78, 101–2.

25. Arist. *Pol.* 2. 6. 11 (1270a): Plut. *Agis* 4, 7; *IG* 5. 1564a; Paus. 3. 17. 6; 3. 8. 1; 6. 1. 6; 5. 8. 11. The daughters of Polycrates of Argos were Panathenaic victors in the early second century B.C. (*IG* 2 ² 2313, 2314).

26. Arist. *Pol.* 1. 5. 6–7 (1260a).

27. For *gynaikonomoi* in Athens and other cities, see C. Wehrli, "Les gynécon-omes," and Vatin, *op. cit.*, pp. 254–61.

28. Arist. *Pol.* 6. 5. 13 (1322b–1323a); 4. 12. 3 (1299a); 4. 12. 9 (1300a).

29. W. S. Ferguson, *Hellenistic Athens*, p. 89.

30. Stob. 16. 30.

31. Zeno: Diog. Laert. 7. 131. Later views on marriage: Stob. 57. 25.

32. Polyb. 36. 17; Tarn and Griffith, *op. cit.*, pp. 100–104.

33. Holger Thesleff, *The Pythagorean Texts of the Hellenistic Period*, pp. 142–45 = Stob. 4.28.10. Translated by Flora R. Levin. On the female students of Pythagoras: Porph. *Pythagoras* 19, and Diog. Laert. 8.41–42. On Neopythagorean-ism: Thesleff, *An Introduction to the Pythagorean Writings of the Hellenistic Period.*

34. Diog. Laert. 10. 119.

35. Diog. Laert. 6. 72.

36. Diog. Laert. 6. 97–98.

37. L. Moretti, ed., *Iscrizioni Agonistiche Greche*, no. 63 = Pleket, no. 9. Cf. H. A. Harris, *Sport in Greece and Rome*, pp. 178–79.

38. R. Calderini, "Gil *agrammatoi* nell'Egitto greco-romano," p. 23, See *P. Oxy-rhynchus* 1467 (A.D. 263) for a woman who demands special consideration because she is literate.

39. Erinna: *Palatine Anthology* 7. 11. 2.

40. Greek text in Page, *Literary Papyri: Poetry*, pp. 486, 488. Translated by Marylin Arthur.

41. Slater, *op. cit.*, pp. 63–65.

42. *Palatine Anthology* 7. 712; cf. 7. 710.

43. *Palatine Anthology* 7. 13.

44. Angel, "Ecology and Population," p. 100 and Table 28.

45. Tarn and Griffith, *op. cit.*, pp. 100–104; Vatin, *op. cit.*, pp. 230–33.

46. *P. Oxyrhynchus* 37 (A.D. 49) for rearing a foundling; *P. Oxyrhynchus* 744 (1 B.C.) on exposing a daughter.

47. Hyperides, fragment B, 45, "Against Demetria"; Tarn and Griffith, *op. cit.*, p. 105.

48. Ps.-Dem. 59.30–32

49. *OGIS* 2.674. I owe this reference and interpretation to M. G. Raschke.

50. Athenaeus, Machon, Alciphron, and Lucian are important sources of infor-mation about courtesans in different periods. On Phryne, see also Ferguson, *op. cit.*, p. 88.

51. On Agathoclia, see Ath. 13. 577 and Polyb. 15. 31–33.

52. See Otto J. Brendel, "The Scope and Temperament of Erotic Art in the Greco-Roman World"; K. Clark, *The Nude*, especially pp. 23–145; and Havelock, *op. cit.*

53. Thuc. 1. 6. 5; cf. Hdt. 1. 10.

54. Pl. *Republic* 5. 452A–B.

55. Hdt. 1. 8–12.

56. See K. J. Dover, "Classical Greek Attitudes to Sexual Behavior." Professor Dover has brought to my attention a very rare representation of a woman making the conventional homosexual chin-chucking gesture to another woman on a plate from Thera, ca. 620 B.C., published in Arnold von Salis, *Theseus und Ariadne*, p. 10 and Plate 7, and in Gisela Richter, *Korai*, p. 24 and Plate 8c.

57. T. B. L. Webster, *Athenian Culture and Society*, pp. 139–40; this finding is not readily verified, and remains controversial. I am grateful to Ann Sheffield for this reference.

58. Ael. *VH* 4. 3; Pliny, *HN* 35. 58.

59. Paoli, *op. cit.*, pp. 20–23. Elpinice, though a member of the upper class, was poor and notorious; thus her modeling for Polygnotus was irregular (Plut. *Cimon* 4).

60. Pliny *HN* 35. 61; Cic. *De Inventione* 2. 1. 1.

61. On Praxiteles' Aphrodite, see, e.g., Pliny, *HN* 36. 20; Ath. 13. 590.

62. Brendel, *op. cit.*, pp. 41–54.

63. Arist. *Gen. An.* 1. 20 (728a–b).

64. Ov. *The Art of Love* 2. 719–32.

## Chapter VIII

1. For Roman women, especially of the upper classes, see J. P. V. D. Balsdon, *Roman Women: Their History and Habits*. For an account of the political activities of women, especially between 60 B.C. and A.D. 14, see R. Syme, *The Roman Revolution*.

2. For Cornelia, see Plut. *Tiberius Gracchus* 1.4 and *Gaius Gracchus* 4, 19, and App. *Civil Wars* 1. 20; on her statue, see Pliny *HN* 34. 31, and the base in A. Degrassi, ed., *Inscriptiones Italiae* 13.3 ("Elogia"), no. 72, pp. 51–52. A shorter inscription is reported in Plut. *Gaius Gracchus* 4. 3: "Cornelia, mother of the Gracchi."

3. R. Taubenschlag, *The Law of Greco-Roman Egypt in the Light of the Papyri: 332 B.C.–640 A.D.*, pp. 48–49, 176–77.

4. For the Lex Claudia de tutela, see G. Rotondi, *Leges publicae populi romani*, pp. 467–68; on literacy, Calderini, *op. cit.*, pp. 30–31.

5. Dionysius of Halicarnassus attributed this feature to marriages concluded "with ritual," implying the existence of marriages without *manus* even in the days of Romulus (*Ant. Rom.* 2. 25).

6. Livy 1. 26.

7. Livy 3. 44–58; Dion. Hal. *Ant. Rom.* 11. 28–49; Diod. 12. 24.

8. Alan Watson, *The Law of Persons in the Later Roman Republic*, p. 110.

9. Val. Max. 6. 3. 9. The ideal that a woman must not drink survived so that even in A.D. 153 a woman donor to a man's *collegium* made herself one of the recipients of the cash distributions from her fund, but excluded herself from the drinking for which she had also donated money (*ILS* 7213. 12).

10. Aul. Gell. 10. 23; cf. Livy 34. 2. 11. Watson, *op. cit.*, p. 28, accepts Cato's testimony.

11. Plut. *Roman Questions* 6 also suggests that a reason for married women's habit of kissing their blood relatives on the lips was the desire of the men to maintain surveillance over the women's drinking. Cf. *Mor.* 265b.

12. Dion. Hal. *Ant. Rom.* 2. 25. 4.

13. Plut. *Romulus* 22. 3.

14. Dion. Hal. *Ant. Rom.* 2. 25. 6.

15. Pliny *HN* 14. 89–90.

16. Livy 39. 18. 6.

17. Plut. *Roman Questions* 108.

18. Plut. *Pompey* 9.

19. Plut. *Caesar* 14. 4–5.
20. Plut. *Pompey* 44.
21. Plut. *Sulla* 35.
22. T. P. Wiseman, *Cinna the Poet*, p. 181.
23. Ulp. *Digest* 1. 12.
24. Paulus *Sententiae* 5. 6. 15.
25. Val. Max. 8. 2. 3.
26. Vell. Pat. 2. 100. 5; Dio 55. 10–14.
27. Polyb. 31. 26.
28. Plut. *Cato the Younger* 25. 52. Cf. Hattie Gordon, "The Eternal Triangle, First Century B.C."
29. Plut. *Sulla* 3. 2.
30. "Turia": *CIL* 6. 1527, 31670 = *ILS* 8393 (in Marcel Durry, ed., *Eloge funèbre d'une matrone romaine*).
31. *Digest* 48. 5. 21 (20); for Julian laws on marriage and adultery, see Rotondi, *op. cit.*, pp. 443–47.
32. *Digest* 48. 5. 1–4.
33. *Digest* 48. 5. 14 (13). 5.
34. *Stoicorum Veterum Fragmenta* 244.
35. Lucan *Pharsalia* 2. 387–88.
36. *Digest* 48. 5. 6. 1.
37. Suet. *Aug.* 101.
38. Tac. *Ann.* 2. 85. 1.
39. *Codex Theodosianus* 9. 9. 25.
40. Livy 1. 57–60.
41. Hor. *Odes* 3. 14. 4; Prop. 4. 11. 36; Lattimore, *op. cit.*, p. 296; Durry, *op. cit.*, p. 9; and Gordon Williams, "Some Aspects of Roman Marriage Ceremonies and Ideals," pp. 23–24.
42. Pliny *Ep.* 3. 16; Dio 60. 16. 5–6; Martial 1. 13. Cf. Pliny *Ep.* 6. 24; Tac. *Ann.* 6. 29; 16. 10.
43. Polyb. 31. 26.
44. Polyb. 18. 35; 31. 22; 31. 27.
45. See John H. D'Arms, *Romans on the Bay of Naples*, pp. 8–12.
46. Val. Max. 4. 4. 1.
47. Tac. *Ann.* 12. 22; Pliny *HN* 9. 117. Cf. G. Rickman, *Roman Granaries and Store Buildings*, pp. 164–65.
48. See Amundsen and Diers, "Age of Menarche," and Keith Hopkins, "The Age of Roman Girls at Marriage."
49. David Daube, *Roman Law*, pp. 102–12.
50. For a different viewpoint, see W. den Boer, "Demography in Roman History." Whether women are enumerated in the census figures at particular periods in Roman history remains unclear, despite the efforts of Joël Le Gall, "Un critère de différenciation sociale," and P. A. Brunt, *Italian Manpower 225 B.C.–14 A.D.*
51. On the names of Roman women, see Iiro Kajanto, "Women's Praenomina Reconsidered."
52. Justin Martyr *Apology for the Christians*, "To Antoninus Pius," 27. I owe this reference to JoAnn McNamara.
53. Degrassi, "L'indicazione dell'età nelle iscrizioni sepolcrali latine," pp. 85–86.
54. In his sample Keith Hopkins found 149 sons and 100 daughters ("On the Probable Age Structure of the Roman Population," p. 262).
55. Watson, *Roman Private Law Around 200 B.C.*, p. 22; Brunt, *op. cit.*, p. 559.
56. Suet. *Aug.* 89. 2; Livy *Per.* 59; Aul. Gell. 1. 6; H. Malcovati, *Oratorum Romanorum Fragmenta*, p. 107.

57. Dio 54. 6. 7.

58. On contraception, see Hopkins, "Contraception in the Roman Empire," and John T. Noonan, Jr., *Contraception*, pp. 23–46. For the possibility of coitus interruptus in Archaic Greece, see the fragment of Archilochus, *P. Coloniensia* 7511.

59. Pliny *H N* 29. 85; Aëtius 16. 17.

60. Soranus 1. 61. The references to Soranus are to his *Gynecology*, translated by O. Temkin (Baltimore: Johns Hopkins University Press, 1956). Hopkins, "Contraception," p. 140, note 47.

61. Lucretius 4. 1269–78.

62. Hopkins, "Contraception," p. 135, note 30.

63. On abortion, see Noonan, *op. cit.;* Krenkel, *op. cit.;* Nardi, *op. cit.*, reviewed by Sheila Dickison in *Arethusa* 6 (1973): 159–66.

64. Ov. *Loves* 2. 14. 27–28.

65. *Ibid.; Fasti* 1. 621–24; *Her.* 11. 37–42. Juvenal 6. 595–97. Sen. *Helv.* 16. 1.

66. *Digest* 48. 19, 39; 48. 8. 8; 47. 11. 4.

67. *Digest* 48. 19. 38. 5. See the discussion in Noonan, *op. cit.*, pp. 44–46, and Hopkins, "Contraception," p. 137 note 35.

68. Soranus 2. 17; 4. 9. On mothers not nursing their children, see Tac. *Dial.* 28. 4–29.

69. Hopkins, "Age Structure of the Roman Population," pp. 260–63.

70. Angel, "Ecology and Population," Table 28.

71. Columella *On Agriculture* 12, Preface 9–10. Cato *Agr.* 143. 1.

72. Tac. *Agr.* 4. For other influential mothers, cf. Aurelia, mother of Caesar; Rhea, mother of Sertorius, Atia, mother of Augustus, in Tac. *Dial.* 28; and Cornelia in Cic. *Brut.* 211.

73. Pliny *Ep.* 5. 16. 3.

74. Quint. 1. 6; Cic. *Brut.* 211.

75. Plut. *Pompey* 55, 66, 74, 76, 78–80.

76. Pliny *Ep.* 4. 19. 4.

77. Quint. 1. 1. 6.

78. Musonius Rufus (ed. Hense), fragment 4.

79. Arrian *Discourses of Epictetus*, fragment 15 = Stob. 3. 6. 58.

80. Sallust *The War with Catiline* 25. Translated by Judith Peller Hallett. On Sempronia, see Syme, *Sallust*, pp. 25–26, 133–35.

81. Juvenal 6.434–56. Translated by Roger Killian, Richard Lynch, Robert J. Rowland, and John Sims.

82. Mentioned by Martial 10. 35. 38.

83. [Tibullus] 3. 13. Translated by Judith Peller Hallett. On Sulpicia, see Esther Bréguet, *Le roman de Sulpicia*, and G. Luck, *The Latin Love Elegy*, pp. 107–16.

84. [Tib.] 3. 11. Translated by Judith Peller Hallett.

85. [Tib.] 3. 16.

86. On the circle of Julia Domna, see G. W. Bowersock, *Greek Sophists in the Roman Empire*, pp. 101–9.

87. A Greek woman who was not an orator but whom necessity forced to make one public address is mentioned in Diod. 12. 18. 4.

88. Val. Max. 8.3; Claudine Herrmman, *Le rôle judiciaire et politique des femmes sous la république romaine*, pp. 100–101, 107–8, 111–15. On Hortensia, see also Quint. 1.1.6.

89. App. *Civil Wars* 4. 33.

90. Sabine women: Livy 1. 13. Coriolanus: Livy 2. 40. Verginius: Livy 1. 26. Contributions to the gods: Livy, *passim.* On women's contribution to the offering of Camillus to Apollo: Val. Max. 5. 6. 8. Poisoning: Livy 8. 18; Val. Max. 2. 5. 5.

91. Livy 22. 56. 4–6; 34. 6. 15; Plut. *Fabius Maximus* 18. 1–2; Val. Max. 1. 1. 15.

The substance of this discussion of the Oppian Law was first presented in my "Women and War."

92. Livy 22. 57. 9–12; 22. 60. 1–3; 34. 3. 7; 22. 61. 1; 23. 48. 8–9. Single women and orphans were not liable for the *tributum*, but paid the *aes equestre.*

93. Daube, *op. cit.*, pp. 71–75; see p. 162 above. For a contrary opinion, see Crook, "Intestacy in Rome."

94. Plut. *Cato the Elder* 18.

95. Polyb. 31. 26. 6–10.

96. Livy 34. 1–8; Tac. *Ann.* 3. 34; Val. Max. 9. 1. 3; Oros. 4. 20. 14; Zonaras 9. 17. 1

97. Livy 24. 18. 13–14; 34. 5. 10; 34. 6. 14.

98. Livy 26.36. Cf. the theme of women's avarice and luxury in Tac. *Ann.* 3.33–34. Juno: Livy 27.37.9–10.

99. Livy 34. 7. 12; but cf. 34. 7. 13, modifying the rhetorical point.

100. Livy 22. 7. 7–13; 22. 60. 2.

101. Livy 25. 2. 9–10.

102. Livy 29. 14. 10–14; Ov. *Fasti* 4. 179–372. Cf. G. Wissowa, *Religion und Kultus der Römer*, p. 318.

103. Livy 26. 36. 5; 27. 51. 9.

104. Livy 34. 1–8. 3.

105. Livy 34. 50. 3–7; Val. Max. 5. 2. 6.

106. Polyb. 9. 11a; Brunt, *op. cit.*, pp. 67–68.

107. Tac. *Ann.* 3. 34.

108. Plut. *Agis* 4; Plut. *Spartan Sayings* 212b.

109. Livy 34. 4. 15–18; 34. 7. 8–10.

110. Plut. *Cato the Elder* 18; H. H. Scullard, *Roman Politics 220–150 B.C.*, pp. 156, 260.

111. Le Gall, "Critère," pp. 281, 285–86.

112. *Hist. Aug.: Elagabalus* 4. 4 and *Aurelian* 49. 6. For a body of women with possibly the same functions as the *senaculum* at Rome, see Angela Donati, "Sull' iscrizione Lanuvina della curia mulierum," and J. Straub, "Senaculum, id est mulierum senatus," p. 229.

113. Plut. *Gaius Gracchus* 4. 3–4.

114. Malcovati, *op. cit.*, p. 220.

115. Plut. *Caesar* 5. 1–2.

116. Suet. *Aug.* 8. 1, 61. 2; Dio 54. 35. 4–5.

117. Ruth Hoffsten, *Roman Women of Rank of the Early Empire as Portrayed by Dio, Paterculus, Suetonius, and Tacitus*, pp. 88–89.

118. Scullard, *op. cit.*, p. 156.

119. Tac. *Ann.* 1. 14. 1–3.

120. Statues: Dio 55. 2. 5; 61. 12. 2; Tac. *Ann.* 14. 61. 1; Pliny *HN* 34. 31. Inscriptions in Pleket, *passim.*

121. Plut. *Antony* 10; C. Babcock, "The Early Career of Fulvia"; Vell. Pat. 2. 74. 2.

122. W. W. Tarn, "Alexander Helios and the Golden Age."

123. Alexandra of Judaea: Josephus *Jewish Antiquities* 15 [3. 1] 40. Aba at Olba in Cilicia: Dio 49. 44. For Cleopatra, see *Cambridge Ancient History*, vol. 10.

124. See, e.g., Finley, "The Silent Women of Rome."

## Chapter IX

1. P. R. C. Weaver, *Familia Caesaris;* Susan Treggiari, *Roman Freedmen During the Late Republic.*

2. Columella *On Agriculture* 12, Preface, 9.

3. On these jobs, see Treggiari, "Women in Slavery" and "Domestic Staff at Rome in the Julio-Claudian Period, 27 B.C. to A.D. 68"; Mima Maxey, *Occupations of the Lower Classes in Roman Society;* Le Gall, "Métiers de femmes au *Corpus inscriptionum Latinarum.*"

4. Cato *Agr.* 143. Cf. Columella *On Agriculture* 12, Preface, 8.

5. Aemilia: Val. Max. 6. 7. 1. Cato: Plut. *Cato the Elder* 21, 24. Augustus: Dio 54. 19. 3; 58. 2. 5; Suet. *Aug.* 71. 1. Claudius: Tac. *Ann.* 11. 29.

6. *CIL* 1. 1214.

7. *Digest* 23. 2. 8; 2. 14. 2; *Inst.* 1. 10. 10.

8. On slaves bred at home as a source of new slaves, see I. Biezunska-Malowist and M. Malowist, "La procréation des esclaves comme source de l'esclavage."

9. Weaver, *op. cit.,* pp. 109–10; Treggiari, "Women in Slavery."

10. Weaver, *op. cit.,* p. 172; Treggiari, "Women in Slavery." Trimalchio: Petron. *Sat.* 53.

11. *CIL* 1.2. 1221.

12. A seven-year-old is deflowered in Petron. *Sat.* 25. See also Durry, "Le mariage des filles impubères dans la Rome antique," pp. 21, 25.

13. Gaius 1. 19; *Digest* 40. 2. 13.

14. Beryl Rawson, "Family Life Among the Lower Classes at Rome in the First Two Centuries of the Empire."

15. *Digest* 23. 2. 44.

16. Statius *Silvae* 3. 3; Weaver, *op. cit.,* pp. 171, 289–94.

17. *Digest* 24. 2. 11.

18. Ter. *The Self-Tormentor* 300–301.

19. Columella *On Agriculture* 1. 8. 19; cf. Varro *On Agriculture* 2. 1. 26.

20. *Code Iust.* 5. 4. 3.

21. On the Senatusconsultum Claudianum, see Crook, *Life and Law*, p. 62, and Weaver, *op. cit.,* pp. 162–69.

22. Dio 65. 14; Suet. *Vespasian* 3; *Hist. Aug.: Antoninus Pius* 8. On Acte, freedwoman of Nero, see Tac. *Ann.* 13. 12; Suet. *Nero* 28; Dio 61. 7.

23. Herculaneum Tablets 13–30. A.-J. Boyé, "Pro Petronia Iusta."

24. Treggiari, *Roman Freedmen*, p. 214.

25. Brunt, *op. cit.* pp. 558–66.

26. *Ibid.,* p. 565.

27. Lyde and her four slaves: *Monumentum Liviae* 4237, 4275, 4276, cited by Treggiari, "Women in Slavery."

28. Plut. *Antony* 9. 5. Servius, on Virgil Eclogue 10. Freedwomen at bachelor parties: Cic. *Letters to His Friends* 9. 26. 2.

29. *IG* 2² 1553–78. Cf. M. Tod, "Epigraphical Notes on Freedmen's Professions," pp. 10–11.

30. *CIL* 1.2.1211. Cf. Durry, *Eloge funèbre*, p. 9.

31. Suet. *Aug.* 73.

32. Maxey, *op. cit.,* p. 31. The weighing of wool is the only supervisory job as yet attested for slave women in an upper-class household (Treggiari, "Women in Domestic Service in the Early Roman Empire").

33. On Pompeii, see H. H. Tanzer, *The Common People of Pompeii,* and Michele D'Avino, *The Women of Pompeii.*

34. Helen Jefferson Loane, *Industry and Commerce of the City of Rome (50 B.C.–200 A.D.),* pp. 103–5, 110–11.

35. See J.-P. Waltzing, *Etude historique sur les corporations professionnelles chez les Romains jusqu'à la chute de l'Empire d'occident,* 1: 348–49, and 4: 254–57; Guido Clemente, "Il patronato nei collegia dell'impero romano."

36. On the price of prostitutes, see Richard Duncan-Jones, *The Economy of the Roman Empire*, p. 246.

37. Ramsay MacMullen, *Roman Social Relations 50 B.C. to A.D. 284*, pp. 86–87.

38. Exemptions from *operae:* prostitutes, *Digest* 38. 1. 38; high status, 38. 1. 34; over fifty, 38. 1. 35; married to patron, *Code Iust.* 6. 39; married with patron's approval, *Digest* 38. 1. 48.

39. Suet. *Aug.* 65. 2.

40. *CIL* 6. 8958.

41. Juvenal 11. 172–73. Hor. *Epist.* 1. 14. 21; *Sat.* 1. 2. 30.

42. On the doles and assistance programs, see A. R. Hands, *Charities and Social Aid in Greece and Rome*, who gives English translations of the relevant texts; Duncan-Jones, *op. cit.*, *passim;* and Denis Van Berchem, *Les distributions de blé et d'argent à la plèbe romaine sous l'empire*, who cites one woman recipient of public grain. She is Mallia Aemiliana, known from *ILS* 9275, who availed herself of the right of some male member of her family, or was granted an extraordinary privilege, or, as Van Berchem (pp. 42–43) suggests, was the recipient of special charity as a widow.

43. On the *curia mulierum* of *ILS* 6199, see Chapter VIII, note 112 above.

44. Augustus: Suet. *Aug.* 41. Trajan: Pliny *Pan.* 26, 28. 1–3.

45. Duncan-Jones, *op. cit.*, p. 301.

46. *ILS* 977.

47. Pliny *Ep.* 7. 18

48. *ILS* 6278. Cf. Duncan-Jones, *op. cit.*, pp. 27, 144–45.

49. *Hist. Aug.: Antoninus Pius* 8. 1; *Marcus Aurelius* 7. 8; 26. 6.

50. *CIL* 14. 4450. Cf. Duncan-Jones, *op. cit.*, pp. 228–29, no. 641.

51. Treggiari, "Libertine Ladies," p. 198.

52. Kajanto, "On Divorce Among the Common People of Rome."


## Chapter X

1. Cic. *Letters to His Friends* 14. 4.

2. On the numerous cults of Fortuna—many of which are not specific to women—see W. H. Roscher, *Ausführliches Lexikon der griechischen und römischen Mythologie;* Wissowa, *op. cit.;* Jean Gagé, *Matronalia;* and Robert E. A. Palmer, "Roman Shrines of Female Chastity from the Caste Struggle to the Papacy of Innocent I."

3. Arn. 2. 67; a relief on the Ara Pacis of Augustus shows a young girl clad in a toga on a ceremonial occasion.

4. On Matuta, see Ov. *Fasti* 6. 475–768; Plut. *Roman Questions* 16, 17; *Mor.* 492d; and Robert E. A. Palmer, "Cupra, Matuta, and Venilia Pyrgensis," pp. 295–96.

5. Livy 10. 23; Prop. 2. 6. 25.

6. Livy 10. 31. 9.

7. Livy 2. 40. 12.

8. Val Max. 8. 15. 12; Pliny *HN* 7. 120; Solinus 1. 126.

9. Livy 10. 23; Festus 270L.

10. Juvenal 6. 306–48. Translated by Roger Killian, Richard Lynch, Robert Rowland, and John Sims.

11. Freud, *op. cit.*, p. 51.

12. Robert E. A. Palmer, *The Archaic Community of the Romans*, p. 153 note 1; Kurt Latte, *Römische Religionsgeschichte*, pp. 108-11.

13. Zosimus 5. 38.

14. Dion. Hal. 1. 76-78.

15. Livy 22. 57. 2.

16. Aristotle: see Chapter III, above. Theopompus: Ath. 12. 517. Livy 1. 57. 6 on the contest between a Roman and an Etruscan wife. Juvenal 6. Tac. *Germania* 19.

17. Suet. *Dom.* 8. 3-5; Pliny *Ep.* 4. 11. 5-16; Robert E. A. Palmer, "Roman Shrines."

18. Peter Garnsey, *Social Status and Legal Privilege in the Roman Empire*, pp. 57-58.

19. Cic. *Cat.* 3. 9; Plut. *Crassus* 1 and *Mor.* 89e.

20. On the affair of 114 B.C., see, most recently, Erich S. Gruen, *Roman Politics and the Criminal Courts, 149-78 B.C.*, pp. 127-32.

21. Gaius 1. 145.

22. Aul. Gell. 1. 12. 9-12; Plut. *Numa* 10.3.

23. Suet. *Aug.* 44. 2-3; Vitruvius 5. 6.

24. Aul. Gell. 1. 12. 9.

25. Dio 55. 22. 5.

26. Plut. *Romulus* 22.3; Henri Le Bonniec, *Le culte de Cérès à Rome*, pp. 86-88. On controversial issues, I have followed Le Bonniec's interpretations.

27. Latte, *op. cit.*, pp. 141-43.

28. Cyril Bailey, *Phases in the Religion of Ancient Rome*, p. 197.

29. For further reading, see J. Leclant, *Inventaire bibliographique des Isiaca (IBIS)*, A—D, and other works in the series "Etudes préliminaires aux religions orientales dans l'Empire romain" (Leiden: Brill, in progress).

30. Plut. *Isis and Osiris* 372e-f, 382c.

31. This inscription is dated third or fourth century A.D. by V. Tran Tam Tinh, *Le culte des divinités orientales en Campanie*, p. 77, but first or second century A.D. by L. Vidman, *Sylloge inscriptionum religionis Isiacae et Sarapiacae*, no. 502 = *CIL* 10. 3800; cf. no. 42.

32. Diod. 1. 27.

33. *P. Oxyrhynchus* 11. 1380. 214-16.

34. Vera Frederika Vanderlip, ed., *The Four Greek Hymns of Isidorus and the Cult of Isis*, p. 35, lines 33-34.

35. Juvenal 6. 511-41. Translated by Roger Killian, Richard Lynch, Robert Rowland, and John Sims.

36. The virgin of Isis: Vidman, *op. cit.*, no. 62 = *IG* 7. 3426. Prop. 2. 33; cf. 4. 5. 34.

37. For a full description of the ceremonies, see Tran Tam Tinh, *Le culte des divinités orientales à Herculaneum*, pp. 29-49.

38. The freedman's daughter is Usia Prima, daughter of Rabirius Postumus Hermodorus, in *CIL* 6. 2246; cf. Treggiari, *Roman Freedmen*, p. 205. The social and economic backgrounds of followers of Isis are analyzed by Michel Malaise, *Les conditions de pénétration et de diffusion des cultes égyptiens en Italie*, pp. 127, 136-37.

39. R. E. Witt, *Isis in the Graeco-Roman World*, pp. 70-72, 222.

40. Malaise, *op. cit.*, pp. 94, 99.

41. Val. Max. 1. 3. 4.

42. Dio 47. 15. 4.

43. Hor. *Epode* 9. 13-14.

44. Tac. *Ann.* 2. 85; Suet. *Tiberius* 36; Josephus *Jewish Antiquities* 18. 65-80.

45. Witt, *op. cit.*, pp. 223-54; A. Roullet, *The Egyptian and Egyptianizing Mon-*

*uments of Imperial Rome*, pp. 23–35. The proximity of the temple of Isis of the Campus Martius no doubt contributed to the idolatry of Santa Maria sopra Minerva, whose church was built over a temple of Minerva beside the great Iseum.

46. Malaise, *op. cit.*, p. 94.

## Epilogue

1. Dio 54. 16. 2; *eugeneis* may mean "freeborn" rather than "upper-class."

# WORKS REFERRED TO

Adler, A. *Understanding Human Nature*. New York: Greenberg, 1930.

Ahlberg, Gudrun. *Prothesis and Ekphora in Greek Geometric Art*. Studies in Mediterranean Archaeology, vol. 32. Göteborg: Aströms, 1971.

Alexiou, Margaret. *The Ritual Lament in Greek Tradition*. London: Cambridge University Press, 1974.

Amundsen, D. W., and Diers, C. J. "The Age of Menarche in Classical Greece and Rome." *Human Biology* 41 (1969): 125–32.

———. "The Age of Menopause in Classical Greece and Rome." *Human Biology* 42 (1970): 79–86.

Angel, J. Lawrence. "Ecology and Population in the Eastern Mediterranean." *World Archaeology* 4 (1972): 88–105.

———. "Geometric Athenians," appendix to *Late Geometric Graves and a Seventh-Century Well in the Agora*, by Rodney S. Young. *Hesperia*, Supplement 2, pp. 236–46. Athens: American School, 1939.

———. "Paleoecology, Paleodemography, and Health." Paper delivered at 9th International Congress of Anthropological and Ethnological Sciences, August 28–September 8, 1973, Chicago and Detroit.

Babcock, C. "The Early Career of Fulvia." *American Journal of Philology* 86 (1965): 1–32.

Bailey, Cyril. *Phases in the Religion of Ancient Rome*. Berkeley: University of California Press, 1932.

Balsdon, J. P. V. D. *Roman Women: Their History and Habits*. London: Bodley Head, 1962.

Beauvoir, Simone de. *The Second Sex*. Reprint. New York: Bantam, 1961.

Beazley, J. D. *Attic Red-figure Vase-painters*. 2d ed. Oxford: Clarendon Press, 1963.

Bell, Clive. *Civilization*. New York: Harcourt Brace Jovanovich, 1928.

Berger, A. *Encyclopedic Dictionary of Roman Law*. Philadelphia: American Philosophical Society, 1953.

Best, E. E. "Cicero, Livy and Educated Roman Women." *Classical Journal* 65 (1970): 199–204.

Biezunska-Malowist, I., and Malowist, M. "La procréation des esclaves comme source de l'esclavage." In *Mélanges K. Michalowski*, pp. 275–80. Warsaw: Panstowe Wydawnictwo Naukowe, 1966.

Birt, T. *Frauen der Antike*. Leipzig: Quelle and Meyer, 1932.

Boer, W. den. "Demography in Roman History." *Mnemosyne*, 4th ser. 26 (1973): 29–46.

Bothmer, D. von. *Amazons in Greek Art*. Oxford: Clarendon Press, 1957.

Bowersock, G. W. *Greek Sophists in the Roman Empire*. Oxford: Clarendon Press, 1969.

Bowra, C. M. *Greek Lyric Poetry*. Oxford: Clarendon Press, 1961.

———. *Sophoclean Tragedy*. Reprint. London: Oxford University Press, 1965.

Boyé, A.-J. "Pro Petronia Iusta." In *Mélanges Henri Lévy-Bruhl*, pp. 29–48. Paris: Sirey, 1959.

Braunstein, O. *Die politische Wirksamkeit der griechischen Frau*. Leipzig: August Hoffman, 1911.

Bréguet, Esther. *Le Roman de Sulpicia*. Geneva: University of Geneva Press, 1946.

Brendel, Otto J. "The Scope and Temperament of Erotic Art in the Greco-Roman World." In *Studies in Erotic Art*, edited by T. Bowie and C. Christenson. New York: Basic Books, 1970.

Brenk, Frederick, S.J. "Hesiod: How Much a Male Chauvinist?" *Classical Bulletin* 49 (1973): 73–76.

Brunt, P.A. *Italian Manpower 225 B.C.–A.D. 14*. London: Oxford University Press, 1971.

Burck, E. *Die Frau in der griechisch-römischen Antike*. Tusculum Schriften. Munich: Heimeran, 1969.

Calderini, R. "Gli *agrammatoi* nell'Egitto greco-romano." *Aegyptus* 30 (1950): 14–41.

Cameron, A. "The Exposure of Children and Greek Ethics." *Classical Review* 46 (1932): 105–14.

Charbonneaux, Jean. *Archaic Greek Art*. New York: Braziller, 1971.

Charlier, Marie-Thérèse, and Raepset, Georges. "Etude d'un comportement social: Les relations entre parents et enfants dans la société athénienne à l'époque classique." *L'antiquité classique* 40 (1970): 589–606.

Clark, Kenneth. *The Nude*. Reprint. Garden City, N.Y.: Doubleday, Anchor, 1956.

Clemente, Guido. "Il patronato nei collegia dell'impero romano." *Studi classici e orientali* 21 (1972): 142–229.

Coldstream, J. N. *Greek Geometric Pottery*. London: Methuen, 1968.

Crook, J. A. "Intestacy in Rome." *Proceedings of the Cambridge Philological Society* 199, n.s. 19 (1973): 38–44.

———. *Law and Life of Rome*. London: Thames & Hudson, 1967.

D'Arms, John H. *Romans on the Bay of Naples: A Social and Cultural Study of Villas and Their Owners from 150 B.C. to A.D. 400*. Cambridge, Mass.: Harvard University Press, 1970.

Daube, David. *Roman Law: Linguistic, Social and Philosophical Aspects*, Edinburgh: Edinburgh University Press, 1969.

Davies, J. K. *Athenian Propertied Families 600–300 B.C.* Oxford: Clarendon Press, 1971.

D'Avino, Michele. *The Women of Pompeii*. Naples: Loffredo, 1967.

Degrassi, A. "L'indicazione dell'età nelle iscrizioni sepolcrali latine." *Akte des IV internationalen Kongresses für griechische und lateinische Epigraphik*, pp. 72–98. Vienna: Böhlau, 1964.

———, ed. *Inscriptiones Italiae*.

Desborough, V. R. d'A. *Protogeometric Pottery*. Oxford: Clarendon Press, 1952.

Deubner, L. *Attische Feste*. 1932. Reprint. Hildesheim: Olms, 1962.

Deutsch, Helene. *The Psychology of Women.* Vol. 1. New York: Grune & Stratton, 1947.

Diehl, E. *Anthologia Lyrica Graeca.* 3d ed. Leipzig: Teubner, 1949–52.

Donati, Angela. "Sull'iscrizione Lanuvina della curia mulierum." *Rivista storica dell'antichità* 1 (1971): 235–37.

Dover, K. J. "Classical Greek Attitudes to Sexual Behavior." *Arethusa* 6 (1973): 59–73.

Duff, A. M. *Freedmen in the Early Roman Empire.* Oxford: Clarendon Press, 1928.

Duncan-Jones, Richard. *The Economy of the Roman Empire: Quantitative Studies.* London: Cambridge University Press, 1974.

Durry, Marcel. "Le mariage des filles impubères dans la Rome antique." *Revue des études latines* 47 *bis* (1970): 17–25.

———, ed. *Eloge funèbre d'une matrone romaine.* Paris: Budé, 1950.

Ehrenberg, Victor. *The People of Aristophanes.* Oxford: Blackwell, 1943. Reprint. New York: Schocken Books, 1962.

Ember, M. "Warfare, Sex Ratio, and Polygyny." *Ethnology* 13 (April 1974): 197–206.

Engels, Frederick. *The Origin of the Family, Private Property and the State.* Reprint. New York: International Publishers, 1972.

Erdmann, W. *Die Ehe im alten Griechenland.* Münchener Beiträge zur Papyrusforschung und antiken Rechtsgeschichte, vol. 20. Munich: Beck, 1934.

Farnell, L. *Cults of the Greek States.* Oxford: Clarendon Press, 1896–1909.

Ferguson, W. S. *Hellenistic Athens: An Historical Essay.* London: Macmillan, 1911.

Finley, M. I. "Archaeology and History." *Daedalus* 100 (1971): 168–86.

———. "The Silent Women of Rome." *Horizon* 7 (1965): 57–64. Reprinted in *Aspects of Antiquity: Discoveries and Controversies,* pp. 129–42. London: Chatto & Windus, 1968.

———. "Marriage, Sale and Gift in the Homeric World." *Revue internationale des droits de l'antiquité* 2 (1955): 167–94.

———. *Studies in Land and Credit in Ancient Athens, 500–200 B.C.: The Horos Inscriptions.* New Brunswick, N.J.: Rutgers University Press, 1952.

———. "Utopianism Ancient and Modern." In *The Critical Spirit: Essays in Honor of Herbert Marcuse,* edited by K. Wolff and B. Moore, Jr., pp. 3–20. Boston: Beacon, 1967.

———. "Was Greek Civilization Based on Slave Labour?" *Historia* 8 (1959): 145–64. Reprinted in Finley, *Slavery in Classical Antiquity,* pp. 53–72. Cambridge, England: Heffner, 1969.

Fitton, J. W. "That Was No Lady, That Was ..." *Classical Quarterly* 64 n.s. 20 (1970): 56–66.

Flacelière, R. "D'un certain féminisme grec." *Revue des études anciennes* 64 (1962): 109–16.

———. "Le féminisme dans l'ancienne Athènes." *Comptes rendus de l'Académie des Inscriptions et Belles-Lettres* (1971): 698–706.

———. *Love in Ancient Greece.* New York: Crown, 1962.

Forrest, W. G. *A History of Sparta.* London: Hutchinson, 1968.

Förtsch, Barbara. *Die politische Rolle der Frau in der römischen Republik.* Würzburger Studien zur Altertumswissenschaft, vol. 5. Stuttgart: Kohlhammer, 1935.

Freud, Sigmund. *Civilization and Its Discontents.* London: Hogarth, 1957.

Friedl, Ernestine. "The Position of Women: Appearance and Reality." *Anthropological Quarterly* 40 (1967): 97–108.

Fromm, E. *The Forgotten Language.* New York: Grove Press, 1972.

Gagé, Jean. *Matronalia: Essai sur les dévotions et les organisations cultuelles des femmes dans l'ancienne Rome.* Collection *Latomus,* no. 60, 1963.

Garnsey, Peter. *Social Status and Legal Privilege in the Roman Empire.* Oxford: Clarendon Press, 1970.

Gernet, Louis. *Anthropologie de la Grèce antique.* Paris: Maspero, 1968.

Gomme, A. W. "The Position of Women in Athens in the Fifth and Fourth Centuries B.C." *Classical Philology* 20 (1925): 1–25. Reprinted in Gomme, *Essays in Greek History and Literature,* pp. 89–115. Oxford: Blackwell, 1937.

Gordon, Hattie. "The Eternal Triangle, First Century B.C." *Classical Journal* 28 (1933): 574–78.

Greer, Germaine. *The Female Eunuch.* New York: McGraw-Hill, 1971.

Gruen, Erich S. *Roman Politics and the Criminal Courts, 149–78 B.C.* Cambridge, Mass.: Harvard University Press, 1968.

Hadas, Moses. "Observations on Athenian Women." *Classical Weekly* 39 (1936): 97–100.

Hallock, Richard T. *Persepolis Fortification Tablets.* Chicago: University of Chicago Press, 1969.

Hands, A. R. *Charities and Social Aid in Greece and Rome.* London: Thames & Hudson, 1968.

Harris, H. A. *Sport in Greece and Rome.* Ithaca, N.Y.: Cornell University Press, 1972.

Harrison, A. R. W. *The Law of Athens: The Family and Property.* Oxford: Clarendon Press, 1968.

Harrison, Evelyn B. "Athena and Athens in the East Pediment of the Parthenon." *American Journal of Archaeology* 71 (1967): 27–58.

Harrison, Jane. *Prolegomena to the Study of Greek Religion.* 3d ed. 1922. Reprint. New York: Meridian, 1955.

Havelock, Christine. "The Nude in Greek Art." Paper delivered at Women in Antiquity conference, April 26, 1973, State University of New York at Buffalo.

Hawkes, Jacquetta. *Dawn of the Gods.* London: Chatto & Windus, 1968.

Herfst, P. *Le travail de la femme dans la Grèce ancienne.* Utrecht: Oosthoek, 1922.

Herington, C. J. *Athena Parthenos and Athena Polias.* Manchester, England: Manchester University Press, 1955.

Herrmann, Claudine. *Le rôle judiciare et politique des femmes sous la républiqué romaine.* Collection *Latomus,* no. 67, 1964.

Herter, H. "Die Soziologie der antiken Prostitution im Lichte des heidnischen und christlichen Schrifttums." *Jahrbuch für Antike und Christentum* 3 (1960): 70–111.

Hignett, C. *A History of the Athenian Constitution to the End of the Fifth Century B.C.* Oxford: Clarendon Press, 1952.

Himes, Norman E. *Medical History of Contraception.* 1936. Reprint. New York: Schocken Books, 1970.

Hirvonen, Kaarle. *Matriarchal Survivals and Certain Trends in Homer's Female Characters.* Annales Academiae Scientiarum Fennicae, Series B, vol. 152. Helsinki: Suomalainen Tiedeakatemia, 1968.

Hoffsten, Ruth. *Roman Women of Rank of the Early Empire as Portrayed by Dio, Paterculus, Suetonius, and Tacitus.* Philadelphia: University of Pennsylvania Press, 1939.

Hopkins, Keith. "Contraception in the Roman Empire." *Comparative Studies in Society and History* 8 (1965): 124–51.

———. "On the Probable Age Structure of the Roman Population." *Population Studies* 20 (1966): 245–64.

Jacoby, F., ed. *Die Fragmente der griechischen Historiker.* Leiden: Brill, 1923–58.

Jebb, R., ed. *Sophocles.* Vol. 3, *The Antigone.* London: Cambridge University Press, 1962.

Kaibel, G., ed. *Epigrammata Graeca.* Berlin: Reimer, 1878.

Kajanto, Iiro. "On Divorce Among the Common People of Rome. *Revue des études latines* 47 bis (1970): 99–113.

———. "Women's Praenomina Reconsidered." *Arctos* n.s. 7 (1972): 13–30.

Kaser, Max. *Roman Private Law.* 2d ed. London: Butterworth, 1968.

Kiefer, O. *Sexual Life in Ancient Rome.* London: Routledge & Kegan Paul, 1934.

Kitto, H. D. F. *The Greeks.* Harmondsworth, England: Penguin, 1951.

Krenkel, W. A. "Erotica 1: Der Abortus in der Antike." *Wissenschaftliche Zeitschrift der Universität Rostock* 20 (1971): 443–52.

Kühner, R., and Gerth, B. *Ausführliche Grammatik der Griechischen Sprache.* Vol. 2. Hanover: Hahnsche, 1904.

Kurtz, Donna C., and Boardman, John. *Greek Burial Customs.* Ithaca, N.Y.: Cornell University Press, 1971.

Lacey, W. K. *The Family in Classical Greece.* Ithaca, N.Y.: Cornell University Press, 1968.

———. "Homeric *Hedna* and Penelope's *Kurios.*" *Journal of Hellenic Studies* 86 (1966): 55–68.

Latte, Kurt. *Römische Religionsgeschichte.* Munich: Beck, 1960.

Lattimore, R. *Themes in Greek and Latin Epitaphs.* Illinois Studies in Language and Literature, vol. 28. Urbana: University of Illinois Press, 1942.

Le Bonniec, Henri. *Le culte de Cérès à Rome.* Paris: Klincksieck, 1958.

Leclant, J. *Inventaire bibliographique des Isiaca (IBIS). Répertoire analytique des travaux relatifs à la diffusion des cultes isiaques, 1940–1969.* Etudes préliminaires aux religions orientales dans l'Empire romain. Leiden: Brill, 1972.

Lefkowitz, Mary. "Critical Stereotypes and the Poetry of Sappho." *Greek, Roman and Byzantine Studies* 14 (1973): 113–23.

Le Gall, Joël. "Un critère de différenciation sociale." In *Recherches sur les structures sociales dans l'antiquité classique,* pp. 275–86. Paris: Centre national de la recherche scientifique, 1970.

———. "Métiers de femmes au *Corpus inscriptionum Latinarum.*" *Revue des études latines* 47 bis (1970): 123–30.

Leipoldt, J. *Die Frau in der antiken Welt und im Urchristentum.* 2d ed. Leipzig: Köhler and Ameland, 1955.

Lewis, Naphtali. "On Paternal Authority in Roman Egypt." *Revue internationale des droits de l'antiquité* 17 (1970): 251–58.

Licht, Hans [P. Brandt]. *Sexual Life in Ancient Greece.* New York: American Anthropological Society, 1934.

Liddell, H. G., and Scott, R., eds. *A Greek-English Dictionary.* 9th ed., rev. by H. S. Jones. Oxford: Clarendon Press, 1925–40.

Lilja, Sara. *The Roman Elegists' Attitude to Women.* Annales Academiae Scientiarum Fennicae, Series B. vol. 135, fascicle 1. Helsinki: Suomalainen Tiedeakatemia, 1965.

Loane, Helen Jefferson. *Industry and Commerce of the City of Rome (50 B.C.–200 A.D.).* Baltimore: Johns Hopkins University Press, 1938.

Lobel, E., and Page, Denys L., eds. *Poetarum Lesbiorum Fragmenta.* Oxford: Clarendon Press, 1955.

Luck, G. *The Latin Love Elegy.* 2d ed. London: Methuen, 1969.

McClees, Helen. *A Study of Women in Attic Inscriptions.* New York: Columbia University Press, 1920.

MacMullen, Ramsay. *Roman Social Relations: 50 B.C. to A.D. 284.* New Haven: Yale University Press, 1974.

Macurdy, Grace. *Hellenistic Queens.* Baltimore: Johns Hopkins University Press, 1932.

Malaise, Michel. *Les conditions de pénétration et de diffusion des cultes égyptiens en Italie.* Leiden: Brill, 1972.

Malcovati, H. *Oratorum Romanorum Fragmenta.* 2d ed. Turin: Paravia, 1955.

Maxey, Mima. *Occupations of the Lower Classes in Roman Society.* Chicago: University of Chicago Press, 1938.

Michell, H. *Sparta.* London: Cambridge University Press, 1964.

Mill, John Stuart. *On the Subjection of Women.* 1869. Reprint. New York: Fawcett, 1971.

Moretti, L., ed. *Iscrizioni agonistiche greche.*

Motto, A. L. "Seneca on Women's Liberation." *Classical World* 65 (1972): 155–57.

Mulder, J. J. B. *Quaestiones Nonnullae ad Atheniensium Matrimonium Vitamque Coniugalem Pertinentes.* Utrecht: Bosch, 1920.

Müller, C., ed. *Fragmenta Historicorum Graecorum.* Paris: Didot, 1841–73.

Mylonas, G.E. *Eleusis and the Eleusinian Mysteries.* Princeton: Princeton University Press, 1961.

Nardi, E. *Procurato aborto nel mondo greco–romano.* Milan: Giuffrè, 1971.

Neumann, Erich. *Amor and Psyche: The Psychic Development of the Feminine, A Commentary on the Tale by Apuleius.* Bollingen Series, vol. 54. Princeton: Princeton University Press, 1956.

———. *The Great Mother: An Analysis of the Archetype.* Bollingen Series, vol. 47. Princeton: Princeton University Press, 1955.

Nilsson, M. P. *Geschichte der griechischen Religion.* Vol. 1. Munich: Beck, 1955.

Noonan, John T., Jr. *Contraception: A History of its Treatment by the Catholic Theologians and Canonists.* Reprint. New York: Mentor, 1967.

North, Helen. *Sophrosyne: Self-Knowledge and Self-Restraint in Greek Literature.* Ithaca, N.Y.: Cornell University Press, 1966.

Page, Denys L. *Corinna.* London: Society for the Promotion of Hellenic Studies, 1953.

———, ed. *Alcman: The Partheneion.* Oxford: Clarendon Press, 1951.

———, ed. *Literary Papyri: Poetry.* London: Heinemann, 1941.

———, ed. *Sappho and Alcaeus.* Oxford: Clarendon Press, 1955.

Palmer, L. R. *The Interpretation of Mycenaean Greek Texts.* Oxford: Clarendon Press, 1963.

Palmer, Robert E. A. *The Archaic Community of the Romans.* London: Cambridge University Press, 1970.

———. "Cupra, Matuta, and Venilia Pyrgensis." *Illinois Studies in Language and Literature,* vol. 58 (1969): 292–309.

———. "Roman Shrines of Female Chastity from the Caste Struggle to the Papacy of Innocent I." *Rivista storica dell'antichita* 4 (1974): 113–59.

Panofsky, D. and E. *Pandora's Box: The Changing Aspects of a Mythical Symbol.* Bollingen Series, vol. 52. New York: Pantheon, 1962.

Paoli, U. E. *La donna greca nell'antichità.* Florence: Le Monnier, 1953.

Pembroke, Simon. "Last of the Matriarchs: A Study in the Inscriptions of Lycia." *Journal of the Economic and Social History of the Orient* 8 (1965): 217–47.

———. "Women in Charge: The Function of Alternatives in Early Greek Tradition and the Ancient Idea of Matriarchy." *Journal of the Warburg and Courtauld Institute* 30 (1967): 1–35.

Peradotto, John. *Classical Mythology: An Annotated Bibliographical Survey.* Urbana, Ill.: American Philological Association, 1973.

Pleket, H. W., ed. *Epigraphica II: Texts on the Social History of the Greek World.* Leiden: Brill, 1969.

Pomeroy, Sarah B. "Andromache and the Question of Matriarchy." *Revue des études grecques* (forthcoming).

——. "Women and War." Paper delivered at the Sixth International Congress of Classical Studies, 1974, Madrid.

——. "A Classical Scholar's Perspective on Matriarchy." In *Liberating Women's History*, edited by B. Carroll. Urbana: University of Illinois Press, 1975.

——. "Feminism in Book V of Plato's *Republic.*" *Apeiron* 8 (1974): 32–35.

——. "Selected Bibliography on Women in Antiquity." *Arethusa* 6 (Spring 1973): 125–57.

Préaux, Claire. "Le statut de la femme à l'époque hellénistique, principalement en Egypte." Recueils de la Société Jean Bodin. Vol. 11, *La femme* (1959): I: 127–75

Raubitschek, Anthony E. *Dedications from the Athenian Acropolis.* Cambridge, Mass.: Archaeological Institute of America, 1949.

Rawson, Beryl. "Family Life Among the Lower Classes at Rome in the First Two Centuries of the Empire." *Classical Philology* 61 (1966): 71–83.

Richter, Donald C. "The Position of Women in Classical Athens." *Classical Journal* 67 (1971): 1–8.

Richter, G. M. A. *The Archaic Gravestones of Attica.* London: Phaidon, 1961.

——. *Korai: Archaic Greek Maidens: A Study of the Development of the Kore Type in Greek Sculpture.* London: Phaidon, 1968.

Rickman, G. *Roman Granaries and Store Buildings.* London: Cambridge University Press, 1971.

Robert, J. and L. "Bulletin épigraphique." *Revue des études grecques* 76 (1963): 121–92; 81 (1968): 420–549.

Robinson, D. M., and Graham, J. Walter. *Excavations at Olynthus 8: The Hellenic House.* Johns Hopkins University Studies in Archaeology, vol. 25. Baltimore: Johns Hopkins University Press, 1938.

Roscher, W. H. *Ausführliches Lexikon der griechischen und römischen Mythologie.* 6 vols. Leipzig: Teubner, 1884–1937.

Rostovtzeff, M. I. *Greece.* 2d ed., revised by E. Bickerman. London: Oxford University Press, 1963.

Rotondi, G. *Leges publicae populi romani.* 1912. Reissued Hildesheim: Olms, 1962.

Rougé, Jean. "La colonisation grecque et les femmes." *Cahiers d'histoire* 15 (1970): 307–17.

Roullet, A. *The Egyptian and Egyptianizing Monuments of Imperial Rome.* Leiden: Brill, 1972.

Ste. Croix, G. E. M. de. "Some Observations on the Property Rights of Athenian Women." *Classical Review,* n.s. 20 (1970): 273–78.

Salis, Arnold von. *Theseus und Ariadne.* Berlin and Leipzig: de Gruyter, 1930.

Samuel, A. E.; Hastings, W. K.; Bowman, A. K.; and Bagnall, R. S. *Death and Taxes.* American Studies in Papyrology, no. 10. Toronto: Hakkert, 1971.

Schaps, David. "Women and Property Control in Classical and Hellenistic Greece." Ph.D. dissertation, Harvard University, 1972.

Scullard, H. H. *Roman Politics 220–150 B.C.* Oxford: Clarendon Press, 1951.

Segal, C. "Sophocles' Praise of Man and the Conflicts of the *Antigone.*" In *Sophocles,* edited by T. Woodard. Englewood Cliffs, N.J.: Prentice-Hall, 1966.

Seltman, Charles. "The Status of Women in Athens." *Greece and Rome,* Series 2, 2 (1955): 119–24.

——. *Women in Antiquity.* London: Thames & Hudson, 1956.

Slater, Philip. *The Glory of Hera.* Boston: Beacon Press, 1968.

Smithson, Evelyn Lord. "The Protogeometric Cemetery at Nea Ionia." *Hesperia* 30 (1961): 147–78.

——. "The Tomb of a Rich Athenian Lady, ca. 850 B.C." *Hesperia* 37 (1968): 98–103.

Straub, J. "Senaculum, id est mulierum senatus." In *Bonner Historia Augusta Colloquium 1964–65*, pp. 221–40. Bonn, 1966.

Syme, R. *The Roman Revolution.* Oxford: Clarendon Press, 1939.

———. *Sallust.* Berkeley: University of California Press, 1964.

Tanzer, H. H. *The Common People of Pompeii.* Johns Hopkins University Studies in Archaeology, no. 29. Baltimore: Johns Hopkins University Press, 1939.

Tarn, W. W., and Griffith, G. T. *Hellenistic Civilization.* 3d ed. London: Arnold, 1952.

Taubenschlag, R. *The Law of Greco-Roman Egypt in the Light of the Papyri: 332 B.C.–640 A.D.* 2d ed. Warsaw: Panstowe Wydawnictwo Naukowe, 1955.

Thesleff, Holger. *An Introduction to the Pythagorean Writings of the Hellenistic Period.* Aabo: Aabo Akademi, 1961.

———, ed. *The Pythagorean Texts of the Hellenistic Period.* Aabo: Aabo Akademi, 1965.

Thompson, W. E. "Athenian Marriage Patterns: Remarriage." *California Studies in Classical Antiquity* 5 (1972): 211–25.

———. "The Marriage of First Cousins in Athenian Society." *Phoenix* 21 (1967): 273–82.

Thomson, George Derwent. *Studies in Ancient Greek Society.* Vol. 1, *The Prehistoric Aegean.* New York: International Publishers, 1949.

Tod, M. "Epigraphical Notes on Freedmen's Professions." *Epigraphica* 12 (1950): 3–26.

Tran Tam Tinh, V. *Le culte des divinités orientales à Herculaneum.* Leiden: Brill, 1971.

———. *Le culte des divinités orientales en Campanie.* Leiden: Brill, 1972.

Treggiari, Susan. "Domestic Staff at Rome in the Julio-Claudian Period, 27 B.C. to A.D. 68." *Histoire sociale; Revue canadienne* 6 (1973): 241–55.

———. "Libertine Ladies." *Classical World* 64 (1971): 196–98.

———. *Roman Freedmen During the Late Republic.* Oxford: Clarendon Press, 1969.

———. "Women in Domestic Service in the Early Roman Empire." Paper delivered at the Berkshire Conference on the History of Women, October 26, 1974, Cambridge, Mass.

———. "Women in Slavery." Paper delivered at the Women's Caucus of the American Philological Association meeting, December 1973, St. Louis.

Tritsch, F. F. J. "The Women of Pylos." In *Minoica: Festschrift Sundwall*, edited by Ernst Grumach, pp. 406–45. Deutsche Akademie der Wissenschaften zu Berlin, Schriften der Sektion für Altertumswissenschaft, 12. Berlin: Akademie Verlag, 1958.

Ucko, Peter J. *Anthropomorphic Figurines of Predynastic Egypt and Neolithic Crete with Comparative Material from the Prehistorical Near East and Mainland Greece.* Royal Anthropological Institute, Occasional Paper No. 24. London: Andrew Szmidla, 1968.

Van Berchem, Denis. *Les distributions de blé et d'argent à la plèbe romaine sous l'empire.* Geneva: Georg et Cie., 1939.

Vanderlip, Vera Frederika, ed. *The Four Greek Hymns of Isidorus and the Cult of Isis.* American Studies in Papyrology, no. 12. Toronto: Hakkert, 1972.

Vatin, Cláude. *Recherches sur le mariage et la condition de la femme mariée à l'époque hellénistique.* Paris: E. de Boccard, 1970.

Ventris, Michael, and Chadwick, John. *Documents in Mycenaean Greek.* London: Cambridge University Press, 1956.

Vidal-Naquet, Pierre. "Esclavage et gynécocratie dans la tradition, le mythe, l'utopie." In *Recherches sur les structures sociales dans l'antiquité classique*, pp. 63–80. Paris: Centre national de la recherche scientifique, 1970.

Vidman, L. *Sylloge inscriptionum religionis Isiacae et Sarapiacae.* Berlin: de Gruyter, 1969.

Vogt, Joseph. *Von der Gleichwertigkeit der Geschlechter in der bürgerlichen Gesellschaft der Griechen.* Akademie der Wissenschaften und der Literatur in Mainz, Abhandlungen der Geistes und Socialwissenschaft. Wiesbaden: Steiner, 1960.

Waldock, A. J. A. *Sophocles the Dramatist.* London: Cambridge University Press, 1966.

Waltzing, J.-P. *Etude historique sur les corporations professionnelles chez les Romains jusqu'à la chute de l'Empire d'occident.* Vols 1 and 4. Louvain: Charles Peeters, 1895–1900.

Watson, Alan. *The Law of Persons in the Later Roman Republic.* Oxford: Clarendon Press, 1967.

———. *Roman Private Law Around 200 B.C.* Edinburgh: Edinburgh University Press, 1971.

Weaver, P. R. C. *Familia Caesaris: A Social Study of the Emperor's Freedmen and Slaves.* London: Cambridge University Press, 1972.

Webster, T. B. L. *Athenian Culture and Society.* Berkeley: University of California Press, 1973.

Wehrli, C. "Les gynéconomes." *Museum Helveticum* 19 (1962): 33–38.

Weiss, K. *Demographic Models for Anthropology. American Antiquity* Memoir. no. 27. 1973.

Wender, Dorothea. "Plato: Mysogynist, Paedophile, and Feminist." *Arethusa* 6 (Spring 1973): 75–90.

Willetts, R.F. *The Law Code of Gortyn. Kadmos,* Supplement 1, 1967.

Williams, Gordon. "Some Aspects of Roman Marriage Ceremonies and Ideals." *Journal of Roman Studies* 48 (1958): 16–29.

Winnington-Ingram, R. P. "Clytemnestra and the Vote of Athena." *Journal of Hellenic Studies* 68 (1948): 130–47.

Wiseman, T. P. *Cinna the Poet.* Leicester: Leicester University Press, 1974.

Wissowa, G. *Religion und Kultus der Römer.* 2d ed. Munich: Beck, 1912.

Witt, R. E. *Isis in the Graeco-Roman World.* Ithaca, N.Y.: Cornell University Press, 1971.

Wolff, H. J. "Marriage Law and Family Organisation in Ancient Athens." *Traditio 2* (1944): 43–95.

Wright, F. A. *Feminism in Greek Literature: From Homer to Aristotle.* 1923. Reprint. Port Washington, N.Y.: Kennikat, 1969.

Wycherley, R. E. *How the Greeks Built Cities.* Garden City, N.Y.: Doubleday, 1969.

# INDEX